Published by Building Community Books,
5 Dryden Street, London WC2E 9NW.

ISBN 1 85416 000 1

Cover photo by Arif Hasan
Designed by Andrew Haig
Graphics by Ross Foley based on originals
by Habitat Forum Berlin
Typesetting by Intertype
Printed in Great Britain by E.G. Bond

Building Community

A Third World Case Book

A summary of the Habitat International
Coalition Non-Governmental Organization's
Project for the International Year of Shelter
for the Homeless, 1987, in association with
Habitat Forum Berlin.

Edited by Bertha Turner

Foreword by Dom Helder Camara

Introduction and Conclusions
by John F.C. Turner

BCB/HFB

To J.G. (Han) van Putten
Founder and Past President of HIC

Contents

Acknowledgements

The Habitat International Coalition Project (HIC) would never have happened and this book would not exist without the help of a great many people and organizations from all parts of the world. To list them all is impossible. The major contributors, of course, are the tens of thousands of low-income people whose achievements are the subject matter. Hundreds of these active community builders have given their scarce and precious time to help those who gathered the information for the case studies summarized in this book. Many other people have carried out the extra work of the project in addition to their normal daily jobs, and we offer them our deepest gratitude.

The community based organizations (CBOs) and non-governmental organizations (NGOs) which prepared the case studies and data bases, their sponsors, their advisors and those responsible for preparing this book are all listed, either below, or on the title pages of individual case study texts, along with those who sponsored the project or programme described. We have made every effort to avoid omissions or errors, since we know how offensive this can be to those who have contributed. We hope that anyone inadvertently left out will accept our sincere apologies.

The United Nations Centre for Human Settlements (UNCHS) Nairobi, was the first of our sponsors to come forward. Their financial contribution early in 1984 allowed the HIC Project to take off. AHAS, GRET and PGC carried out the large scale, worldwide survey identifying 341 cases of which 194 were from Third World countries. This collection of materials has had extensive use, helping funding organizations to identify likely projects for their sponsorship, and providing subject matter for the International Year of Shelter for the Homeless (IYSH '87) publications and events in many parts of the world.

We are deeply grateful to the sponsors listed below who supported the preliminary, larger survey and the in-depth documentation of the 20 cases.

This book is dedicated to J.G. (Han) van Putten, Founder and Past President of the Habitat International Coalition, to whom a very special vote of thanks must go. Han, along with Peter Slits and their colleagues, have carried the increased administrative burden of the HIC Secretariat, in addition to their own work for the International Union of Local Authorities (IULA) in The Hague.

The HIC Steering Group which shaped and guided the HIC NGO Habitat Project was as follows: J.G. van Putten, Chairman, Habitat International Coalition (HIC), The Hague, Netherlands; John F.C. Turner, HIC Project Co-ordinator, Co-director of Alternative Habitat for Another Society (AHAS), London, United Kingdom; Dieter Baldeaux, Deutsche Entwicklung Stiftung Wohnen (DESWOS), Köln, Federal Republic of Germany; Yves Cabannes, HIC Project Case Advisor, Groupe de Recherches et d'Echanges Technologiques (GRET), Paris, France; David Hall, President of HIC and Director, Town and Country Planning Association (TCPA), London, United Kingdom; Geoffrey Payne, Director, Centre for Development and Environmental Planning (CENDEP), Oxford Polytechnic, Oxford, United Kingdom; David Satterthwaite, International Institute for Environment and Development (IIED), London, United Kingdom; Han Verschure, HIC Project Case Advisor, Director, Post Graduate Centre-Human Settlements (PGC-HS), Catholic University of Leuven, Belgium.

The Researchers and Producers of the admirable case studies, monographs, photographs and visual materials for the HIC NGO Habitat Project were: Laique Azam and Quaratul Ain Bakhteari, Karachi, Pakistan; M. Barbier-Wiesser, Ministry of Co-operation, Paris, France; Somsook Boonyabancha, Bangkok, Thailand; Paul Bottelberg, International Association of Building Companions Development Co-operation (COOPIBO), Leuven, Belgium; K. Cappon, Wevelgem, Belgium; Centre for Housing and Human Settlements Studies (CHHSS) and HSF and the Klong Toey Community Group, Bangkok, Thailand; Centro Co-operativista Uruguayo (CCU), Montevideo, Uruguay; Priscilla Connolly, Centro de la Vivienda y Estudios Urbanos (CENVI), Mexico City, Mexico; Co-operativa 20 de Junio and Centro Experimental de la Vivienda Economica (CEVE), AVE/CEVE/SEHAS, Córdoba, Argentina; A. G/Egziabher, Y. Halu, T. Tekle, T. Debas, c/o Redd Barna (Norwegian Save the Children), Addis Ababa, Ethiopia; Arif Hasan, Karachi, Pakistan; Harrington Jere, Marijke Vandersuypen Muyaba, Francis Ndilila, Human Settlements of Zambia (HUZA), Lusaka, Zambia; Sister Lydia Kalaw, Domus Mariae Foundation, Manila, Philippines; Benedict Lambal, Ufulal, Senegal; Rocio Lombera G., Centro Operacional de Vivienda y Poblamiento (COPEVI), Mexico City, Mexico; Andrew Maskrey, then of Centro Investigación Domumentatión y

Asesoria Poblacional (CIDAP), Lima, Peru; Ruth McLeod, Women's Construction Collective (WCC), Kingston, Jamaica; S.K. Mohandas, Centre for Development Studies and Activities (CDSA), Poona, India; P. Nicholas, Evelyn Waas, M. Gaye, ENDA-RUP, Dakar, Senegal; Gustavo Riofrio, Marcela Riofrio, (CIPUR), Lima, Peru; T. Schilderman, Projet Pozzolana, Chaux Tourbe, (PCCT), Ruhengeri, Rwanda; Johan Silas, Institute of Technology Surabaya (ITS), Indonesia; Phillipe Theunissen and the Equipe du Certificat inter-universitaire sur l'Habitat rural et urbain dans les Pays en Développement, Catholic University of Louvain, Belgium; Brother Servatius Tjondrohartanto, YSS, Semarang, Indonesia; M.A. Windey, S.J. Village Reconstruction Organization (VRO), Hyderabad, India.

Sponsors of the HIC NGO Habitat Project:
Australian Development Assistance Board (ADAB), Canberra City, Australia; International Association of Building Companions Development Co-operation (COOPIBO), Leuven, Belgium; Groupe de Recherche et d'Echanges Technologiques (GRET), Paris, France; Habitat International Coalition (HIC), The Hague, Netherlands; Human Settlements of Zambia (HUZA), Lusaka, Zambia; Institute of Technology Surabaya (ITS), Indonesia; International Development Research Centre (IDRC), Ottawa, Canada; Marian Housing Foundation, Manila, Philippines; Misereor, Aachen, Federal Republic of Germany; Planning Committee for Non-governmental Organization Activities, World Conference on the United Nations Decade for Women, New York, NY, United States of America; Post Graduate Centre-Human Settlements (PGC-HS), Leuven, Belgium; United Nations Centre for Human Settlements (UNCHS), Nairobi, Kenya; Village Reconstruction Organization (VRO), Hyderabad, India.

The Habitat Forum Berlin 'wallnewspaper' production team: Rainer W. Ernst, Ludwig Thürmer: Directors; Ulla Kroog-Hrubes: Organization; Wolf-Rudiger Gericke: Editor Project Studies; Bruno Bakalovich, Thomas Schneider, Ludwig Thürmer: Visual Concept and Graphic Design; Andrew Maskrey, Bertha Turner, John F.C. Turner (AHAS); Yves Cabannes (GRET); Jean-Francois Mabardi, Philippe Theunissen (Habitat et Participation); Rainer W. Ernst, Ludwig Thürmer (HFB); Han Verschure (PGC-HS); Ulli Hellweg (S.T.E.R.N.): Advisors and Editors in Chief.

Sponsorship for printing and publication
Since this book was not planned in the original HIC NGO Habitat Project proposal and budget, no funds were set aside to cover the time and costs of origination carried out by AHAS during 1987.

Special thanks are therefore due to those individuals and organizations who made this work possible through their contributions and advance orders for copies of the book. In alphabetical order, they include: the Aga Khan Award for Architecture, Geneva, Switzerland; Ahrends, Burton and Koralek, Architects, London; William Doebele of the Graduate School of Design, Harvard University, Cambridge, Massachusetts, USA; the German Appropriate Technology Exchange (GATE), Eschborn, Federal Republic of Germany; the International Development Research Centre (IDRC), Ottawa, Canada; the Lucis Trust, London; the Swedish Association for Development of Low-cost Housing (SADEL), Lund, Sweden; and the United Nations Centre for Human Settlements (UNCHS), Nairobi, Kenya.

Special thanks are also due to those who carried out the actual design and production: Andrew Haig, Ross Foley and Martyn Partridge for design, graphics and typesetting respectively. And finally, a special vote of thanks for their enthusiastic feedback and assistance to Louisa Denman and Nick Wates of Building Communities Bookshop, and for their agreement to share responsibility for publishing this book with Bertha Turner and John F.C. Turner in their new joint venture: Building Communities Books.

Editor's Preface

This book describes major breakthroughs in housing, being made today by the poor of Third World countries. Living under governments which cannot afford to house them, and unable to afford market prices, they must build their own communities. Between half and three-quarters of all new homes in most Third World cities are built by low-income people. When they have access to available resources and are free to use them in their own ways, people and their community-based organizations can build up to five times more than their governments with the same funds, and to similar or better standards.

How can such poor people build so much with so little? What are the keys to success? What lessons do they teach for building fulfilling and sustainable societies in rich and poor countries alike?

Building Community addresses these questions with authority. Selected from over 300 cases, the 20 presented in this book have been edited from in-depth documentation by researchers working at the grass roots. They highlight the potentials as well as the problems and show what can and must be done in rich countries as well, where so many people are discovering and reclaiming their forgotten need and capacity for community building. This sea change of ideas is reflected in the community architecture and participatory planning movement in the United Kingdom, as well as in Europe, the United States of America and Canada.

The book shows how people can win their rights to resources for housing and the freedom to act for themselves; how governments can enable people by supporting local initiative; and how the essential changes in understanding can come about.

The turning point for this new understanding was the memorable Open Forum at Vancouver, Canada in 1976. Held in parallel with the United Nations Habitat Conference on Human Settlements that year, it was the first major event at which people of the non-governmental 'third sector' came together from different parts of the world to share their experience. Encouraged by its success, the organizer, Han van Putten, set up the Habitat International Council – HIC, the non-governmental organizations' (NGO) Committee on Human Settlements. Perseverance of a few members over the past decade ensured that, through HIC, NGOs worldwide established their presence and gained a voice at the United Nations'

Commission on Habitat. And, during the United Nations' International Year of Shelter for the Homeless, 1987 (IYSH '87), HIC finally became truly global, changing its name to Habitat International *Coalition*, the NGO *Alliance* on Human Settlements. Representatives of 57 NGOs and community-based organizations (CBOs) from 40 countries on all continents attended the HIC NGO Seminar in Limuru, Kenya, in March 1987, and formulated the Declaration included in this book. This historical document was confirmed at the subsequent NGO Global Forum in Nairobi in April and at Habitat Forum Berlin in June, which also saw the start of an action programme.

The project on which this book is based started back in 1983. The NGO Habitat Project was HIC's contribution to IYSH '87, with the aim of drawing worldwide attention to: **the underestimated contribution and underused potentials of NGOs (non-governmental organizations) and CBOs (community-based organizations) in home and neighbourhood building, improvement, management and maintenance by and for people, especially (by and for) those with low incomes and who are vulnerable to discrimination or disasters.**

During the Project's first year, a preliminary survey covering 341 cases of NGOs and CBOs in 75 countries on all continents was carried out, funded by the United Nations Centre for Human Settlements. This was followed by in-depth documentation of 20 selected cases. It was decided at this stage to limit selection to Third World countries where homelessness is most acute and in order to ensure comparability. Although selection was further influenced by the availability of funds, sponsors and local researchers, the final selection demonstrates the immense variety of CBO and NGO approaches to home and neighbourhood building. The 20 cases in this book cover a wide range of geographic, social and economic conditions and span a spectrum of scales – from small village and neighbourhoods to relatively large townships. The projects selected also show widely different ways in which environmental improvements serve as vehicles for social and economic development.

The cases present many useful examples of ways and means for locally self-managed home and neighbourhood building, improvement and management. These are the useful precedents to be found in this book, as they are far more likely to be adaptable and transferable to other situations than whole programmes. Programmes are courses of action composed of selected options for the component tasks – from initial group of community organizing to the management and maintenance of the improvements. The great variety of programmes illustrated by the cases highlights a key issue discussed in the Conclusions: the common but vain search for 'replicable programmes' to be administered by central authorities. Every successful programme is uniquely adapted to its place, time and people, as it must be if it is to match people's needs and priorities. This book is not intended as a catalogue of model programmes to be adopted by agencies and imposed on people, therefore. Rather, it is a source of 'tools for community building' – ideas and methods for use by local people and those working with them, to plan and carry out their own programmes.

Building Community will be of interest to everyone searching for alternatives to the unsustainable or unworkable systems dominated by the market or state. The cases point to new directions in housing that can lead to a sustainable future, directions that are paralleled by those emerging in the fields of food, health, learning and many other vital activities. The evidence in the book will be of equal importance to policy-makers and the professionals who serve them; to those who design and carry out local projects; and to students.

The **Foreword** by Dom Helder Camara, edited from his keynote speech at Habitat Forum Berlin in 1987, sheds light on the material, social and spiritual meaning of the struggles of people all over the world toward a decent life for themselves and their children. No one is better qualified to provide this global view. Dom Helder has won international acclaim as the outspoken Archbishop Emeritus of Olinda and Recife, Brazil and he has suffered personally for his courageous defence of the poor.

The **Introduction** is by John F.C. Turner, Co-ordinator of the HIC NGO Habitat Project and a pioneer since the 1950s in promoting community participation in both Third and First World countries. He provides insights into the viewpoint which shaped the Project's initial design and subsequent implementation.

The **cases** form the heart of *Building Community*. They are arranged alphabetically by continent and name, for easy reference. They are designed for use also as separate, individual reprints with the relevant credits on the title page of each one. They were prepared from the extensive documentation provided by people working in the field, according to the Steering Group's guidelines which specified a detailed schedule of data relevant to the

key issues, a monograph and audio-visual material. As funds become available, more of this research material will be edited and published under separate cover.

The **Issues and Conclusions** section is based on a paper which John F.C. Turner has evolved through a number of presentations and feedback at various meetings and workshops leading up to and during IYSH '87. It was first presented in preliminary form to the Development Advisory Group of the Organization for Economic Co-operation and Development (OECD) in October 1986. Progressively refined versions were contributed as discussion papers for meetings during 1987.

The **Directory of Sources** provides a selection of references of special interest to promotors and enablers, leaders and participants in community-based programmes. It is based on users' knowledge, rather than exhaustive research, and inevitably subject to the limitations of time and space.

The Limuru Declaration, drawn up in Kenya in April 1987, is reproduced as it echoes the spirit and content of this book. It was formulated by people from 40 countries in all world regions, representing 57 NGOs, 45 of which are based in Third World countries. Their joint Declaration reflects the wisdom of many experienced people, hard-won through long years of committed work, personal sacrifice and in some cases, personal suffering.

HIC conceived, planned and organized the overall project, obtained financial sponsorship for case studies by local researchers, and provided guidance. HIC members (AHAS, GRET, PGC-HS) and others listed in the credits section of each case, wrote the condensed, edited texts and provided the photos and information necessary for 16 of the 'wallnewspapers' designed and produced by the Habitat Forum Berlin team. These exhibition-format posters were displayed at the Berlin Forum and at many other IYSH '87 events. In addition to posters on 16 of the cases in this book, the set includes 6 on 'Changing the City'; these are especially appropriate for institutional use, complementing and complemented by this book. Texts for 4 additional case studies which did not appear as 'wallnewspapers' were especially written for this book by AHAS: El Augustino, Peru; Saarland Village 1, the Philippines; Yayasan Sosial Soegiyapranata, Indonesia; and the Village Reconstruction Organization Programme, India.

Bertha Turner, Co-director, AHAS, London   January 1988

Foreword

This Foreword is an edited version of the keynote address given by Dom Helder Camara, Archbishop Emeritus of Olinda and Refice, Brazil, on the occasion of the Habitat Forum Berlin Conference, 'Learning from One Another', held in Berlin, Federal Republic of Germany, in June 1987. Translated from the Portuguese by the HFB staff, it is here edited by Bertha Turner and reproduced with the kind permission of Dom Helder.

Dear Brothers and Dear Sisters,
We come here from different parts of the world seeking to deepen our knowledge of one of the major problems of our time: homelessness.

We are aware that in our time, with its great technical and scientific progress, there still exist millions and millions of homeless people, or people with dwellings which do not deserve the name 'home'. (We must) examine the connection between homelessness and its consequences – the way in which this problem aggravates other major problems of our time.

The home plays a major role in human life. However, it is not enough just to have a house. Sometimes a man comes home, having lost his job, but lacking the courage to tell his family the bad news. He hopes to get a new job soon. It is terrible for the head of the family to come home bringing nothing! Sometimes, he (eventually has to) go far away from home to look for work.

Terrible, too, is the problem of lack of education, not being able to send the children to school, watching them grow up with no preparation for adult life. I remember when education seemed to be the big problem of the European world. After this came the question of food. Now it is housing.

Why is the world in a situation where more than two-thirds of humanity live in sub-human conditions more fit for animals than for humans?

My country, my dear Brazil, is almost the size of a continent and could contain Germany 30 times over. Yet it is unbelievable that this huge country remains in the hands of only eight per cent of its population.

A woman from a very rich, industrialized country (once) advised me: 'Tell your people to do as we have done: to use their heads, to work hard, to be honest and they will achieve what we have already achieved'. Her thinking contains three basic misunderstandings: first, that we are unintelligent; second, that we do not have the will to work hard; and third, that we are dishonest. Honesty is there, especially among the poor. In our countries, the lack of honesty usually derives from a dictator. Intelligence is not lacking, nor are the people short of honesty and humility, so what is lacking?

The problem comes from the traditional injustice in external politics and trade. When there is exchange between our countries, the prices of both the raw materials and of the industrial products we need have always been and still are determined in the major decision-making centres of the world. It is clear that our raw materials have an ever-decreasing value, while industrial products an ever-increasing one.

'But you do not take into account the aid you receive'. Yes, we do. We are grateful. But we reach a point where aid, on its own, is not enough.

We must have the courage and confidence to say that there are signs of the times which are very positive. A first such sign is that today, within the more developed countries, there are ghettos, pockets of the Third World. Often there is a shortage of work, particularly for the young. Often, exiled people arrive because dictators dislike people who speak clearly and openly. And often so-called 'illegal immigrants' arrive.

Once (when I was) in the USA, they were celebrating their Founding Fathers, who left England because of religious persecution. At the same time, there was a project in another part of the country to expel 10,000 'illegal immigrants' who enter the country without proper documents. To a large audience, I said: 'My friends, I find this country celebrating its Founding Fathers. (Their deeds were) a noble act, born of love of liberty. But while we respect (them), when they came, they were met by the natives of this country. And the Founding Fathers were unable to show them any documents. So we should have the humility to acknowledge that many who settled in America are the descendants of illegal immigrants!'

Who are the masters of the world empire today? Once there was the Roman Empire. Portugal, Spain and Holland once held empires, too. When I was a child, Great Britain ruled the seas. After the First World War, it seemed there would be one great power: the United States of America. After the Second World War, there seemed to be two great powers: the United States of America and the Soviet Union.

When the First Industrial Revolution took place in

England, the steam-engine brought so much hope (that) everyone would have a comfortable life, a human life. However, these hopes soon encountered serious problems. Instead of serving everyone, the First Industrial Revolution benefitted only a small group of people.

Today we are watching the Third, the Fourth Industrial Revolution, with automation and robots. Once again, it seems that instead of being for all, it will benefit only a small group. Meanwhile, at the same time, even in industrialized countries, the lack of jobs continues.

It is terrible that our century, having already seen two World Wars, is now going through so-called 'conventional wars'. They differ from the two World Wars only in the fact that nuclear, chemical and biological weapons are not used. However, more people have been killed by conventional warfare since the end of the Second World War than were killed in the whole of that war.

Conventional wars induce countries who are unable to eliminate the hunger of their own people to buy weapons. The prime example of this is Brazil, with its great resources, which has not yet solved the problems of starvation and the deaths of many of its own people, and yet is today one of the major producers and sellers of conventional weapons.

The United Nations tells us that what is spent every year on the weapons race is more than enough to eliminate starvation and misery on earth. Nevertheless, the misery grows day by day.

The weapons race is now so mad that even military superpowers cannot afford the costs. They must now receive covert assistance from the big trans-national companies. (Many years ago) Eisenhower noted this tendency. As he was leaving the White House after his second term as President of the United States, he denounced the connection between economic and military power. Today, the masters of the world empire are the great multi-national corporations.

When trans-nationals come to our underdeveloped countries, they predict miracles. They will bring modern technology, strong and stable money, (and) generate many new jobs. The reality is quite different. There rapidly develops a natural connection between the small group of the rich in our countries and the trans-nationals. And the misery continues, this scandal which occurs on an international level and which is repeated in our countries: the rich get richer and the poor get poorer.

(Yet technology and the multi-nationals could have a positive role to play). We have to believe in the power of truth and justice. We have to respect the people and to believe in their becoming organized. As this Forum's title states, we are 'learning from one another'. More and more, we are learning the importance not only of working **for** the people, but **with** the people. When we work only **for** the people, we are the ones with the ideas, the projects, the social influence, the power, the money, and we go to help those poor people. But when we work **with** people, it is different. We trust the people, and it is easy to see that the people who do not know how to read or write because they had no schooling in their childhood, **do** know how to **think**, and that they understand their own problems better than any technician.

All these problems exploding and causing trouble even in the rich, industrialized countries bring our attention to the results of a research study headed by Willy Brandt and conducted by the United Nations. After visits to industrial countries, Third World countries and some areas of great deprivation and misery and discussions with many high-level technicians, a conclusion was reached: **that the rich, industrialized countries of the Northern hemisphere must use their abilities not only to give aid to the Third World, since aid alone does not resolve problems.**

(Instead, there must be) a genuine attempt to develop the countries of the South, the Third World. (If this were not done) the countries of the North would be unable to maintain their present position of wealth, tranquility and progress.

It is easy to see that the rich countries are in a dangerous position. Why try to suppress the internal debts? Governments can do so, but with dangerous consequences. We cannot ignore the fact that developed countries already have problems of unemployment. Rich countries with a high level of production: to whom will they sell? To other rich countries, which also have a high level of production? To the Third World, already burdened with debt? Today the debt problem is being studied by experts. They verify the point that our fantastic debts are, to a large extent, the result of forgetting the ethics of economic problems.

The problems are reaching the point of absurdity. What can we do about them? We must try to convince the rich, industrialized countries that, along with making use of human intelligence, they must also take into account God's plan. We persist in speaking about the First, Second, Third and Fourth Worlds. Yet God has not created several different worlds, He has created only one, with one family.

How can we link and join together, no matter where we are? Through all religions there is now a movement toward mutual understanding, to discover what joins us together, rather than what separates us. Three months ago, in Córdoba, Spain, Jews, Christians and Muslims meeting together were all asking: 'How can we work together toward a more humane and fair world?' Different religions working together can create a world with less violence, less war for the children of today.

Recognizing the importance of this Forum, I hope that instead of being an end, it is a beginning. We already know of the very grave problem of homelessness: billions of God's children without shelter, human beings like us; of the problem of starvation, of unemployment, of debts. This Forum is (not only) about housing, but also about several different options toward development. A rich country calling attention to the need for re-examining this problem (of genuine development for the Third World), has a very powerful voice, and the world will listen. **Either we are saved together, or we will sink together.**

An Introductory Perspective

The eye of the beholder

Some years ago, when almost all politicians and professionals regarded urban settlements built by low income people as 'slums', 'eyesores', 'cancers' and so on, two Englishmen were standing on a hillside overlooking a huge 'barriada', or self-organized and rapidly developing squatter settlement, on the outskirts of Lima, Peru. One Englishman was myself, an architect in the process of being de-schooled and re-educated by the experience of working with these city builders. The other was a visiting Minister of the British Government, who had asked for a guided tour, to see for himself what he had heard about such settlements. Working with the 'barriada' builders had already taught me much of what I know about housing and local development, and they had affirmed my faith in the immense capabilities of people, however poor they may be. I naively expected the visiting Minister to be as encouraged as I was by the sight of so many people doing so much with so little. But the Minister was appalled. He viewed it as a monstrous slum, threatening civilization itself, while I saw a vast building site and a developing city. We returned to the Embassy in mutually bewildered silence. Only some time afterwards did I realize that what we see depends on where we stand. One person's problem is another person's solution.

The cases in this book describe the activities of similar people in all parts of the world. They are presented as evidence of the immense, but largely ignored and often suppressed, potential of people with hope for the future. The personal experience described above illustrates the viewpoint which I shared with the other members of the HIC Project Steering Group in selecting the case studies in this book. The selection illustrates ways in which this potential can be realized – especially with the institutional support of governments and the often essential assistance of non-governmental organizations (NGOs).

Today, more informed people share this appreciation of the vast achievements of low- and very low-income people who are actually building most homes and neighbourhoods in many Third World cities. Yet even now, twenty-five years after the episode in Lima, and the first publications suggesting that the so-called 'problems' are also solutions, there are still many who feel disgust and pity for the poor, rather than respect for how they survive, and admiration for what they do despite truly appalling hardship. Those who know, at first hand, the people whose actions are described in this book will also know that they do what they do because they have hope. However, many governments still fear people's own organizations and actions, on which real development and the world's future depend. The overt suppression of local initiative by openly repressive regimes, and its inhibition by covertly repressive government are to be expected from those who equate development with centralization of power and wealth. Those who are genuinely concerned about global and local inequities can be truly caring by supporting people's hopes and their own action – by far the greatest resource for overcoming despair and grinding proverty.

Most donations from the general public are still given mainly in response to images of despair. Using patronising titles such as 'Give Me Shelter', the media still tends to present the poor as objects of pity, clutching begging bowls, and in helpless, dependent poverty. These insults to the poor probably do extract larger gifts from the conscience-stricken but uninformed populations of rich countries. Until awareness of both sides of the reality is more widespread, fund-raising for development and emergencies may still depend on such appeals. But increasingly, the mass-media have been communicating what many voluntary aid organizations already know and what bi-and multi-lateral agencies are fast learning: that relieving sudden emergencies and the on-going disaster of poverty depend on complementing, instead of ignoring the victims' own resources and priorities.

People do more with less

The cases in this book show that the continuing disasters of generalized proverty and vulnerability can be mitigated and eventually eliminated. They point to ways and means by which the more dramatic forms of homelessness following earthquakes and floods, famines and wars can be drastically reduced, even if they can never be eliminated altogether. By concentrating attention on the human resources of the poor, rather than on their often appalling conditions, the cases highlight the necessity of supporting locally self-managed action. Only through government policies which enable people can the immense potential for development by people be realized. Knowledge of what even very poor people are capable of doing and of what even very rich states fail to do for those who cannot afford market prices, undermines the false claims of those who would have us believe that either the state or the market can substitute for the community-based initiative of the people. Those who sacrifice people on the altars of the marketplace or the state can no longer claim that happiness tomorrow depends on frustration today. In fact, policies that inhibit personal and local initiative abort the community-building on which our very future depends.

The poor build for themselves an enormously greater number of homes and neighbourhoods than can ever be provided by public welfare and private charities. Between half and three-quarters of all urban settlement and homebuilding in the rapidly growing cities of the Third World are built by and for the poor themselves. This majority, usually four-fifths of the population, have no access to new housing supplied by commercial developers or public agencies. Donors to housing charities vastly outnumber those who are eventually sheltered by their gifts.

Most of the well-off, in rich and poor countries alike, must still be confronted with these simple facts. And these facts must be seen against the backdrop of one, overwhelming fact: that all life on our already badly-damaged planet depends on all of us doing far more with much less. When we see great numbers of low-income people building and improving their communities, and at costs three or five times lower than those built **for** them, we must admit that we have a great deal to learn from those builders and from their enablers.

Current policies usually frustrate and disable people. As an Argentinian squatter-builder once said, and as millions more, squatters or not, know only too well: 'There is nothing worse than being prevented from doing what one is able to do for oneself.' Enablement is the key. Neither bureaucratic mass-housing nor the uncontrolled market can build communities and eliminate homelessness. But **people** can, when they have access to essential resources and when they are free to use their own capabilities in locally-appropriate ways.

The word 'people' means everyone: infants and children, youth, the aged, and women as well as men. The achievements described are mainly community initiatives, not the products of any one age or sex group. The cases show that specific needs according to gender, age, health, ethnicity or culture are far more likely to be served through community-based programmes than through commercial developments or through government schemes in which people have no significant part. The cases also show how home and neighbourhood building depend more on women than on men, who almost always dominate the paternalistic forms of market- and state-based housing provision. Centrally managed organizations tend to be hierarchic and authoritarian. Community-based organizations, on the other hand can be directly democratic, and have little need for elaborate lines of command or representation. As long as their territories are clearly defined, community organizations have more to gain from co-operation than from the competitive pursuit of empire building or from internecine communal conflicts.

Only people can build community

By approaching housing as an activity, a process involving everyone, along with most of the resources on which life depends, we have a paradigm for the world as a whole. This may seem far fetched to those whose views are limited to the political and economic rivalry of market and state-based systems. But the perspective through which these Third World initiatives are viewed reveals that there are three interlocking and interdependent systems, not two. The cases show us clearly that the answer to the housing question is no longer simply a choice between or combinations of speculative commercial developments and categorical government programmes (that is, programmes that supply officially determined categories of goods and services to officially determined categories of consumers). The conventional view of politics simply as conflict and compromise between free markets and central governments is a gross oversimplification of reality, leading to incomprehensible explanations. It is impossible to paint realistic pictures of the world as we see it with two primary colours, but with all three, it is relatively easy.

A true perspective shows all three dimensions. The new politics are about new relationships between the three interdependent systems: state, market and community-based systems which are non-governmental and non-commercial. The perspective and principles can be seen more clearly in the harsher realities of the Third World, and they are the same as those now widely reported and discussed in the fields of food production and nutrition, medicine and health maintenance, education and other spheres of vital human activity. Many terms coming into current use already refer to the emerging third system, or to aspects of it: 'civic society', 'the voluntary sector', 'the informal sector', 'la société civile' and 'el sector popular' among others. It may not be a mere coincidence that our political vocabulary has no widely recognized term for the 'third sector' or system and that pyramidally-organized societies inhibit and largely ignore the role of women – the natural leaders of the vital third system. A new balance of powers at all levels and in all basic social activities is vital, for a workable and sustainable future.

As in any other view of real experience, the cases confirm the generally overlooked fact that most human, material and even financial resources are invested in homes and neighbourhoods. Dwelling environments occupy the greater part of all built-up areas. Most lifetime is spent in the home and neighbourhood. More energy is used for servicing, maintaining and building homes and local facilities than for everything else together.

Collectively, of course, we spend more money on and in the home and neighbourhood than everywhere else combined. So how we build and live locally is inseparable from the issues of human, economic and environmental degradation and development. 'Housing', conceived as a sector, like a slice of cake, is a dangerous abstraction. It is part of the mystifying jargon so effectively used by those who can profit from it, as long as the third system fails to express its autonomy and allows the state and market to take over.

When housing is usurped by commercial and political interests and powers, quantities are all that seem to matter. The qualities of housing, what it does for people, as distinct from what it is, as a commercial or political commodity, have to take second place and are often ignored altogether. This is not due to corporate or bureaucratic perversity but to the fact that no large, centrally-managed organization can possibly cope with the extreme complexity and variability of personal and local housing needs and priorities – demands that must be met if the housed are to invest their own time and effort in the acquisition, improvement and maintenance of their dwellings and surroundings.

It is only when people have sufficient choices and are free to make their own decisions as to where they shall live, in what kind of dwelling, and with what form of tenure, that a sufficient variety can evolve. And it is only when people exercise these necessary freedoms that the planning and building or the improvement, management and maintenance of homes and neighbourhoods can become vehicles for community building.

The evidence presented in this book endorses the claim that my co-authors and I published some years ago in **Freedom to Build** (Macmillan, New York, 1972): *'When dwellers control the major decisions and are free to make their own contributions in the design, construction or management of their housing, both this process and the environment produced stimulate individual and social well-being. When people have no control over nor responsibility for key decisions in the housing process, on the other hand, dwelling environments may instead become a barrier to personal fulfilment and a burden on the economy.'*

Housing economy depends on local autonomy
If the satisfaction of a society's housing needs depends on the economic use of available resources, then it depends on people's own personal and local knowledge. As politicians are fond of saying, people are society's principal resource. But as politicians are less inclined to declaim, the use of that resource depends on enabling policies that free and encourage people to use what they know and to do what they can. Individual and collective satisfaction depends on the release of personal and local knowledge, skills and initiatives.

Knowledge depends on one's experience and, as stated earlier, on what one can see from where one stands. What an insider sees, looking outwards and up from a personal and local situation, is quite different from what an outsider sees, looking down from the expert's professional altitude. While the connections between one small place and its surroundings are clearly seen from above, they are not easily seen from within. Conversely, the vital details are difficult to see or too numerous to cope with when seen from above. When outside experts are responsible for making detailed housing decisions for centrally administered multi-family developments, they are bound to generalize, however much they may have studied their 'target populations'. The managements are also bound to limit the variations, in order to minimize their costs. These are the so-called 'economies of scale', which become diseconomies when inappropriate scales are adopted for the job. On the other hand, when people make their own personal and local decisions without due regard for the larger environment, substantial losses may also occur, for them, for their neighbours, or for the city and society as a whole.

These complementary kinds of essential expertise must work in co-operation, in order to achieve an economic, convivial and environmentally sound use of non-polluting, renewable or long-lasting material resources. The relationship between the insiders and outsiders is critical. As their influence or effective authority over resource use is complementary and equal in practice, there must be sufficient equality to ensure mutual respect.

Local autonomy depends on central supports

Autonomy means inter-dependent self-management, not independent self-sufficiency, as those who confuse it with autarchy believe. People's own underused capacities and those of community-based organizations cannot be used as excuses to off-load governmental responsibilities. When government fails to use its unique powers to ensure access to resources and services so that people cannot provide for themselves or through their own local organizations, their essential contributions will be inhibited or even perverted. And the same happens when government abuses its powers through centrally administered provision, instead of supporting and enabling locally self-managed production.

The fact that so many people have done so much with so little in low-income countries, while so little is done for low-income people with so much by their governments, demonstrates the necessity of the radical policy changes which are already taking place. Increasingly, with some and perhaps vital assistance and encouragement from international agencies and NGOs, Third World government policies are changing over from vain attempts to supply public housing to the support of locally self-managed initiatives. The necessity of enabling policies is not so obvious in countries whose governments can afford to subsidize all who cannot pay current market prices. But as the longer-term social and economic costs of depriving people of their freedom of choice and responsibilities turn people's demands to be housed into demands to house themselves, we become increasingly interested in Third World experience and what it can teach.

In his address to the United Nations Commission on Human Settlements in Istanbul on May 5, 1986, Dr. Arcot Ramachandran, Executive Director of the UN Centre for Human Settlements, declared that:

'Our agenda for the next 10 years must be to find the necessary capacities to apply (these) enabling strategies: (while we cannot be sure of success) we can only give a guarantee of failure for any other kind of strategy.'

Internationally, there is a growing acceptance of the fact that market-based, state-based and mixed housing supply policies have failed. The only alternatives are those based on the third sector or system which can be supported and enabled, instead of being suppressed and disabled by market and state monopolies.

In the necessarily general and question-begging terms that one has to use in a summary, an enabling policy has to create a new balance between the complementary powers of the three systems – even where the third, people and community-based system is badly eroded and weak as in Britain and most other highly industrialized and institutionalized countries. Dr. Ramachandran's agenda implies a recognition of local capacities for deciding what to do locally, and of central capacities for enabling local self-management by ensuring access to resources and for setting the limits to what may be done by people and their own community-based organizations and enterprises. Partnerships between these kinds of authority involve negotiation. The existence of mediating structures is therefore a pre-requisite for an enabling policy.

NGOs and the community-based organizations (CBOs) which they serve are essential. Only they can build up the necessary political pressures and only they can successfully balance opposing interests. Individuals and small groups are generally dependent on mediating organizations for successful negotiation. Ideally, these are their own community-based organizations, but more often, people and their own CBOs depend on third party NGOs to assist in two vital ways:

– to help people to organize, to articulate their demands, to assess their own resources, to plan and implement their own programmes and to manage and maintain their own homes and neighbourhoods; and
– to act as mediators between people and their CBOs in their negotiations with the commercial enterprises and government agencies.

Only very small minorities can depend on NGOs to provide them with homes or to improve their communities – even smaller numbers than those who can expect government to do the same. In other words, NGOs can and do make essential contributions to changes of policy, through the demonstration of alternative ways and means of home and neighbourhood building – ways and means that show what industry and government can and must do in order to enable people to build a just and sustainable society.

John F.C. Turner, London, January 1988.

NGO promotes community development

Documentation:
Marijke Vandersuypen Muyaba
Harrington Jere
Francis Ndilila
c/o HUZA, PO Box 50141
Lusaka, Zambia.

Human Settlements of Zambia

Advisor: John F.C. Turner
AHAS, UK.

Text: Bertha Turner and
Andrew Maskrey
AHAS, UK.

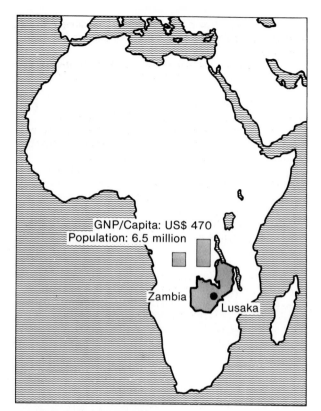

GNP/Capita: US$ 470
Population: 6.5 million

Zambia

Lusaka

Population Lusaka (1980): 536,000
Population Lusaka squatter areas where HUZA is involved
(1986): over 250,000

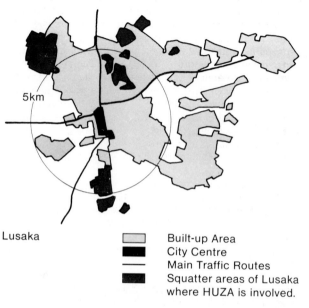

Lusaka

5km

	Built-up Area
	City Centre
	Main Traffic Routes
	Squatter areas of Lusaka where HUZA is involved.

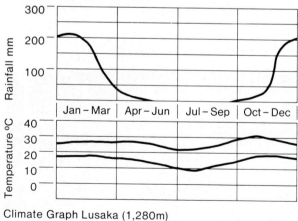

Climate Graph Lusaka (1,280m)

Lusaka 1975

Since 1975, due to inflation (800% since 1976) and the devaluation of the national currency (250% in 1985), income patterns have changed drastically.

Squatter areas of Lusaka

Percentage Distributions of Population by Income Level
S=when 85% of household income must be spent on food

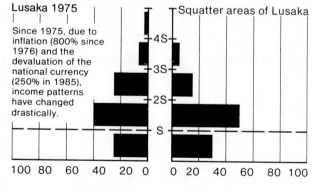

Human Settlements of Zambia (HUZA) is a national non-governmental organization (NGO) acting in the three main areas of Zambian development: economic, social and political. Working independently between the grass roots and the authorities, HUZA influences the direction and quality of development. In 1964, the government invited the American Friends Service Committee (AFSC) to participate in the self-help housing economic and social development of Zambia, and again, in 1974 to promote community participation in the Lusaka settlement up-grading and sites-and-services programme. In 1982, AFSC Zambia became Human Settlements of Zambia (HUZA) by handing over to Zambian staff. With the redirection of Zambia's declining copper-based economy toward agricultural development and small-scale industry, HUZA's programme has changed. The focus is now on promoting income-earning activities, improving nutrition and health and reducing living and house-building costs - all with the participation of women and youth.

A one-party, participatory democracy
Zambia's United National Independence Party operates under a well-defined set of guidelines and the republican constitution. At the same time, it also encourages self-criticism and innovative ideas.

The Party framework is designed to maximize 'bottom-up' participation:

1. Everyone belongs to a Section of 25 households, represented by 4 men, 4 youths and 4 women.

2. 10 Sections form a Branch represented by 4 youths, 4 women and 4 men.

3. Branches are grouped in Wards whose Chairmen are elected by all registered voters. Ward Chairmen, who also serve as local District Councillors, preside over the Ward Committee of 8 men, 8 women and 8 youths.

4. District Councillors send delegates to Provincial Councils.

Abbreviations:

AFSC   American Friends Service Committee
EDF   European Development Fund
NHA   National Housing Authority
HPU   Housing Project Unit
HUZA   Human Settlements of Zambia
LCC   Lusaka City Council
LUDC   Lusaka Urban District Council
RPG   Road Planning Group

5. The Provincial and District Councillors, along with Members of Parliament, form delegations to the Central Committee.

6. The Central Committee is elected every 5 years by the National Council and headed by the President of Zambia.

The institutional framework
Projects undertaken in a particular Section must be supported by that Section's Chairman and his committee. Projects involving 10 Sections or more are appraised by the Branch Chairman and committee. Projects requiring legislative approval are channelled through the Ward Committee whose Chairman, as a member of the District Council, can present this to the District and Provincial Committees for legal backing. This is the institutional framework in which HUZA operates. Experience suggests that it does generate a consensus and does enable popular participation.

Housing needs in Lusaka
The AFSC programme which launched HUZA was a supportive government response to the housing needs of the rapidly growing population of Lusaka. By 1974, ten years after independence, Lusaka's population had grown to well over quarter of a million, nearly half of whom lived in the peripheral, unserviced settlements.

Before HUZA started.

PHOTO: HUZA, LUSAKA, ZAMBIA

HUZA

Rural-urban migration
In 1974 nearly 90 per cent of adult residents of Lusaka's peri-urban settlements were migrants from the following areas of Zambia:

Eastern Zambia	50 per cent
Northern Province	21 per cent
Central Province	7 per cent
Western Province	5 per cent
Luapala Province	4 per cent
Southern Province	4 per cent
North-western Province	2 per cent
Copperbelt	0.4 per cent

Primary Sample Survey, HPU 1974
Only 10 per cent had lived in Lusaka before 1960.

The population was and still is a socio-economic mix: about two-thirds of the households had (and continue to have) very low incomes, at or near subsistence level, needing to spend at least three-quarters of their income on food and fuel alone. The other third have varying savings margins with a significant number in the lower-middle income bracket, needing to spend no more than one-third of their income on food and fuel.

Sites without services
Most peri-urban settlement dwellings in 1974 had 2-3 rooms with sun-dried mud brick walls and corrugated sheet roofs of asbestos cement or galvanized steel. There were no utilities, few community facilities and roads were ungraded with no surface-water drainage. Residents provided themselves with wells, pit latrines and some garbage pits. The settlements were dispersed, imposing long journeys to work for many.

Moving toward a support policy

Facing up to realities
By the early 1970s, the authorities had accepted that 'squatter compounds' could not be eradicated. It was equally impossible to relocate their people in rural areas or in publicly subsidized housing. Influenced by Peruvian legislation of 1961 which allowed for the regularization of improvable squatter settlements and the provision of sites with minimal services, the Zambian government passed a similar Act in 1974, the first of its kind in Africa.

Upgrading planned without participation
In the same year work began on up-grading unserviced 'squatter compounds'. The norms and procedures were negotiated with the programme's co-funder, the World Bank. People's participation took place indirectly, through the involvement of two organizations: American Friends Service Committee and UNICEF. The programme was to provide households with 30-year occupancy licenses; water piped to outdoor stand-pipes, shared by 25 houses; improved roads; street-lighting and refuse removal. Community facilities such as schools, health and community centres and markets were also included, along with building material loans to improve or build homes.

NGO assists achievements
By 1978 about 160,000 people in 27,000 households had been served by the up-grading projects in three large settlements (Chawama, George and Garden/Chaisa/Chipata) about three-quarters of their total population. Another 7,550 households had been provided with minimally serviced plots, including the 5,400 households who had been displaced by the improvements. Credits for building materials were given to a total value of US$3 million.

Achieving community participation
Due to community involvement in the implementation phase, no serious opposition occurred during the four years of field activity. The relocation of 4,000 houses to make way for roads and services was accepted along with the relocation of 8,000 households and the disruptive effects of major infrastructure construction. Community participation in carrying out official plans was achieved by the Housing Project Unit (HPU) within the Lusaka City Council. Four of the six staff members were AFSC personnel bringing with them their previous experience of working with local community groups on AFSC's successful 1969 Kafue self-help housing project.

Using existing decision-making structures
The Section was chosen as the unit of communication and organization. Later it was found to lack the overview necessary to plan large areas and it also carried insufficient political weight. So Branches were used rather than Wards, since at that time, their effectiveness was not yet fully developed.

HUZA

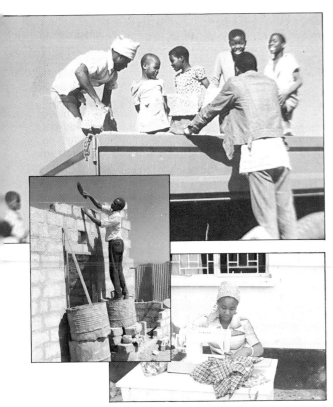

Involving the community

Public meetings using oral communication along with films, radio spots, posters, music groups and visits to completed areas gained support for the project. Evening and week-end meetings were held at Section level to accomodate working people, over a period of 5 months. Everyone was informed directly instead of getting second-hand messages through Party leaders, which, like most word-of-mouth messages, are subject to distortion. At Section level, layouts of resettlement blocks and the location of standpipes was decided. Face to face, direct local communication at meetings allowed the different interests to reach consensus and encouraged leaders to develop a more responsive attitude toward the community. Section leaders then took their proposals to Branch level meetings.

RPGs: a forum for community decisions

The Road Planning Group (RPG) was the main body for making community decisions. RPGs included community leaders and party officials. With the help of HPU and by 'road walks', physically marking the area with pegs, they planned the layout of road routes, school sites and decided which houses were in the path of works. If families could not afford to move, alternatives were worked out.

Limitations and unfulfilled expectations

The HPU had made tremendous efforts to involve the residents of up-grading areas in the planning and project implementation. As a result, residents' expectations were and continue to be that other local authorities in the country would follow that example. Accordingly, in 1976 the National Housing Authority drew up another proposal for a second World Bank-assisted urban improvement project for six other areas.

Despite substantial time and effort put into the programme, external, uncontrollable factors caused the economy to be weakened. Reduced employment and inflation had their effect on the programme, causing it to slow down and eventually to be suspended indefinitely. The programme was based on the principle of full cost recovery and on unrealistic assumptions about low-income people's priorities. Private renting and resale of houses was restricted along with other ways in which low-income people earn their livings. The collapse of world copper markets and the decline of national and personal incomes accelerated the inevitable paralysis. By 1986, Zambian currency was devalued by 250 per cent. In 1973, 80 per cent of residents were owner

HUZA

occupiers, but by 1976, this had dropped to 54 per cent and by 1986 to 40 per cent. As participation benefitted owners more than renters, it declined, slowing improvements and ruining maintenance. The government's rising foreign debt and its people's declining real incomes compounded Lusaka City Council's problems in recovering payments for improvements. The ineffective servicing and maintenance by the LUDC caused even more reluctance to pay. Debts rose and authority was eroded. By 1978 less than half the payments due were being collected.

Decentralization and co-operation

In 1980, in keeping with long-standing, stated policies of self-help and self- reliance, the government introduced a decentralization policy, to meet local priorities and to mobilize under-used resources. The copper industry was operating at a loss, the economy was worsening and there was a need to increase small-scale industry and agriculture. These changes shaped HUZA's role as promotor of community organization and enterprise and as a mediator between people and government.

Complementing limited government powers
HUZA now concentrates on community-based activities, maximizing local resources, since NGOs are better placed to promote these vital grass-root activities than government. HUZA also recognizes that it must act in ways that match, enhance and complement local government services and programmes. Early success of the up-grading programme was largely due to AFSC. But by raising people's awareness, expectations and demands, the problem of government's limited capacity to respond was aggravated. HUZA, as AFSC's successor, now responds to this problem. HUZA's initiatives show how more can be achieved with less, building community without imposing personal or national debts.

The case of the incinerator
Some common institutional barriers to local projects and the comparative advantages of NGOs' roles are illustrated by the case of the incinerator. The Chawama Urban Health Clinic was built by Lusaka Urban District Council with government funds in 1984. But the incinerator for the maternity wing was not in the plans and the clinic could not be used until one was provided. As it was not in the Ministry's budget, local councillors were told that an incinerator could not be built until the next financial year. So the clinic, a large investment

on which lives depended, was held up for want of a very small expenditure. Fortunately, HUZA was able to mediate, negotiating permission for the community to build the incinerator themselves, mobilizing resources that government cannot reach.

Reducing expenses and increasing incomes

Three overlapping areas of action
HUZA promotes self-help and self-reliance for development in human settlements. In a low-income country with few international market prospects, reducing costs-of-living and increasing incomes are complementary. HUZA promotes local income-earning training and local enterprise, helping people to get more from their own resources and to improve their health. HUZA works in three complementary programmes that often overlap: Shelter Provision and Improvement through technical assistance and training; lending tools; community leadership training and education in finance, law and land. For example, the Chawama skills training centre provides courses in construction and is developing the production of fibre-cement roofing sheets.

Health, Nutrition, and Gardening through health education; nutrition and cookery training; tools and technical assistance for food growing. For example, in addition to many individual garden plots 20 hectares of land adjacent to the Jack community have been allocated for crops.

Promotion of Productive Enterprise through skills training for local entrepreneurs; loans from a revolving fund; promoting appropriate technologies; research and evaluation of informal sector activities and potentials. For example, the Chawama centre runs courses for clothing design and making, and technical and marketing assistance is provided for women's co-operative clothing and soap manufacturing enterprises.

Economies depend on women
Women are acknowledged as a major force in HUZA programmes. Women combine child-bearing and rearing with managing the household economies. It is they who introduce changes of health practices and nutrition. Women are the principal gardeners, urban farmers and market traders. Most of the income-generating co-operative enterprises, for soap-making and clothing, for instance, are by and for women. The management of home-building and much of the labour is provided by the women.

Community–based urban development in Ethiopia

Documentation:
A. G/Egziabher, Y. Hailu,
T. Tekle, T. Debas
Redd Barna, PO Box 6589,
Addis Ababa, Ethiopia.

Kebele 41

Sponsor:
International Development
Research Centre (IDRC),
Canada.

Advisor and Text:
Yves Cabannes,
GRET, France.

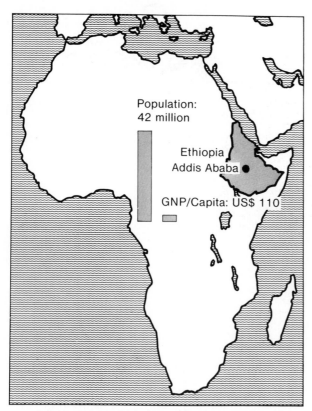

Population:
42 million

Ethiopia
Addis Ababa ●

GNP/Capita: US$ 110

Population Addis Ababa (1984) : 1.4 million
Population Kebele 41 (1984) : 4,157

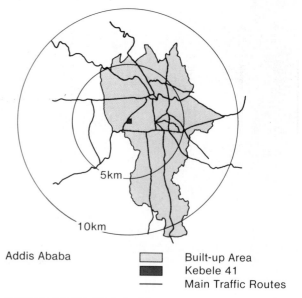

Addis Ababa

	Built-up Area
	Kebele 41
	Main Traffic Routes

Climate Graph Addis Ababa (2,400m)

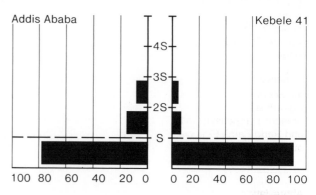

Percentage Distributions of Population by Income Level
S=when 85% of household income must be spent on food

Kebele 41 before the start of the project. No drainage, no waste disposal, no water supply. Bridges and roads were in very bad repair.

The project's history 1981-86

Fundamental changes have taken place since the 1974 Ethiopian Revolution. Urban people have been organized into dwellers' associations (kebeles) and urban land is no longer a commodity for sale or exchange, as speculation has been abolished (Land Nationalization).

Initially, a community representative contacted one of the members of the Municipality of Addis Ababa's International Co-ordination Committee (ICC), requesting permission to present a proposal to an ICC meeting. Permission was given, and Redd Barna-Ethiopia expressed an interest in carrying out the urban development project, due to the large number

Abbreviations:

ICC   International Co-ordination Committee
Redd Barna   Norwegian Save the Children

of children who would benefit. The proposal was accepted and the ICC assisted in drafting the project document. The agreement between Redd Barna-Ethiopia and the Municipality was signed in April 1981.

Kebele 41, near the market and one of the poorest of Addis Ababa's 285 kebeles, was chosen for the project, supported by a 1980 socio-economic and physical study and a 1981 house-to-house survey. Since 1981 the ICC has kept up the necessary contacts on the government side. Redd Barna and the Municipality have been working closely together, with increasing Municipal support, especially since the project began to show positive results.

In 1986 the programme was phased out and the activities introduced with Redd Barna's support are now managed by institutions at community, kebele, Municipality and central government levels. Redd Barna is currently concentrating its efforts in another extremely poor kebele, behind the railway station.

A community-based, integrated approach

Since the beginning of its urban development programme in Kebele 41, Redd Barna-Ethiopia has used a community-based, integrated approach consisting of four major components interlinked with one another.

Physical upgrading deals with the problems of housing, latrines, communal kitchens and community programme buildings.

Income-generating activities are a means of improving the social and economic standards of the community.

Preventive health programmes emphasize mother and child care.

Building the social awareness and participation of the community ensures the smooth running and continuity of the programme, along with long-term and profound social benefits to the people.

The major achievements of the project over the past five years are largely due to having such a well-organized community.

Four committees link the Project with the kebele structure

A zone co-ordinating committee consists of members from the kebele administration and representatives from each zone. In its weekly meetings, it co-ordinates the overall programme, participation and organizes collective labour activities.

A health committee meets twice a week and is made up of members from the kebele administration and representatives from each zone. Its main function is to activate and encourage mothers to participate in the various health programmes. Sometimes this committee organizes environmental clean-up campaigns in the kebele.

The social welfare committee deals with those having social problems and helps them to help themselves.

An education and literacy committee meets whenever necessary. Its responsibility is to activate and mobilize the community to participate, for instance, in the literacy classes. It also identifies those children needing help in their education.

Community awareness and participation
From the start, Redd Barna has involved the community in identifying its own problems, decision-making and overall planning. At present, the level of awareness and participation is very high, enhanced through taking part in the various committees.

Youth and Children Programme
Various activities have been specifically designed to benefit children, as part of the integrated approach:

Literacy classes were opened to 100 children (6 to 10 years) who were unable to attend regular classes.

A kindergarten for 80 children in the kebele's school, soon to be transferred to its own building.

Vegetable gardening was introduced to 80 children, along with crafts, such as woodwork, carpet making, needle work.

Preventive health programme

As poor health damages both individual and community development, special attention was given to having a safe and clean water supply through 3 stand-pipes which are run by the kebele administration.

Environmental health was improved through better latrines, dry waste disposals and showers. In future the City Council will pay the 'sanitary guards' who were subsidized by Redd Barna, to maintain these systems.

The vaccination programme began immunizations in 1982. After coverage of Kebele 41, the programme was extended to 5 other kebeles.

The mother and child health care programme includes pre-natal, post-natal and new-born infant physical examinations along with family planning. Traditional birth attendants (midwives) are also participating and assist many mothers.

Nutrition: Dry ration distribution - sorghum, powdered milk, cooking oil, for instance - to mothers and children under 5 years of age and demonstrations of nutritious food preparation are two ways to show the importance of a healthy diet.

Health Education: Audio-visuals are the most effective way to reach people. Communicable disease control has allowed the identification of cases of tuberculosis and venereal diseases.

First Aid service is given 24 hours a day and is run by the Kebele Health Committee and 120 youngsters.

Physical upgrading

Site: The major roads of Kebele 41 are under construction, since this is a project area of the World Bank.

Housing: The gradual improvement of housing conditions through repairs (118 houses); temporary relief houses (39 units); new houses (51 units).

Communal kitchens: All 52 communal kitchens repaired or newly built.

Sanitation: 24 newly built communal latrines will complement the existing ones which were maintained or closed. By building 6 public areas for showering, Redd Barna increased the number of personal hygiene facilities, helping to improve health.

Garbage collection: A system of garbage collection was implemented. Metal containers, each shared by 25 households, are regularly emptied into one of the 6 central collection points.

Public facilities: In order to develop the income-generating activities, various structures were built: a food processing plant, a grain mill, a garment-making workshop. Educational buildings such as a kindergarten, a nursery, a literacy campaign centre or a library and other health facilities were newly built or upgraded from existing structures.

Income-generating activities

Communal activities which include the grain mill, the laundry facility, a shower room and water stand-pipes are all managed by the Kebele 41 administration and are generating income for the kebele revolving fund.

A food processing plant has provided employment for 30 mothers. They work at cleaning, splitting and packing horse-beans, peas and lentils for sale.

The garment-making unit created 31 jobs for unmarried mothers and school drop-outs.

It can be done

The day-to-day achievements of the Kebele 41 programme have proved that a community-based integrated approach was possible in Addis Ababa, even in the early 1980s, a time of tension and rapid social change. The work at kebele level has become a successful reality, dispelling the doubts of the programme's early days.

Fruitful co-operation

Through its achievements, Redd Barna has gained recognition from various Ministries (Health, Housing, Urban Development and others) and from the Municipality of Addis Ababa. Redd Barna is a member of the International Co-ordination Committee of Addis Ababa City Council.

Around the end of 1982, other external aid agencies began to show an interest in working on kebele development programmes. In fact, NGOs like Concern, Oxfam and the American Save the Children Fund have asked for documents and ideas. Some of them are in the process of starting to work in other kebeles.

Though the relationship between Redd Barna-Ethiopia and the university was only in the project's initial phase (1980-81), the achievements of Kebele 41 are attracting increasing interest from various training institutions.

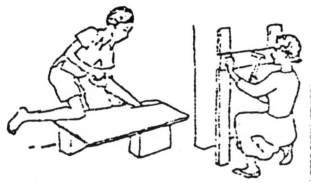

Training and education

The aim is to help young people to acquire skills to increase their employment opportunities. In 1986, 10 students were enrolled in a technical institute, 6 others have places in a job training scheme and 31 received financial help so that they could continue their education.

The people of Kebele, involving men and women ...

PHOTOS: PETER MYHREN, REDD BARNA, ETHIOPA

Kebele 41

Physical Improvements

From community awareness to government acceptance

1	15 Dwelling houses
2	Kitchens
3	Sewage and sanitation units
4	Income generating
5	Nursery
6	Food processing plant
7	Health post
8	Kindergarten
9	Nutrition kitchen
10	Kebele Hall
11	Mill house
12	Library
13	Weavers' house
14	S.C.B. and F.R.C. production shade
15	S.C.B. making room
16	Store
17	Literacy campaign rooms
18-22	Houses
23	Communal latrines
24	Test house no. 2
25	Test house no. 1
26, 27	Houses
28, 29	New latrines and kitchens
30	Communal latrines

... improved their physical environment ...

... and the level of services.

Three lessons and an open question

Upgrading versus urban renewal
The Kebele 41 Urban Development Project has clearly demonstrated that upgrading is the most feasible way to improve highly congested and densely populated low-income settlements. The alternative, urban renewal, is unaffordable to the poor and disruptive to their already precarious lives.

Role of the community
The success of Redd Barna's approach has proved the importance of integrating the social, economic and physical improvements upgrading both the environment and the lives of low-income settlers at the same time. It has also indicated the need for integrating training, education and skills improvement together with physical improvements.

The community is effective through organization
The Kebele 41 project shows the effectiveness of the community, organized through the kebeles and the zonal co-ordination committees. Effectiveness follows when the organized community participates in identifying its needs and planning, implementing and controlling its social, economic and environmental development.

Replicability
Limited attention was paid to cost recovery, since social benefits were of equal importance to the physical improvements. The project required nearly US$2 million, met mainly by subsidies.

Addis Ababa today has 284 other kebeles which need full or partial improvement. Replicability of the project might be limited in the absence of a budget allocation or a grant. An optimum use of subsidy will have to be worked out.

New structures were erected, local jobs created ...

... and health centers opened.

PHOTOS: PETER MYHREN, REDD BARNA, ETHIOPA

A local alternative to Portland cement in Rwanda

Documentation:
T. Schilderman, c/o PPCT
Post Box 32
Ruhengeri, Rwanda.

Pozzolana Cement Project

Co-Sponsors:
COOPIBO and PGC-HS
Belgium.

Advisor and Text:
Han Verschure, PGC-HS
KULeuven, Belgium.

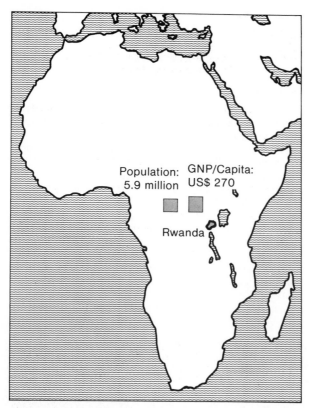

Population:
5.9 million

GNP/Capita:
US$ 270

Rwanda

Population Ruhengeri Province: 600,000
Population Kigombe District: 40,000
Population Ruhengeri Town: 15,000

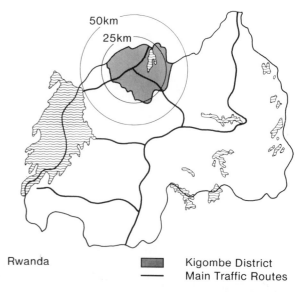

50km
25km

Rwanda

Kigombe District
Main Traffic Routes

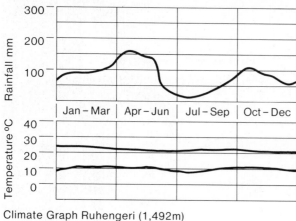

Climate Graph Ruhengeri (1,492m)

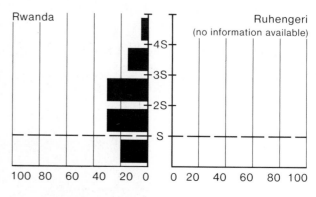

Percentage Distributions of Population by Income Level
S=when 85% of household income must be spent on food

Abbreviations:

COOPIBO   IBO Development Corporation Belgium
OPC   Ordinary Portland cement
PPCT   Projet Pouzzolane, Chaux, Tourbe
          Projet Pozzolana, Lime, Peat

Rwanda is a very densely populated and mainly agricultural country. Urbanized areas amount to only 6.4 per cent and there are no really big cities.

Traditionally people lived scattered in the hills, each family on its own plot. The houses were bee-hive shaped and built from organic materials. Owing to a scarcity of materials and to foreign influence, they were gradually replaced by round houses with walls of clay and roofs structurally separated from the walls. These houses are still to be found in the countryside, while the original type has almost disappeared.

The house is situated in an enclosure, the rugo, in which are also, at the back, a kitchen, a store-house, and sometimes a latrine. Under a century of foreign influence, the houses have become rectangular, allowing for the use of new materials such as corrugated iron and roofing tiles. These enhance the status of the owner and there are now more

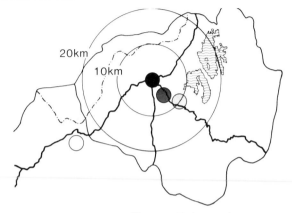

Kigombe District

- ● Ruhengeri
- ○ Pozzolana Deposit
- ◔ Lime Quarry
- ◕ Production Unit
- — Main Traffic Routes
- —·— National Volcano Park

20km
10km

PHOTO : COOPIBO, BELGIUM

A traditional dwelling.

PPCT

rectangular houses than round ones. The majority of houses are still constructed of wattle-and-daub, but mud bricks are becoming more popular, as wood is scarce and expensive. The better off also use burnt bricks, natural stone, and, occasionally, cement blocks for building. In regions with good clays, burnt roofing tiles are used. The most popular roofing material, however, is corrugated iron, now produced in Rwanda.

Housing in Rwanda is affected by the weather, which is often cold and damp. These conditions cause rapid deterioration, especially in houses made of mud. Common problems are: damage to foundations by ground surface water or splashing rain water; erosion of the walls, mainly by rain; cracks in the walls, providing shelter for vermin; damp earthen floors; cold and noise penetrating beneath sheet-iron roofs which have no other ceiling.

The inhabitants try to solve these problems in several ways: by building a base of natural stone and earth (often after the house is built and is already showing deterioration); firming the foundation with cement; building a concrete drain around the house; plastering the outer walls with cement or mortar of inferior quality, giving priority to the facade of the house, as an indication of the householder's status; concreting the pavement; plastering inside with cement or lime and adding a plinth; lime-washing or painting; adding a ceiling; projecting the roof.

Many of these improvements require a good binder. Ordinary Portland cement (OPC) is often too rigid, thus less suitable for improving earth-based constructions. Moreover, OPC remains expensive in Rwanda.

The new school building, using pozzolana-lime binder.

PPCT- a production unit for pozzolan binder

NGO stimulates innovation in local materials

Until 1984 all cement was imported, mainly from Kenya. Erratic supply and difficulties in transport increased its cost, leading Rwanda to produce its own cement. A factory was built, with Chinese assistance, in south-west Rwanda near the largest limestone deposits. Costs remain high owing to the foreign component (fuel); dependence had been shifted rather than diminished.

This development, although important for civil and large construction works, was of little benefit to the small-scale builder. Availability of cement improved, but not its price.

COOPIBO (Development Co-operation IBO), a Belgian NGO, pursued another strategy, based on reliance on local resources. Initially, it stimulated the use of lime and lime-Portland cement mixtures in building, substituting lime for Portland cement to some extent. Later it developed a pozzolanic binder using local resources such as volcanic pozzolanas, limestone and peat.

With the support of the Rwandan authorities, in 1978 in north-west Rwanda, it initiated the Projet Pouzzolane, Chaux (Lime), Tourbe (Peat). PPCT is a research and production centre for an alternative binder, with the aims of: developing a cheaper binder as a partial substitute for Portland cement; using local raw materials, such as volcanic pozzolanas and limestone; promoting peat as an alternative fuel to firewood and imported fuels; creating employment in a region with high un- and under-employment; developing a production centre run on a co-operative basis.

The pilot plant.

The laboratory.

Experiences from the project

An innovative technology
The PPCT project has three phases which partly overlap: research on an alternative binder; development of production technology; installation of a small-scale profitable factory.

Its first two phases have largely been achieved, and a small pilot plant is now producing. Its capacity has yet to be increased in the third phase.

The alternative binder was developed by PPCT, with some assistance from the Post Graduate Centre of University of Leuven, Belgium. It uses two important local materials: volcanic pozzolanas, dried with peat and ground to cement-fineness in a vibrating ball mill; and lime, produced in a vertical kiln, using peat as fuel.

The lime production line.

The binder, however, hardened too slowly and an additive was needed. Tests with various salts showed good strength developments, but presented implementation problems. Ordinary Portland cement emerged as the optimal hardening accelerator. The composition of the binder currently produced is 25 per cent Portland cement, 12.5 per cent hydrated lime and 62.5 per cent pozzolanas, ground to a fineness of 3,5000-4,000 Blaine. Research is still going on with other additives: various ashes, organic products and salts.

Considerable research also went into production technology. The small scale of the intended unit and the use of peat as a fuel made it difficult to rely on conventional solutions used in the cement industry, and the NGO input in this field was essential. A lime kiln and pozzolana dryers were designed to use peat as a fuel. The factory layout made use of gravity as much as possible, by setting up on a hillside. The equipment for grinding and mixing is more conventional and not specific to the cement industry. A small pilot plant is now producing 200 tons per month of this binder, which is much below current demand. A capacity of about 500 tons per month is required, for which funding is awaited.

The pozzolana cement thus produced does not reach the same qualities as a Portland cement, notably with respect to strength, but the product is acceptable for most building, and certainly for housing in Rwanda. It is also much cheaper than Portland cement. To reach satisfactory results, richer mixtures should be used, and much attention paid to curing.

A spirit of co-operation
PPCT provides jobs for 60 full-tme workers and an additional 150 temporary labourers who work in the dry seasons quarrying limestone and cutting peat. The latter are usually subsistence farmers, for whom this extra income is essential, since their holdings of 0.5 hectares average, are too small to provide an adequate living.

To provide them with work, PPCT tries to rely more on labour-intensive methods than on machines for producing its cement.

In the past, a lot of attention was paid to workers' education via literacy and other courses. These helped to increase their skills and participation, but had to be discontinued, mainly due to the lack of further subsidies.

It is as yet uncertain whether PPCT as a whole will become a self-managing co-operative. Parts of it might work on a co-operative basis, but the overall project requires managerial and technical skills beyond the level of the average worker. A more conventional organizational structure may be required.

A struggle for financial support
After some initial research in another project, PPCT was started by the Belgian-based NGO COOPIBO, with the support of the Rwandan authorities, and the financial backing of the Appropriate Technology Fund of Belgium. These funds covered only the initial research phase.

In October 1984, Belgium and Rwanda agreed to implement a second, much larger phase. It would include an in-depth feasibility study, followed by investment in a profitable production unit. So far, Belgian funds have not been forthcoming, despite the facts that real progress has been made and the project is running relatively well. External interests seem to prohibit its expansion.

Faced with such a situation, a small NGO is relatively powerless. Since October 1984, COOPIBO has continued its research and feasibility study and increased production from about 350 (1984) to 2,100 (1986) tons a year, using its limited resources, and with some assistance from other NGOs such as Oxfam. The Rwandan authorities are backing the project, but have so far have failed to unblock the situation.

Towards the application of pozzolan binder

Patterns of use
The cement is produced for a variety of uses: in public buildings; development projects; and in the private sector, mainly for housing. Most often it is used for plastering, but also for pavements, masonry and joints.

Setting formal standards
Establishing norms and standards for materials is usually a requirement of the authorities. PPCT carried out testing and experimental applications on nearby building sites, as well as negotiations with public authorities. Thus a set of realistic standards proposed by PPCT were accepted. These are comparable to those for masonry cements elsewhere, and thus far below the strength level of a Portland cement, yet acceptable for most building in Rwanda. Establishing the level of standards to be attained posed fewer problems in Rwanda, where authorities take a realistic attitude, than with the official funders who often insist on a higher quality product.

Housing improvement in the private sector
Local builders and ordinary people build most of the houses in the private sector and not to strict, established standards. Scarcity of funds and the resultant economizing lead to poor safety levels and high risks. It is more difficult to introduce a new product here, as failure will give rise to bad publicity and rejection of the product. Thus PPCT made a special effort to research and popularize its product. The first step was a technical study (including an analysis of application methods, mixtures, etc.) on the use of other house-building binders in north-west Rwanda, notably Portland cement and lime.

Testing followed within PPCT, substituting pozzolan cement for the original products in their various uses, and in identical quantities. These tests indicated the potential uses and disadvantages of the new product.

Recently the methods thus established have been circulated among people building or improving their houses. The aim was to see whether similar results would be obtained under less controlled conditions.

PHOTOS: COOPIBO, BELGIUM

The conclusions were that pozzolan cement fits in well with housing construction habits and that it can replace other binders in masonry, jointing, pavement, bricks, stones, drains and plastering.

Although improvements are still possible, the research has helped PPCT to establish criteria and utilization techniques for its binder and to increase its use among builders.

Improved finishing with pozzolana-lime rendering.

Application to stairs and base course.

PPCT

Lessons to be learned

To develop PPCT was beyond local capacities and not in the interests of the conventional cement industry. This gap was successfully filled by an NGO.

Some unique and innovative technology has been developed within PPCT. Yet it was impossible not to rely on imported technology for some elements, notably grinding and mixing. This influences the scale and complexity of production, and probably puts the management beyond the capacities of a workers' co-operative.

It has proved to be difficult to continue research while simultaneously developing a production unit.

Safety margins with pozzolan cement are narrower than with Portland cement, which is the binder people know best. Correct building techniques and curing of the new product must be disseminated to its users, as well as information on its shortcomings.

In Rwanda, it proved acceptable to develop a local binder of substantially lower quality than Portland cement. Though adequate for most building, project funders prefer to maintain higher standards and this is inhibiting progress.

A small NGO finds itself in a weak negotiating position vis-á-vis public authorities when applying for funds.

Rural people improve their housing in Tanzania

Documentation and Text:
Paul Bottelberg
c/o COOPIBO
Naamsestenweg 573
3030 Leuven, Belgium.

Tarime Development Project

Co-sponsors:
COOPIBO and PGC-HS,
Belgium.

Advisor and Text:
Han Verschure, PGC-HS
KULeuven, Belgium.

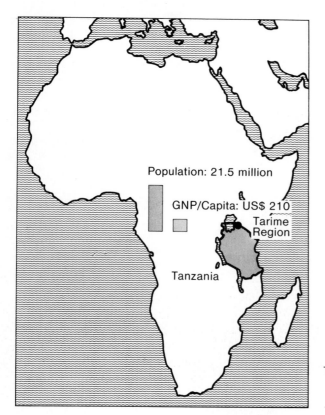

Population: 21.5 million

GNP/Capita: US$ 210

Tarime Region

Tanzania

Population Tarime District: 300,000

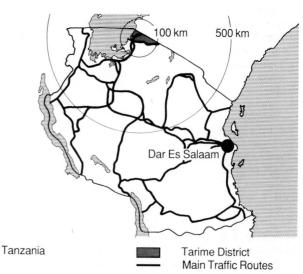

Tanzania

Tarime District
Main Traffic Routes

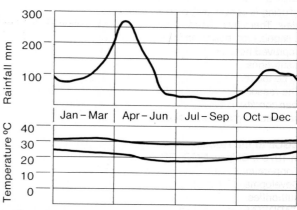

Climate Graph Tarime District (1,200m)

Income Distribution:
Detailed statistics on income distribution are not available. Only a small percentage of the Kuria people in the Highlands earn less then subsistence income, whereas among the Luo people of the Lowlands, this group is larger (between 10 and 20%).
In both areas the majority of peasants earn up to twice the subsistence income, and only a small fraction more than that.

Abbreviations:

CDTF   Community Development Trust Fund
COOPIBO   IBO Development Co-operation
Nyumba Bora   Improved Housing Campaign
TARDEP   Tarime Rural Development Project

Bordering on Lake Victoria, Tarime District is a three-day trip away from the Tanzanian capital and business centre, Dar es Salaam. Poor communications along with critical shortage of fuel and transport, materials and household goods increase Tarime's isolation.

Ninety-six per cent of the District's 300,000 people live in villages and engage predominantly in subsistence agriculture. The two major ethnic groups have different housing arrangements, but most of the villagers' houses have mud-and-pole walls and grass thatched roofs, which last about seven years. Traditional building materials are now becoming increasingly scarce and villagers aspire to a modern house of industrially produced materials. The need for shelter can no longer be satisfied in the usual way; demands for industrial materials and new skills are increasing.

Government policies fall short of aims
Tanzanian development policies are guided by the principle of 'ujamaa' and self-reliance. The efforts of the government towards villagers' participation have proved valuable in political, educational and medical matters. But as far as housing is concerned, official policies did not achieve their aims. There have been various efforts such as the 'villageization policy' and the 'Nyumba Bora Campaign' for improved housing, as well as the setting up of national institutions. Although well-meant, these programmes proved to be too formal. The effects, therefore, have been minimal. The reasons were mainly a shortage of building materials, loan conditions set too high, poor information to the villagers, understaffing and poor staff motivation.

NGOs to the rescue
In 1979 a Belgian NGO, COOPIBO (IBO Development Cooperation) and a Tanzanian NGO, CDTF (Community Development Trust Fund) joined forces to assist local authorities. The Tarime Rural Development Project (TARDEP) took off, emphasizing improvement of housing and living conditions.

PHOTO : COOPIBO, BELGIUM

Typical rural housing in Tarime district.

A consistent participatory approach

TARDEP contains a strong foreign presence in the form of both COOPIBO volunteers and funding. The District Authorities provide local staff, intending senior members to take over when COOPIBO withdraws, ensuring integration of the project and its management with local government. The project team of local and foreign personnel works with village governments and groups in preparing, implementing and evaluating development plans.

A variety of houses: traditional, improved, modern.
Left: the much preferred, but scarce, corrugated iron roof.

Phase one 1979-82: identifying and tackling the problems

The team started in selected villages, surveying housing and discussing related problems with the villagers. Problems were identified as low cash incomes, a scarcity of industrially produced materials, lack of transport and skills. Particular attention was paid to the villagers' own priorities, when looking for solutions. 'Bottom-up' participation was stimulated by regular meetings with villagers. This led to activities which made the 'Nyumba Bora' campaign a reality in the selected villages.

The Supply of Industrial Materials Section used a revolving fund to provide villagers with materials at controlled prices. It also supplied basic carpentry and masonry tools to local craftsmen. A lorry was made available for transport. Training was provided to local craftsmen in order to improve their skills and to organize village building. Finance was provided in innovative ways. As the Tanzanian Housing Bank caters mainly for urban people, programmes had to be developed which would identify income-generating projects and to achieve savings through self-managed building and the economic use of materials and skills.

First results

Previously, government action alone had very little impact on housing improvements in Tarime's rural areas. TARDEP enabled about 300 households in 10 villages to obtain durable houses by the end of 1982. In addition, the animation, motivation and training of village leaders and craftsmen undoubtedly contributed to their becoming more skilled and better informed.

The TARDEP experience in its first phase has shown that government policies can benefit by the presence at grass-roots level of a well-equipped organization specializing in a participatory approach which worked through animation and motivation of the local people. Government departments operate on a less urgent, larger scale and at a physical and social distance from the people they serve. Without an intermediary, communications break down and conflicts often arise, resulting in a deadlock. These problems are mainly structural, resulting from two differerent and conflicting scales of organization. TARDEP is able to provide this linking function, co-operating successfully with many individual officials.

TARDEP strengthens its mediation role between government and villagers

During the first phase of its intervention in Tarime, COOPIBO paid great attention to safeguarding the continuity of the project by integrating with the governmental set-up. TARDEP was able to gain the goodwill of both government and villagers and to collect the information necessary for formulating more appropriate policies.

A 1983 assessment by the TARDEP team confirmed that reliance on formal 'top-down' channels of participation and the concentration on scarce and expensive industrial materials and related skills led to the promotion of a house type which is out of reach for most rural people. The critical condition of the Tanzanian economy and the goodwill generated by TARDEP led the team to challenge existing views on housing. TARDEP would focus on spreading information on the production and use of local materials and would seek to increase the participation of the people in greatest need.

A many-sided programme

Phase two 1982-7

TARDEP's new programme, which was supported by COOPIBO up to the end of 1987, was certain to face resistance, as local materials do not conform to existing ideas of socially acceptable improvements, and as people do not expect a 'foreign' organization to deal in 'second-hand technologies' (their view of local materials). Using local materials has its own drawbacks. For instance, small-scale, clay tile production requires physical exertion, improved organization and consumes scarce firewood.

TARDEP felt its earlier course to be an unworkable basis for realizing the aims of district and national housing policy, and thus initiated the new programme. It started to organize villagers into newly created housing groups, according to the different house types used (mud-and-pole, adobe blocks and mud bricks). Initiatives were developed as follows:

Animation/Motivation: more emphasis was given to showing villagers that it was both possible and necessary to use a variety of materials and techniques and to organize themselves locally.

Access to materials: the supply of industrially produced materials is continued, recognizing, however, the critically low production in Tanzania. Small-scale, clay tile production units were set up in two villages, as well as production units for bricks and sisal-cement tiles. Reafforestation in several villages reflects the trend towards the production of local materials, as well as concern for the environment.

Access to transport: the use of TARDEP's lorry is greatly constrained by the scarcity and high cost of fuel and spare parts. Research concentrates on ox-carts and wooden wheelbarrows. The latter are produced in the villages by trained craftsmen.

Access to skills: central to TARDEP's programme is training for craftsmen, builders and group leaders. Together with the District and the Ministry of Education, COOPIBO

helped to set up a Folk Development College. Group leaders are invited to seminars on organization, leadership and book-keeping skills. Craftsmen and builders take part in courses with special emphasis on the quality and durability of traditional technologies (mud-and-pole, adobe blocks and others). Training is also provided on the manufacture of sisal-cement tiles, burnt bricks, wheelbarrows and on reafforestation.

Access to finance: the project concentrates on promoting economic use of materials and on self-help building, thus reducing costs. Some job opportunities are created in house building. Women are assisted in running reafforestation and protecting the spring water supply.

The new programme assessed

A provisional assessment of TARDEP's new programme, after three years of operation, is positive. The number of houses built reaches previous levels and the programme is more appropriate to the needs of the majority of the rural people. It is doubtful, however, that the authorities will change their preference for top-down participative structures. Besides, one has to take into account that at the time of COOPIBOs withdrawal, the organizational structure of the public sector will still exist.

As TARDEP is aware of these problems, it is now ensuring its relative autonomy from the governmental framework in the future through the continued presence of a local NGO. It has yet to be seen whether CDTF, a party to the TARDEP agreement, will agree that an operational Tanzanian NGO can contribute to the successful implementation of participatory development policies.

TARDEP demonstrates locally produced clay tiles on an improved mud-and-pole house.

Training has resulted in better skilled craftsmen.

Women participating in the process, concentrating on the protection of the environment.

PHOTOS: COOPIBO, BELGIUM

Experiences from a rural district

NGOs can promote
As 'modern', industrially produced materials are at first sight considered more desirable by village people, there is a great need to provide information about the availability of local materials and to demonstrate their use, especially as regional resources are limited. The implications of whether to use local or industrially produced materials should be carefully considered before any housing action is initiated. Concentrating on industrially produced materials in an economic environment of severe production and transport bottlenecks conflicts with the policy of self-reliance, and might further endanger the traditional housing activities of the majority of rural people. However, the promotion of local materials and related techniques still needs thorough investigation to overcome organizational and technical constraints.

NGOs can help to implement
NGOs are essential, even in popular governments having their people's interests at heart. Although Tanzanian policy is based on participation, a rigid and centralized approach was imposed on people from above. A 'foreign' NGO working at a local level could stimulate a consistent, participative approach, enabling a more effective implementation of policies. From their vantage point as a neutral, impartial body, TARDEP was free to comment on the severe scarcity of resources, not sufficiently taken into account by official policies.

NGOs can complement policies
Housing policy implementation in Tanzania should make use of NGO assistance in dealing with problems which the government has been unable to solve alone.

There is need to improve 'bottom-up' participation of rural people. Existing village organizational structures should be considered, but not used unquestioningly. The Building Research Unit, the Centre for Housing Studies, government departments and NGOs should operate as a network, to disseminate information obtained through research into local materials and their related techniques, providing a range of appropriate low-cost materials and techniques as an alternative to costly 'modern' housing materials.

TARDEP

Young people develop their community in Senegal

Documentation:
Benedict Lambal
Ufulal, Oussouye
Senegal and P. Nicholas,
E. Waas, M. Gaye
ENDA-Tiers Monde (RUP)
BP 3370 Dakar, Senegal
and M. Barbier-Wiesser
Ministére de la
Coopération, 1 bis
Avenue de Villars
750007 Paris, France.

Ukanal-Fé

Advisors:
Yves Cabannes,
Guillaume Chantry
GRET, France.

Text:
Equipe du Certificat inter-
universitaire sur l'Habitat
rural et urbain dans les
Pays en Développement
Catholic University of
Louvain, Belgium.

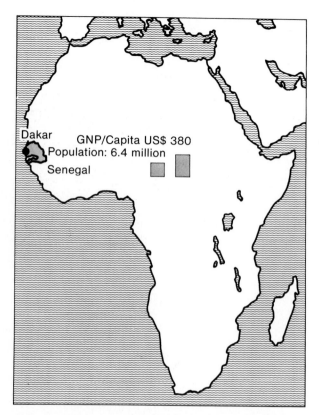

Population Oulouf: 6,000
Population Oussouye: 4,000

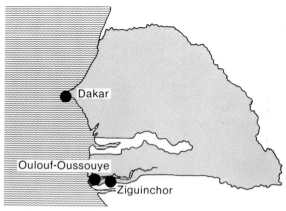

Oulouf plateau consists of six villages:

Community of Oussouye:	Oussouye Kalobone
Rural Community of Oukout.	Sengalene Kahinda Djivant Ediongou

85% of people in Oulouf, the majority, earn their living from agriculture. The remaining 15% are in the public service, work as artists or in commercial enterprises.

Abbreviations and names:

ENDA-TM	Environment Development in the Third World
ILO	International Labour Office
Ufulal	Let us go out
Ukanal-Fé	Let us achieve everything

'Don't be astonished'
In 1961, a group of young people still at school in Oussouye decided to gather together in their free time. This initiative soon brought together all the young people of the village, irrespective of religion, into the association 'Djacoume Djidiahale' which means 'Don't be astonished'. Its main function was to organize dances and other social events.

A year later it changed its name to 'Umentalal' (Hope), and opened branches in Ziguinchor and Dakar, where migration takes many of Oussouye's young people. Apart from organizing leisure activities, the group had a role in assisting those families who had remained in Oussouye.

1973: Ufulal
During a seminar in Dakar, the group changed its name to 'Ufulal'(Let us go out), in honour of a great sorcerer who had resisted colonial penetration. This signified a new and more

Oussouye

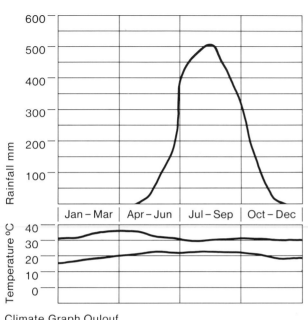

Climate Graph Oulouf

(Rainfall mm — y-axis: 100, 200, 300, 400, 500, 600)
(x-axis: Jan – Mar | Apr – Jun | Jul – Sep | Oct – Dec)
(Temperature °C — y-axis: 0, 10, 20, 30, 40)

open approach. Ufulal became an association with a statute, internal regulations and an elected board. On February 16, 1973, Ufulal was officially recognized by the Ministry for Internal Affairs of the Republic of Senegal. On that occasion, Ufulal undertook to make educational and recreational facilities available to everyone.

1976: Becoming aware of the aims
Seminars in Oussouye and Dakar revealed the determination of the young people of Ufulal to go beyond mere social and cultural events, and to direct their efforts toward development activities. In order to meet the needs of the women of Oussouye, the association and its supporters mobilized to find the funds necessary for setting up a kindergarten.

1978: First concrete results
During the rainy season, the first kindergarten, using the rooms of the primary school, opened its doors to welcome 130 children. The results were startling: infant mortality, which had been between five and ten children per rainy season, fell to zero. This decisive success persuaded the women to set up their own group 'Aidjidjo', to take on the job of running the kindergarten. They also began to cultivate the market gardens and collective fields of the village, providing both finance for the project and more nutritious food for their children.

1979-1986: Ukanal-Fé
Ufulal's main aim was to bring everyone together in an on-going alliance: women and men, old and young, people from the village and from Dakar, and to help the whole village community to accept the challenge of progress. With this

aim, representatives of Ufulal, who had met Mr. Barbier-Wiesser in Dakar, worked out a two-stage programme: 'Ukanal Fé' (Let us achieve everything). The programme will be presented to aid organizations when applying for their financial assistance.

Uniting to be strong
In the course of seven years, numerous projects were brought to fruition. Villagers were mobilized for the construction of community facilities (kindergarten, camp, workshop), to work out a suitable building plan and to initiate income-generating schemes. The intentions were twofold: to meet the needs of the community and to 'prime the pump of development' by creating jobs and enterprises whose profits would then be re-invested in the village.

Yesterday's social life
Traditionally, the young people met only to work in the fields, to hold popular festivities and to pray with the local fetish sorcerer. Since World War II, the young men have gone to secondary school in Dakar and St. Louis. Even if the young women do not study, they still go to town to work as servants. The consequences are the disintegration of the extended family, neglect of the rice fields, and the abandoning of certain traditions. On the other hand, those who leave the village to work usually send part of their earnings back to their parents, so there is an increase in cash income.

Today's youth
The influence of city life, especially on the young, seems to be the reason for the proliferation of small associations or clubs for the young. They bring together practically all the youth of Oussouye, both male and female. Their experiences in Dakar have widened their social contacts, transcending religious divisions.

Ufulal: from dance to development

Setting up Ufulal
Ufulal was especially successful in bringing together young people from Oussouye who are now in Dakar. A recreational atmosphere is provided where members can meet, funds for leisure activities are raised, and members can organize to help each other during the rainy season. But very soon, the association began to devote itself to community activities in Dakar as well as in Oussouye, with a view to improving living conditions of the village community.

With official recognition in 1973, Ufulal's members decided to re-organize the association, structuring it to carry out more formal community work. This also increased their chances to obtain project funding and grants. The association could now negotiate with the local authorities and the state from a position of strength and was recognized as a legitimate partner in development projects.

Community work
From the beginning, Ufulal attached great importance to the involvement of local people: in voluntary work as well as in contributions both in kind and in money. Ufulal formed links with the various partners: local leaders, local and national governments, and international agencies.

Tasks and goals
Ufulal aimed to develop the village of origin, Oussouye, by starting income-generating projects, while at the same time safeguarding traditional cultural values. Both the tasks to be undertaken and the budget worked out are based on real needs expressed by local people. Their ability to organize themselves is viewed as vitally important.

Ukanal-Fé does not depend exclusively on the participation of the village people. It also brings together the administrative and political authorities, the technical assistants and the Friends of Oussouye. Thanks to their involvement at various levels, all aspects of the project were successfully achieved.

The kindergarten
The usefulness of an association such as Ufulal was better appreciated in 1978 when the kindergarten was opened in Ossouye.

Mothers of very young children could now work in the rice fields with an easy conscience, knowing that their children were being well cared for. In that year, the women came together to form their own association, 'Aidjidjo', in order to play an active part in the organization of the kindergarten and in the cultivation of the community plots used as market gardens. Parental contributions supported the daily functioning of the kindergarten, either in the form of money (a subscription) or in the form of food (niebe beans, rice, palm oil, sweet potatoes, honey, or peanuts). The kindergarten's longer term finances were met from members' cash subscriptions, the proceeds from benefit theatrical performances and dances organized by Ufulal and gifts from the village or from a Dakar group, 'Partage' (Sharing).

The tourist camp.

The workshop.

The kitchen of the tourist camp.

Construction begins

In 1981 the association began constructing the new kindergarten building. It was both an example of the dynamic quality of local life and a demonstration project for the use of local materials. Completing this project required a combination of local participation, help from the authorities and financial aid from FAC (French Fund for Help and Cooperation) of the United States, and from ENDA.

The camp

With a second grant from FAC and with help from the State Board of Tourism, Ufulal began building the ninth integrated tourist camp in the Casamance. The system of building teams (mutual aid) was once more successful. From the start, the older people took an active part in the construction of the large, traditionally styled building. The camp has earned substantial profits which are then re-invested in local small businesses.

Productive activities

This next phase of the project was financed by the Overseas Mission Secretariat, an NGO. Several projects were set up simultaneously: a carpenter's shop equipped with two machines supplied by the ILO and financed by the camp's profits; the manufacture of furniture for the kindergarten; the construction of the welcoming house; and a fishing project. Work teams produced all these results, combining collective production and individual responsibility.

Housing and village lay-out

The building techniques which had proved successful in the construction of the kindergarten and the camp were to be disseminated in this phase.

At the request of the Ministry for Town Planning and Housing, ENDA and Ufulal co-operated with the residents of Oulouf in re-examining the town planning project of Oussouye village.

The plan put forward a new way of organizing the area, taking into account both current conditions and traditional concepts such as land rights, respect for traditional meeting places, and holy forests. Intensive discussion was required with the older inhabitants who knew the old land rights.

Change takes its own time

Ufulal has been working as a community development association for fourteen years, with many concrete achievements to its credit. Community initiatives are sometimes short-lived but Ufulal owes its healthy survival to patience, an old fashioned virtue. Sufficient time was allowed by Ufulal for new ideas to take root and to become understood and acceptable to local people. The lesson to be learned is that patience is of the utmost importance if community development projects are to succeed.

The Friends of Ufulal: a decisive factor

Ufulal membership is open to everyone regardless of nationality, creed, race, sex or age. Ufulal's strong desire to meet people produced great benefits in the form of the experience and energy of its technical collaborators. Help was also given by the local authorities (Town Hall and Prefecture) and by donations from fourteen organizations who responded to their appeal: four from France, two from Canada, one from USA, three from Belgium plus Oxfam Belgium, one from Groupe Partage, Dakar, one from the Senegal Government, and one from the Friends of Ufulal organization.

Ukanal-Fé: a worthwhile investment

Local job creation is the first aim of Ukanal-Fé programmes. At first sight the ratio of jobs generated to the large amount of money invested may seem low. But viewing Ukanal-Fé in its own context and over time, it is clear that the local economy is based on indigenous values. The transformed attitudes of the village community and the good use made of both local people and material resources are the key to the project's success.

The drop in infant mortality, improving the lives of women and children along with working conditions in the fields, helping the young adults to return to the village, building facilities and new homes: these offer concrete proof of the development project's worth.

Alternative tourism: a question for the future

Compared with the increasingly dominant form of tourism in Africa, the integrated camp provides an interesting alternative in rural development. Local resources create an opening for international tourism which brings in the foreign currency necessary to make the project self-financing. The symbolic and demonstration value of the Oussouye tourist camp far outweighs the single factor of financial viability alone.

Pakistani women lead a low-cost sanitation project

Documentation:
Quaratul Ain Bakhteari
and Laique Azam
c/o UNICEF
Karachi University
Department of Social
Work, Karachi, Pakistan.

Baldia

Sponsor:
Planning Committee for
NGO Activities: World
Conference on UN
Decade for Women
USA.

Advisor:
John F.C. Turner
AHAS, UK.

Text:
Bertha Turner and
Andrew Maskrey
AHAS, UK.

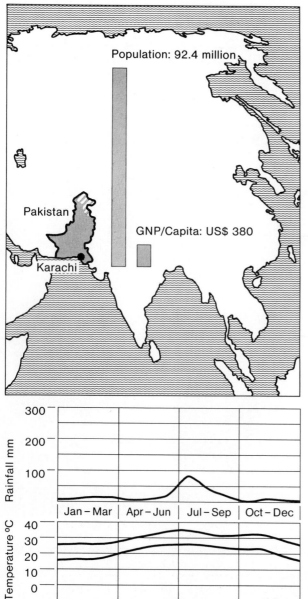

Population: 92.4 million

Pakistan

Karachi

GNP/Capita: US$ 380

Population Karachi (1985) 6.2 million
Population Baldia (1985) 200,000

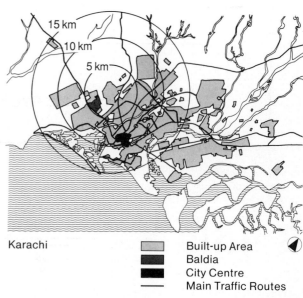

Karachi

	Built-up Area
	Baldia
	City Centre
—	Main Traffic Routes

Climate Graph Karachi (4m)

Rainfall mm

300
200
100

| Jan – Mar | Apr – Jun | Jul – Sep | Oct – Dec |

Temperature °C

40
30
20
10
0

Karachi   Baldia
                          (70% recorded)

4S
3S
2S
S

100 80 60 40 20 0   0 20 40 60 80 100

Percentage Distributions of Population by Income Level
S=when 85% of household income must be spent on food

Abbreviations:

BSPP   Baldia Soakpit Pilot Project
KMC   Karachi Metropolitan Corporation
PHC   Primary Health Care

Before BSPP – lack of sanitation and health information meant high child mortality and endemic diseases.

The Baldia Soakpit Pilot Project (BSPP) is one of two major community based sanitation projects in Karachi, the other is the Orangi Pilot Project. Both have generated remarkable social development but use different technical solutions to problems of sanitation, education and health. In the case of Baldia, the role of women was exceptional.

Baldia: an improving self-built settlement
Baldia Town's 28,000 households comprising 200,000 people are spread over 430 hectares. They migrated directly from rural villages to cluster in the 3 planned and 29 unauthorized 'katchi abadis' (self-built settlements). About two-thirds of Karachi's population live in this type of settlement, drawn together by kinship, tribal, village, ethnic, cultural or occupational ties. Baldia Town's first settlers arrived in 1947, others were relocated by the Karachi Municipal Corporation (KMC) in 1954, and refugees from the India/Pakistan war arrived in 1965. Like most of Karachi's people, they have built their own houses on land illegally occupied from materials obtained locally, and mainly on credit. Over a 25-year period, about 87 per cent of houses were upgraded from mud to concrete block walls. Water, once available for only 1 hour every 2 days, now flows for 2 hours a day, via KMC standpipes.

Karachi's average household income is about Rs1,500. Baldia's people work mainly in low-paid jobs as unskilled labourers or in industry. The average Baldia household income is just Rs700, the combined income of 2 earners to support the average 9 person household. About 25 per cent in Baldia Town earn less than the susbistence wage of Rs500, compared to 10 per cent in Karachi as a whole.

One child in nine dies before age 5
Before the project began in 1979, bucket latrines were used, discharging excreta though holes in the house's outside wall, for irregular removal by sweepers. Urine and waste water ran off into the unpaved street.

Lack of sanitation and of health information resulted in child deaths and endemic diseases. In 1979, BSPP introduced the idea of low-cost, long-life soakpits which need emptying only every 10 to 25 years. People's rural origins made them suspicious of having such disposal systems inside their homes. Involving local people, through their own organizations, in constructing soakpits was expected to bring other physical and social improvements to benefit children. The boost to women's status was an unexpected bonus.

What is a soakpit?

The idea of soakpit latrines is not new, but the type used in Baldia had distinctive design improvements. The pan could be flushed using a bucket of water, and the pit and pit-lining were deeper and built to last.

The soakpit is 14 feet deep and 6 feet across. It can be used by the average family of 9 for about 25 years before it needs to be emptied. Local stone, concrete blocks or a combination of both line the pit, to prevent collapse. To allow liquid to seep out, a tiny gap is left between each block. The pit tapers toward the top to reduce the size of the covering slab needed.

At the house floor level, the top is closed with a latrine pan set in a concrete slab. Care must be taken that the U-shaped bend of the pan always contains water which then ensures a seal between the above- and below-ground areas, thus reducing smells and flies.

The design can be varied by digging the pit to one side and connecting the pan to the pit using a length of pipe.

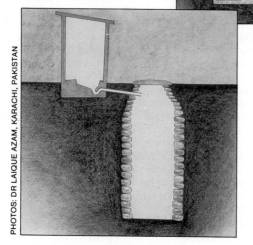

Cross section and plan of a soakpit.

Building a double pit. It can be used for 25 years before it needs to be emptied.

Four times more at lower cost

By January 1984, 200 pit latrines and 3,060 soakpits were built: 430 by UNICEF trainees at Rs1,300 each. Design modifications enabled residents to cut costs down to Rs600 each in the 2,630 soakpits they later built themselves. By 1985, 26 of Baldia Town's 29 'mohallas' (neighbourhoods) had been organized to do their own sanitation. Health and education projects followed, directly improving life for 80,000 people. Building over 1,000 demonstration soakpits with UNICEF funds inspired more than 4,000 soakpit latrines built by the community at an average cost of Rs800 each. Training for 60 masons and 100 families was provided by BSPP. Their methods were adopted spontaneously by 3 'mohallas' outside Baldia, producing 50 additional soakpits. KMC was persuaded to surface roads, streets and pavements and to provide a better water supply and street-lighting and power in 1984.

Breaking down cultural barriers

Build upon existing structures

Technology alone does not solve problems. The project team spent the first year going from house to house on foot. They had no office or vehicle. They explained the soakpit plan, asked for help, identified leaders and organizations and built up a relationship with the community. They built their project on the structure of existing community organizations. It was no accident that BSPP took 18 months to organize the first sanitation committee to build the soakpits. They planned to concentrate on a small area, and let people's enthusiasm take over. Once the idea had taken root, it spread to 20 other communities of over 40,000 people over the following 3 years. Over 2,000 pit latrines were constructed by 12 existing community organizations. Seven new sanitation committees were created, who then persuaded Karachi's Mayor to visit Baldia and to increase the water supply, and to provide roads and electricity. Small-scale demonstration projects ensured understanding of basic principles and produced large-scale results once the ideas were finally understood and accepted.

Home Schools for girls

Female education is discouraged in Pakistan: girls stay at home until marriage. Illiteracy is 78 per cent for women but is also a high 59 per cent among male household heads. Young community women were trained as teachers to operate 107 Home Schools: literally schools in their own homes. They have 2,200 students, 80 per cent of whom are girls and young women who were not allowed to attend other schools. By 1985, 3,000 children were enrolled in Home Schools: half in Baldia, half in 3 other areas. Teachers are paid by the community and have registered their 'Women's Organization of Home School Teachers' with the Government. A Skills Training Centre which is self-managed and controlled, was set up by an NGO with places for 120 girls. The former students, in their turn, teach their skills to others, producing a multiplier effect. A school for 180 children was also set up in a mosque.

Primary Health Care
Twelve Primary Health Care Centres opened and trained 13 Home School teachers as health workers. They immunized about 1,500 children. Over 1,000 mothers registered and one-third were trained to care for infants dehydrated by dysentery through a simple oral rehydration procedure. Growth monitoring has raised 400 children above malnutrition level. Treatment for 20 disabled children was arranged by an NGO. Three family planning centres were set up by the government and an NGO, and now serve 50 mothers referred by PHC workers. A maternity home was also built.

Widening women's horizons
Women, the major clients of BSPP, have an extremely high level of involvement which was not anticipated. Women are both implementors and users of the Home School and PHC. They are learning about health, hygiene and how to use and maintain their own sanitary disposal systems. It took two years of meetings with men's groups to persuade them to give BSPP female workers access to the women of the community. Young women whose tradition allowed them only domestic work and who were not allowed out, now have schools in their homes and conduct adult literacy and other classes outside Baldia.

The involvement of women in the BSPP reached a level which was not anticipated. Traditionally engaged only in domestic work, they have now become involved in community matters. Women run their own home schools and health care centres.

A woman field worker's conclusions

The woman community organizer who has been involved with the Baldia project since the beginning has first-hand experience of the problems and potential of Baldia. She therefore deserves to have the last word on lessons to be learned from the experience.

1. Baldia's people have shown their potential to improve their lives through their own home improvements and their many community organizations.

2. When community social and technical solutions break down, local groups lose confidence in their ability to provide sanitation.

3. Strengthening and improving existing community organizations develops trust and confidence. Working through them ensures acceptance of social and technical aspects, which then take root in the community.

4. Small demonstration models reach and teach more people than lectures and leaflets, generating cost-saving construction by local people. The cumulative effect of a series of small projects will over time become large-scale development.

5. Meet people face to face, in their own places, giving them as much information as possible, and in ways they understand. This creates mutual trust.

6. Women as managers, organizers and users have laid the project's foundations. A woman community organizer motivated both men and women, helping to involve women in the project and related activities.

7. Agencies should enter communities humbly. BSPP started with one community organizer and one part-time engineer. For two years it had no office or vehicle. As work expands, such facilities can then be acquired, responding to community demands.

8. Project funds are better spent on community and human resource development than on subsidized construction or administrative expenses. Most pressing are needs for technical advice, social support and community-based demonstration models.

9. Affordability, usefulness and cost effectiveness must always be kept in mind.

With sanitation as the starting point, the people of Baldia have experienced a fundamental change in the relationships between men and women. The limited relaxation of rigid customs allows men to accept and to benefit from women's newly discovered capabilities. Women feel more fulfilled and confident. Through this changed relationship, their children too will benefit.

External Organizations Involved:

Funds and Overheads for Pilot Phase of the Demonstration Soakpits:
UNICEF, funded by the Dutch Government.

Community Organizer:
Department of Social Work, Karachi University.

Construction Supervision and Training of Masons:
University of Karachi, Pakistan Junior Chamber of Commerce (Jaycees).

Infrastructures:
Karachi Metropolitan Corporation, Umbrella Support of Slum Improvement Committee.

Technical Assistance:
Central Government Agencies and Dutch Advisory Mission (plus additional finance). Water and Waste in Developing Countries, Loughborough University of Technology, UK.

Financial Contributions to the Project 1979-85 in US$

UNICEF, funded by the Dutch Government:		250,000
NGO Contribution, Habib Bank Trust:		
Mosque School	2,500	
Industrial Home	4,500	
Primary Health Care	5,500	
		12,500
TOTAL EXTERNAL CONTRIBUTION		$262,500 (17%)
Community of Baldia:		
Sanitation	413,500	
PHC	16,250	
Education	281,125	
Family planning, maternity homes, Home School Teachers, Welfare combined	552,400	
Community of Baldia Total:		$1,263,275 (83%)
TOTAL		$1,525,775 (100%)
Complementary infra-structural improvements by the government		$84,040,625

Renters take over and transform an Indian slum settlement

Documentation:
S.K. Mohandas, CDSA
Centre for Development
Studies and Activities
PO Box 843
Deccan Gymkhana
Poona 411 004, India.

Ganeshnagar

Sponsor:
MISEREOR
Federal Republic of
Germany.

Advisor:
John F.C. Turner
AHAS, UK.

Text:
Andrew Maskrey and
Bertha Turner
AHAS, UK.

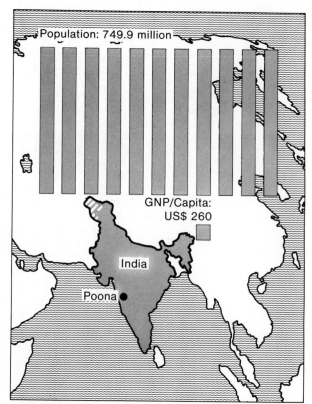

Population: 749.9 million

India

Poona

GNP/Capita: US$ 260

Population Poona (1981): 1.2 million
Population Ganeshnagar: 8,000

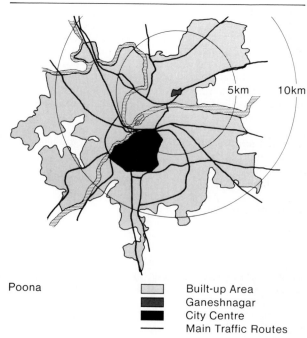

Poona

5km 10km

	Built-up Area
	Ganeshnagar
	City Centre
—	Main Traffic Routes

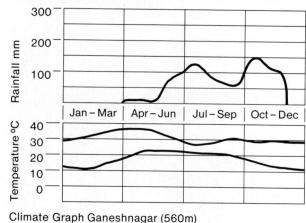

Climate Graph Ganeshnagar (560m)

Rainfall mm
300
200
100

Jan – Mar | Apr – Jun | Jul – Sep | Oct – Dec

Temperature °C
40
30
20
10
0

Poona
(no data available)

Ganeshnagar

4S
3S
2S
S

100 80 60 40 20 0 0 20 40 60 80 100

Percentage Distributions of Population by Income Level
S=when 85% of household income must be spent on food

Ganeshnagar is a slum settlement of some 1,200 families located in the Yerawada area of Poona, a large industrial city in the Maharashtra State of western India. In 1968, slum landlords took over an area of government land and built shanty huts which they rented to migrants. Since 1970, residents have formed their own organization, taken the settlement over from the landlords and carried out an extensive improvement programme. Residents prepared and implemented a new layout plan on their own and then persuaded Poona Municipal Corporation to provide basic services such as water standpipes, latrines, drains, paving of streets and lanes and street lighting. The settlement was officially recognized by the Corporation in 1976, encouraging residents to improve their houses and to carry out additional community projects through their organization. Local participation was remarkably high: at one point over ninety residents were serving on different committees, and the local organization grew in strength.

Living on the subsistence line
The population of Ganeshnagar is typical of slum settlements in Poona. Nearly 60 per cent of the adults were born and had their previous place of residence in Poona City. Around three-quarters of the predominantly nuclear families are Hindus, the rest are a mixture of Buddhists, Muslims, Christians and Bahais. Most working people are labourers and craftsmen, with smaller proportions of clerical workers and traders. Two-thirds of the families have incomes between two and six times the minimum wage (US$22), and only 3 per cent receive less than that amount. The median urban household of 5 members requires about two and a half minimum wages just to buy food. This means that few families have any savings margin for housing improvements.

The costs of not being organized
The 1976 Slum Areas Act allowed the Corporation to carry out a slum census, to recognize settlements officially and to carry out slum improvement schemes. Nonetheless, few slums have achieved such a high degree of improvement as Ganeshnagar.

A striking contrast can be seen in Laxminagar, a slum of some 5,000 households, also located in the Yerawada suburb. It was formed in 1974 on reclaimed marsh land which was not yet sufficiently solid for human habitation. In 1976, people formed an organization and demanded basic services from the Corporation. Drinking water

standpipes, community latrines and open drains were installed. However, the community organization splintered into small groups with no co-ordination between them. Residents were unable to organize themselves to obtain additional services and no further improvements were made. Existing services are not maintained and the environment is deteriorating rapidly as houses gradually sink back into the marsh while quarry pits full of stagnant monsoon and waste water create health hazards.

Making the most of improvements
Ganeshnagar shows the key role autonomous community organization can play in improvement programmes and local development. Only through organizing themselves could Ganeshnagar's residents manage to free themselves from the clutches of the slum-lords, gain Corporation support and carry out a wide range of improvements. Because they were not organized, Laxminagar's residents have been unable to use the basic services which the Corporation provided as a catalyst for further community-based improvements. Ganeshnagar demonstrates the improvement in environmental and social quality which is possible when people are in charge of their own housing programmes, even in very low-income contexts such as India.

Deterioration after improvement – Laxminagar.

PHOTO: S.K. MOHANDAS, CDSA, POONA

Poona: a major industrial centre

Poona is one of the ten metropolitan cities of India and is the third largest city in Maharashtra State. Poona's population has risen steadily from 597,562 in 1961 to 856,105 in 1972 to 1,203,351 by 1981. Nonetheless, the growth rate dropped from 43.27 per cent over the 1961-72 period to 40.56 per cent over the 1972-81 period. The population is expected to reach 1,530,000 people by 1991.

Slum population outnumbers overall urban growth

In 1976, Poona Municipal Corporation carried out a slum census identifying 327 slum settlements occupying about 16 per cent of the Corporation's residential land. About one third of the city's population presently live in these settlements, with an expected rise to about half the population by 1991. In the thirty year period, 1951-81, the slum population of Poona increased by 1,003 per cent, while the overall population of the city increased by only 139 per cent.

Rural famine swells the slums

Slum settlements are spread all over the city and can be classified into three groups. One group is located in the city centre; a second group is located out of the centre, but within the city limits and a third group is on the urban periphery. Most of this latter group of slums are recent, between 15 and 20 years old. The main reasons behind the formation of these peripheral settlements were a famine in rural Maharashtra in the late 1960s and industrial growth in and around Poona. The majority of peripheral slums are located in the Yerawada suburb, to the north-east of the city centre.

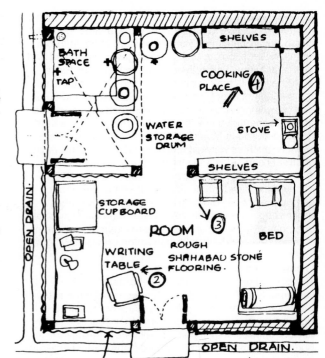

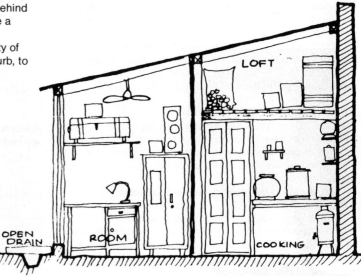

From rented slum to self-managed settlement

An explosion of migrants

In 1968, there was an explosion at a government ammunition factory located in Khadki Cantonment, on the north boundary of Poona. Many affected families moved to Yerawada to form a settlement on government land they called New Khadki. Neither government nor the Corporation took any action on the squatters. This encouraged slum landlords to build shanty huts on more government land nearby. These were rented out to migrants and others affected by the ammunition factory explosion. Ganeshnagar was one of the settlements formed in this way.

The interior of a Ganeshnagar home.

Protection racket

Slum landlords charged not only shanty rent but also protection money, supposedly to protect householders against any threat of eviction or demolition by the Corporation. Hired 'toughs' continually harassed residents. As prices increased and land on which to build additional shanties became scarce, landlords demanded higher rents from the residents. In some cases, residents were forced to leave the settlement and their huts were rented to other households who could pay more. If a family tried to protest against the landlords, their hut was demolished or their belongings destroyed. Housing and environmental conditions deteriorated rapidly as no maintenance and repairs were undertaken by the landlords. With no other alternative, residents had to pay both rent and protection money as well as carrying out repairs and maintenance.

Organizing against the landlords

In 1970, a few households formed a group to resist the landlords, and in a short period, managed to enlist widespread support from other families. They refused to pay rent and despite all efforts to the contrary, landlords lost control over the settlement and were forced to sell the shanties to the occupants. The community successfully pressed for a low price and some families refused to pay. By the end of 1970, Ganeshnagar had completely freed itself from the landlords' control.

Recognition stimulates improvements

First steps toward improvement

In 1971, community leaders decided to consolidate and legitimize the organization by forming an elected committee. The settlement was divided into nine wards, the residents of each one electing a committee member to represent them. The first move of the new committee was to prepare a new layout plan for Ganeshnagar. There were no proper lanes or open spaces in the settlement, hut layout was congested and haphazard and service installation was impossible. The new plan incorporated straight streets and lanes and a large open space at the entrance to the settlement. It was decided that families should keep their existing space allocation and that the number of huts to be demolished should be kept to a minimum. More land was required along the periphery of the settlement to make the layout plan work. The plan was presented to the community for approval and in less than a year, 80 per cent had already been implemented by the residents. Community space was protected by the committee from encroachment.

Feeling the need for services

After implementing the layout plan, residents felt the need for basic services. Drinking water, drains and sewers were non-existent and garbage disposal was also a major problem. In 1973/4, they pressed the Corporation to install services. Meanwhile, the committtee registered itself in order to obtain legal status. In 1975, the Corporation installed water standpipes, street lights, latrine blocks and open lined drains as well as paving streets and lanes. However, although this brought temporary relief, the services problem was far from solved.

Maintenance is as important as installation

Shortly, services became unusable due to lack of maintenance and improper use by residents. The committee decided to collect voluntary contributions from households to pay ten women from the settlement who needed jobs to clean drains, latrines, streets and lanes, as well as dispose of the garbage. This also made residents aware of the problem, ensuring their co-operation in cleaning the settlement. This initiative stimulated the Corporation to provide additional latrine blocks and water standpipes.

PHOTO: S.K. MOHANDAS, CDSA, POONA

Improvement through organization – Ganeshnagar.

Settlement recognition stimulates housing improvement

In 1976, Ganeshnagar was declared a recognized slum settlement by the Corporation, following the city-wide slum census. The land was acquired by the Corporation from government and from the Golf Club. This increased residents' security of tenure and encouraged them to invest savings in house improvement. Households built plinths and foundations for their houses using rubble masonry from local quarries. Using brick or stone for the lower walls and a variety of second-hand building components for the rest of the dwelling, a full-scale housing improvement programme was carried out. In 1979-80, the Corporation took over the maintenance of services as part of a city-wide policy decision. The residents not only helped to maintain cleanliness in the settlement, but also supervised the work of Corporation staff.

Launching new community projects

With settlement recognition and service installation, the committee launched various new community projects. The open space was levelled and raised above ground level and plans were drawn up to build a nursery school, a community temple and a gymnasium. In 1979, the nursery school was built and with the help of the Corporation, put into operation. A women's organization was formed which ran a day-care centre for children of employed parents and also a food programme for malnourished children. Sewing machines were also obtained from the Social Welfare Department of the State Government, to enable women to improve their incomes by doing tailoring work. In 1980, construction of the community temple was started and it was completed in 1984, along with a kindergarten school and the gymnasium.

Improvements strengthen the organization

With the increase in community projects and activities, the committee of nine members became inadequate. It was decided to form ward-level committees, as well as sub-committees for specific projects. In the next elections, ten people were elected from each ward, one of whom would represent the ward on the central committee. In this way, ninety people became involved in carrying out community projects and looking after the community and its services. Sub-committees were formed to look after the temple project, the nursery school and festival celebrations. When it was decided to set up a library, a sub-committee was formed, which also organized educational tours for the residents to other parts of India.

Consolidating the settlement

In the last few years, residents continued to support the community organization and to improve their dwellings and surroundings. Nearly all houses are now of permanent materials. Many have converted their front rooms into shops or small businesses, while the better off have added a second storey to their dwellings. Many residents have paid for individual water and electricity connections and many others share with their neighbours. By August 1986, about 40 per cent of families had individual metered water connections, while there were 20 water standpipes with a total of 50 taps. There were 10 latrines each with 10 seats. There were 5 large garbage bins which are cleaned regularly by Corporation staff, along with the drains and latrines. Nearly all the major streets and lanes in the settlement have been paved.

Before and after improvements.

PHOTOS: S.K. MOHANDAS, CDSA, POONA

Organization and community development

Improving through organizing
Through organizing themselves, even very low income people in a poor country like India have made substantial improvements in their housing and environment. In Ganeshnagar, organizing permitted the community to mobilize and use all their available resources, as well as obtaining support from the government. Locally appropriate solutions were found to local problems because people themselves were in control. In other settlements where people did not organize and were isolated from one another, they were prey to exploitation by landlords and no improvement could take place.

Security as a precondition for improvement
In Ganeshnagar, organizing gave people the confidence and security necessary to start improving their settlement. Obtaining recognition from the Corporation was another particularly important factor which increased people's security and the legitimacy of their organization and encouraged them to carry on investing and improving.

Ganeshnagar is no longer a slum
Eighteen years after its formation, Ganeshnagar is no longer a slum in the true sense of the word. Improvement has not been restricted to rebuilding houses. Through their own organization, people, with the support of the Corporation, have managed to provide a wide range of community services and facilities to satisfy their basic needs. More important still, Ganeshnagar has emerged from these experiences as a community. No one can quantify the improvement in the social quality made in Ganeshnagar, compared to the days when the hapless residents were continually harassed by gangs of hired 'toughs'. No government could have made that improvement unilaterally.

Indonesians participate in inner-city settlement improvement

Documentation:
Johan Silas
and students
Institute of Technology
Surabaya (ITS)
Eddy Indrayana
and colleagues
KIP-KMS, Surabaya
Indonesia.

Kampung Banyu Urip

Advisor:
John F.C. Turner
AHAS, UK.

Text:
Andrew Maskrey and
Bertha Turner
AHAS, UK.

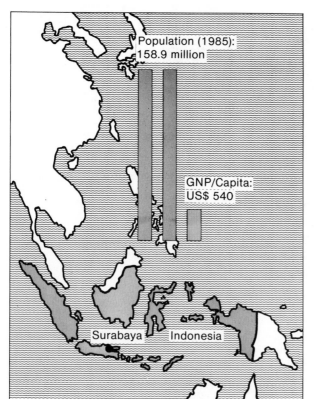

Population (1985):
158.9 million

GNP/Capita:
US$ 540

Surabaya   Indonesia

Population Surabaya (1986): 3 million
Population Banyu Urip (1986): 40,000

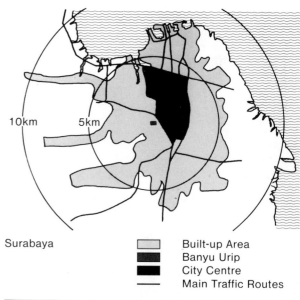

Surabaya

	Built-up Area
	Banyu Urip
	City Centre
—	Main Traffic Routes

10km   5km

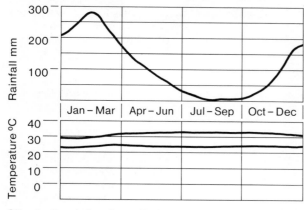

Climate Graph Surabaya (6m)

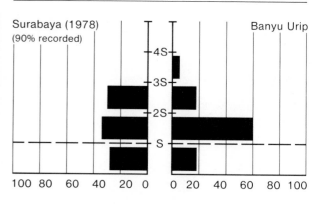

Surabaya (1978)
(90% recorded)

Banyu Urip

Percentage Distributions of Population by Income Level
S=when 85% of household income must be spent on food

Kampung before and after site improvements.

Banyu Urip is a low-income settlement or 'kampung' of 40,439 people in the south-west centre of Surabaya, the second largest city of Indonesia. The original site was an old Chinese graveyard where a few hundred people squatted and made their homes. In 1955, they were joined by ex-'freedom fighters' and their families, who also took up residence on the site. Banyu Urip was initially on the fringe of pre-war Surabaya, but the city has since expanded and grown around it and it is now a typical inner city kampung.

Nearly half the heads of family were born in Surabaya itself. Employment is varied, but with one common characteristic: most family heads have second jobs in the informal sector. The income level is slightly higher than in most kampungs, approximately 55 per cent of the population earn over US$760 a year. The area was subdivided into plots of approximately 7 by 14 metres: one for each family. As in most Surabaya kampungs, the houses are of one storey, most with floor areas between 50 and 75 square metres. Now that all have a water supply, many also have a bath and toilet.

Since colonial times improvements have been carried out in many kampungs by outside agencies, with little or no participation by local people. In Banyu Urip, people were involved right from the start. Since 1972 they had already been carrying out small-scale improvements through their own autonomous neighbourhood organizations. In 1979, due to local pressure, Banyu Urip was incorporated into the Kampung Improvement Programme (KIP), carried out by the local authority of Surabaya, with support from the local university. People participated in the drafting and discussion of the improvement plan, as well as in its implementation.

Abbreviations

KIP   Kampung Improvement Programme
RT   Rukun Tettanga (block level organization)
RW   Rukun Warga (neighbourhood level organization)

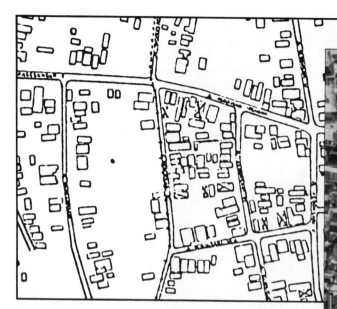

Most Indonesian cities developed through the conglomeration and densification of existing villages. After losing their agricultural land to urban services and higher income housing, the villages were transformed into high-density inner city kampungs.

Villages grow into a city

Most Indonesian cities have grown through a process of densification and conglomeration of existing villages, now kampungs. Today, about three-quarters of the 40 million urban population of Indonesia live in kampungs, many dating from the pre-war colonial period.

After the Second World War, incoming migrants who could not find space in the original kampungs, squatted empty or abandoned areas of land in the cities, forming new kampungs. In Indonesian law, the squatters were able to claim some tenure rights permitting the progressive development of their own homes and neighbourhoods. In Surabaya, almost 70 per cent of the population of 3 million live in kampungs. They are found in all parts of the city, from the central business district to the urban periphery. Nearly one-quarter were formed by squatting, mainly in the post-war period. The rest developed from villages.

Urban services are generally absent from most kampungs. Through the 'Rukun Tetangga' (RTs) and 'Rukun Warga' (RWs) the block and neighbourhood levels of local organization, community facilities such as meeting halls, schools and open spaces are provided. At the same time, a wide range of commercial activities flourish. The houses themselves evolve over time, extra rooms being added to meet additional needs and temporary materials giving way to permanent structures as finances permit. Most kampung houses generate additional income through sub-letting or use as shops or workshops.

Between 1979 and 1982, vehicular roads, footpaths, drainage, water standpipes and public toilets were provided by the KIP at a per capita cost of about US$22 for the 28,000 inhabitants served. Once the works were carried out, the community assumed responsibility for the use and further development of the improvements. Trees, shrubs and flowers were planted; street lighting was installed; a security guard house and meeting halls were built and houses were improved. In 1983 the community's request for the legalization of their tenure was approved.

PHOTOS: MR. ZAENUDDIN, SURABAYA PHOTO CLUB

Most kampung houses generate additional income through subletting or use as shops or workshops.

Participation means caring for improvements

BANYU URIP

Learning from the people

The Banyu Urip experience demonstrates the need for a change of direction. When people participate in the planning, implementation and management of the improvements, the results are far better than when an outside agency carries out a programme using a public works approach, without input from the local community. In Banyu Urip the formal improvements carried out stimulated people's own improvements to their houses and neighbourhood, an ongoing process which multiplies the initial investment made. At the same time, because

people were involved in the KIP right from the start, they adopted the improvements as their own, caring for them and reducing the need for future maintenance.

Banyu Urip is an all too rare example of appropriate supportive actions being taken by local authorities and professionals who have respected the kampung as a positive contribution to Indonesia's urban development. Learning from the people themselves, they have enabled the community and its organizations to tap into its own vast potential for improvement.

The other Surabaya: real estate and public housing

Kampung builders are not the only inhabitants of Surabaya. Commercial and subsidized private developments, co-operative and public housing have all contributed to the city's growth. Housing for the higher income groups occupies most of the available land and receives the best urban services. Kampung dwellers are too poor to afford such housing and are left to fend for themselves.

Government housing policy also gives a low priority to supporting the housing efforts of the poorest. Since 1976 there has been a public building programme to supply low-cost housing. The present Five Year Plan 1984-1989 budgeted US$933 million to build 300,000 houses serving 1,500,000 people. By contrast, only US$13.3 million is budgeted for the improvement of 5,000 hectares of kampung serving 1,500,000 people in 400 different towns and villages. In other words, 70 times more is being spent on housing the better off than on supporting low-income people's own housing initiatives.

Paradoxically, if the budget currently being spent on low-cost public housing were instead allocated to the KIP, it would then be possible to serve some 105,000,000 people. This is more than 3 times the total kampung population of Indonesia. But if the current KIP budget were allocated to low-cost public housing, only 21,425 people would be served.

Typical public housing and a kampung street.

Participation ensures improvement

Big improvements come in small programmes

Since 1972, when Banyu Urip formed its own self-help kampung improvement association, people have carried out small-scale works to strengthen their claims to secure tenure. Through the RTs and the RWs the community built footpaths and public toilets while houses were improved individually. Staff and students of the Department of Architecture of the Institute of Technology of Surabaya, interested in what people were doing, incorporated Banyu Urip in a survey to determine priorities for kampung improvement. They helped the community to press for its inclusion in the Kampung Improvement Programme in 1979. Once the local authority had approved the budget for the KIP in Banyu Urip, a draft plan was drawn up which was discussed with the people. The plan was developed and implemented by a general contractor in consultation with the residents. Greater care was therefore taken to avoid unnecessary demolitions of existing homes, and greater attention was given to detailed design of the many semi-public access paths and the few streets.

Taking part leads to taking care.

Not involving people leads to this.

PHOTOS: JOHN F.C. TURNER

Footpaths as key elements

The most important component of the KIP was the improvement of footpaths, accounting for a third of the total cost of the programme. Not only does the footpath improve accessibility, but it also stimulates house improvement by the residents. In the kampung, the footpath has a key social function. It is used as a playground, street market in the morning, for drying clothes and for street and wedding parties. Defining footpaths helped to define boundaries between private, semi-private and public land, ensuring good maintenance of open spaces and avoiding encroachments. As time passes, the contrast between Banyu Urip and other kampungs, where people did not participate in the improvement programme, becomes more dramatic. In Banyu Urip the residents care for their shared improvements as well as for their own homes. But in other improved kampungs where there was no participation, streets and paths are unswept, drains are often used as rubbish tips and open spaces are neglected. Many improvements deteriorate so seriously that they need rebuilding after a few years.

A resource still untapped

The KIP represents a real alternative to the policies of supplying low-cost housing. Kampung improvements help to generate a supportive housing environment for large numbers of very-low-income people.

Scarce government resources are used to match the needs of the low-income majority and full advantage is taken of otherwise wasted resources which kampung communities already have in their hands. Public housing projects serve the wrong groups: those who least need government subsidy. The KIP in Banyu Urip shows how much can be achieved with a relatively small capital investment and far lower long-term costs.

Participation means caring for improvements.

PHOTO : MR ZAENUDDIN, SURABAYA PHOTO CLUB

A slum community's thirty-year struggle in Thailand

Documentation:
Centre for Housing and
Human Settlements
Studies (CHHSS),
HSF and Klong Toey
Community Group
Bangkok, Thailand.

Klong Toey

Sponsor:
International Development
Research Centre (IDRC)
Canada

Advisor:
Han Verschure
PGC-HS KULeuven
Belgium.

Text:
Somsook Boonyabancha
Thailand.

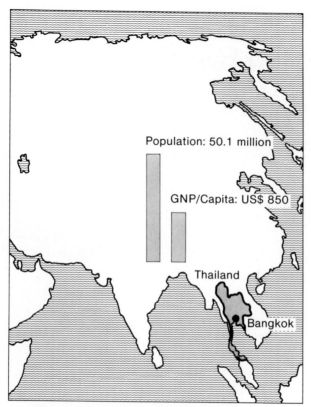

Population: 50.1 million

GNP/Capita: US$ 850

Thailand

Bangkok

Population Bangkok (1985): 5.5 million
Population Klong Toey (1986): 40,000

Income Distribution:

In 1981 the average monthly household income in
Klong Toey was $US64 per month, compared to about
US$226 in the Inner Bangkok Metropolitan Area. In
Klong Toey about 28% of households earned less than
US$35 per month, 16% between US$35 and US$70;
26% between US$70 and US$140; and 9% more than
US$140, The figures for the Inner Bangkok
Metropolitan area are respectively: 1%. 5%, 21% and
73%.

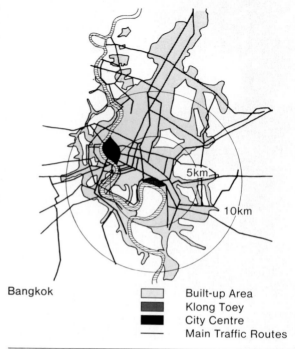

Bangkok

☐ Built-up Area
■ Klong Toey
■ City Centre
— Main Traffic Routes

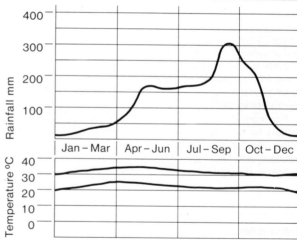

Climate Graph Bangkok (10m)

PHOTO : PGC-HS KULEUVEN, BELGIUM

Klong Toey is the largest of Bangkok's over 1,000 slum and squatter settlements. Approximately 6,000 households have settled on 65 hectares of land belonging to the Port Authority of Thailand (PAT), next to the international harbour and less than 10 kilometres from central Bangkok.

For more than a quarter of a century, Klong Toey settlers have struggled for survival and for the right to stay in the city. Today, they have gained recognition as city dwellers, with full legal rights to stay in the heart of Bangkok, through a land-sharing agreement.

Abbreviations

NHA National Housing Authority
PAT Port Authority of Thailand

A Bangkok slum as symbol

Klong Toey is more than just a squatter area. To some people, it signifies the evils of a decaying social sector in a slum; to others, a creative, even heroic community in a struggle to house itself. Politicians, social workers, researchers and opportunists have all made their own use of Klong Toey, while the inhabitants have endured the changes in attitudes, social norms, policies and experts' views on low-income urban housing during the past decades.

Not only has Klong Toey changed from a rejected squatter settlement to a government show-case, but, more importantly, from the 'unwanted urban poor' to a powerful community, organized at the grass-roots and gaining increased ability to lead other participatory changes in the city.

In 1950, only 200 families lived on the edge of the marsh land. Now around 40,000 people have a home in

The developed village before removal, showing the well-maintained main walkways.

After land-sharing: dismantling a building for re-assembling on a new site.

PHOTOS: PGC-HS KULEUVEN, BELGIUM

Klong Toey; some are migrants from the provinces, others urban residents evicted from other slums. Most families in the community earn their living from various activities related to the harbour. The squatter settlement has, over the years, become one of the largest 'markets' for cheap urban housing for the poor.

Struggle for survival and the right to stay

The constant struggle against eviction by the PAT, together with the formation of a particular 'slum subculture' developed from a spontaneous to a progressively well-organized, community-based movement, strengthened in the early '70s by the involvement of several voluntary agencies. Piecemeal housing solutions had been tried in Klong Toey, from threats (including arson) and sporadic eviction with no rehousing offered, to attempts at resettlement and the construction of 2,098 units in five-storeyed flats by the National Housing Authority (NHA) between 1976 and 1980.

These solutions failed, and only resulted in strengthening the community, as the Klong Toey people learned from their struggle for survival.

The final result of the long struggle came in January 1983, in the form of a unique land-sharing agreement with PAT, granting the dwellers a 20-year, legal lease.

Land-sharing: respecting the rights of slum-dwellers and landlord

Land-sharing has been used since 1982 as a compromise technique, to resolve eviction conflicts between slum-dwellers and landlords in Bangkok. Basically, land-sharing is a plan to partition the former slum areas into two parts: one for re-housing and the other for the landowners' developments. Through recognizing both claims as legitimate, the plan seeks to resolve the conflict by negotiation, to defuse a potentially volatile confrontation, which could lead to social unrest, by taking full advantage of the development potentials of the site, creating conditions where all may benefit. Obviously, land-sharing is a compromise solution.

A land-sharing agreement is the result of a long process of negotiation, rather than a simple, straightforward plan for redeveloping a site. Land-sharing needs strong community organization, as well as the solid support of other agencies, so that the costs of evicting settlers become prohibitive for landlords. Such an agreement is a concrete result of inhabitants' participation and co-operation.

Low-income housing and tenants' legal rights have been secured as the result of a power struggle between conflicting interests: rights of tenure for the squatters against the technical, legal rights of the landlord; the right to stay against development plans of the authorities.

Land-sharing in Klong Toey

The National Housing Authority (NHA) is the government body responsible for housing development, in co-operation with the people's organizations, non-government organizations (NGOs), and others concerned. The scheme, which began in 1981, includes the construction of 1,440 new dwelling units, the relocation of 2,352 dwelling units, the provision of services for those not moved, and changing the layout in the settlements not moved, thus creating 2,465 units. This makes a total of 6,257 units.

Population density has increased by more than half, and so has the expenditure on housing, resulting in an overall improvement in living conditions. The settlement is now better organized and has improved infrastructure. Nearly every household has its own unit, floor-area per household has increased by 77 per cent, and the value of the houses has almost doubled. Land-sharing in Klong Toey has brought an end to the eviction struggle and has provided the poor with the opportunity to use their energy and initiative to develop permanent housing in their settlement.

The houses reassembled in new location.

Combining the roles of the actors

The success of Klong Toey depended on the co-operation of many parties: the people's organizations in their struggle for housing, the NGOs in their supporting role, government agencies as a force for compromise, the landlord, politicians, academics, individuals and the general public. The inhabitants of Klong Toey, in their thirty-year struggle against eviction by PAT, have learned how to survive the sporadic evictions, and how to negotiate. They achieved this despite partial disorganization and the multitude of scattered groups.

In the absence of government services, the role of the NGOs in this project was significant. They reacted directly to the people's problems, on occasion becoming trapped into being day-to-day social relief organizations. However, a particular and very significant type of slum-oriented organization has also emerged, which developed during the process and became community-based organizations. It is interesting to note that some of these well-co-ordinated organizations scattered about the slum area have been transformed into community-based NGOs (CB-NGO). These CB-NGOs have a particularly important role in organizing the people, as they live and work in the slum and are thus able to respond directly to the problems and to develop with the process of struggle. The CB-NGOs, combined with the people's organizations, have become the backbone of the Klong Toey community.

The work of academics helped to publicize the situation during the early '70s. Academic research was followed by the setting up of a student workshop in the slum, and by the first community centre. In this way, politicians, international agencies and the general public learned of Klong Toey's problems and the findings of a study even had a impact on the orientation of the NHA in 1973.

The NHA has broadened its understanding of the range of possible low-income housing solutions from its work in Klong Toey, where it has been involved in the construction of dwellings since 1973, as well as in resettlement and land-sharing. The NHA has no direct political power, nor is it a property developer, but it has, in its role as a third party, mediated in negotiations between landlord and the people's organizations.

In this case the landlord, being ultimately the state, had particular difficulty in evicting people, especially in order to use the land commercially. The growing number of people in certain areas threatened PAT's development project, but its various attempts to evict them failed.

As Klong Toey is the biggest slum, it has always been able to attract the attention of the media, and has used this, combined with the popular movement, to great effect.

The engagement and co-operation of all these people has gradually led through adjustment and direction to a solution. The people of Klong Toey accept the solution, as they themselves have played a role in its formulation.

Impacts of development

The right of the poor to stay in the city
Since Klong Toey has long been a symbol for the slums of Bangkok, the gaining by its people of the right to remain will have a significant effect on the struggle and the rights of squatters elsewhere. It constitutes a landmark in the struggle for recognition of the right of the poor to stay in the city, and will add to its momentum.

Continuity and step-by-step development
In greater Bangkok, more than sixty major and occasionally violent evictions over the years have not succeeded in eliminating the slums. Long-term Klong Toey residents have themselves been evicted an average of 5 times during the last 30 years, managing somehow to reappear in other parts of the area. Evictions only strengthen the resolve of the people and the NGOs not to give up. Later, the problems of sporadic eviction were tackled in a more organized way. Community work assisted by NGOs became problem-oriented, rather than strictly plan-oriented, and problems were solved area by area, case by case, with a consistent and gradual approach. Both the people and the NGOs were able to

digest and to learn from this gradual process, in which their achievements and morale have increased little by little. After the first resettlement, the people's organizations underwent a considerable change, with a move towards legalization. Success in the struggle to remain has promoted further organization and work. After relocation in the land-sharing scheme, the Klong Toey group became the focal group in the organization of 18 other groups in the area, uniting them in the Union of Klong Toey. Later, this Union engaged in various important activities, such as the creation of a drug-free zone.

Negative impacts
Land-sharing in the Klong Toey Project has marked the end of the long and tough struggle for the 'right to stay' in the biggest slum in Bangkok. However, the legal agreement also underlined the change from informal to more organized reconstruction with better facilities. Such a formal change, on the other hand, not only placed an increased economic burden on the people, but it also meant that wealthier people from outside began to show an interest.

Redevelopment by land-sharing may turn out to be another method of eviction, especially in the case of weak people's organizations, by gradual market mechanisms. In Klong Toey, the 'right to stay' is sometimes being sold for about 100,000 Baht, which is about 2 times higher than the 'right for flats'. (Thai Baht 26 = US$1.) Klong Toey people may be faced with a strong financial incentive to sell out their right. This may become the new challenge for the Klong Toey people to answer.

A low-cost
sewer system
by low-income
Pakistanis

Documentation:
Arif Hasan, Consultant to
the Orangi Pilot Project
1/D26 Daulat House
Karachi 41, Pakistan.

Orangi
Pilot Project

Sponsor:
International Development
Research Centre (IDRC)
Canada.

Advisor:
John F.C. Turner
AHAS, UK.

Text:
Andrew Maskrey and
Bertha Turner
AHAS, UK.

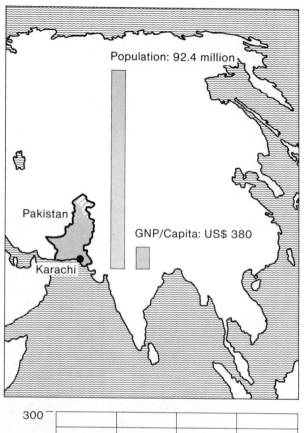

Population: 92.4 million

Pakistan

GNP/Capita: US$ 380

Karachi

Population Karachi (1985): 6.2 million
Population Orangi (1985): 700,000

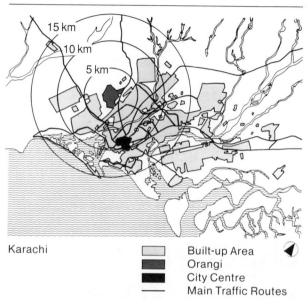

Karachi

	Built-up Area
	Orangi
	City Centre
	Main Traffic Routes

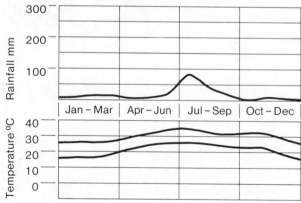

Climate Graph Karachi (4m)

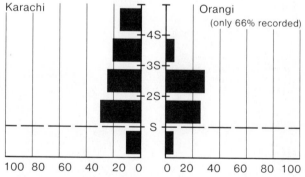

Percentage Distributions of Population by Income Level
S=when 85% of household income must be spent on food

Abbreviations

OPP   Orangi Pilot Project
KMC   Karachi Metropolitan Council

Orangi Pilot Project (OPP) is one of two major community-based sanitation projects in Karachi. The other, the Baldia Soakpit Pilot Project, also generates social development but differs in the technology used - an individual soakaway.

Two in three live in self-built settlements

Orangi (population 700,000) is typical and the largest of Karachi's 362 'katchi abadis'. About 4 million people, two-thirds of Karachi's population, live in these unauthorized squatter- or owner-built settlements. Orangi's settlement began in 1965. Like most of Karachi's citizens, the residents have been building their own houses on initially unserviced land bought from illegal developers, with materials obtained on credit from small local manufacturers and suppliers. Most labour is locally contracted by the households.

Orangi's average household income, Rs1,000, is one third lower than in Karachi as a whole. Most households have two earners each providing the equivalent of an official minimum wage--just enough to feed a family, with nothing left over for housing, clothing, the journey to work and other essentials. Under 5 per cent in Orangi earn even less than one minimum wage, as against 10 per cent in Karachi as a whole.

Before OPP began, primitive forms of excreta disposal, poorly laid drains and the lack of rainwater drainage created a dangerously insanitary environment increasing social conflict as well as disease and mortality.

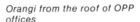

Orangi from the roof of OPP offices

PHOTO: JOHN F.C. TURNER

The lanes were open sewers...

... flooded in the rainy season

Lane residents often installed drains...

Sewers as a vehicle for local development

Sewer line costs for 20,000 households reduced by nearly 80 per cent

Since 1980, Dr. Akhtar Hameed Khan's OPP has enabled low-income people to finance and install sewers serving 20,000 homes housing some 200,000 people for Rs28.5 million. The same works carried out by government contractors would have cost nearly five times as much. The people invested their time and Rs27 million or one month's average income per household served. OPP has invested Rs1.5 million in research, equipment and technical assistance, thanks to Aga Khan Abadi, President of BCCI, the Pakistan-owned Bank of Credit and Commerce.

Based on previous experience and convinced that it is possible for low-income populations to install their own systems at an affordable cost, Dr. Akhtar Hameed Khan started working in Orangi in 1980. Using simple technologies that people can appropriate and develop themselves, work and organization began with the lanes, democratizing the commonly exploitative local leadership and improving neighbourliness along with health and self-confidence.

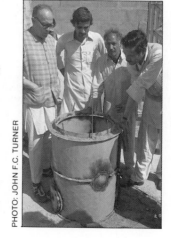

PHOTO: JOHN F.C. TURNER

Akhtar Hameed Khan (left) discusses steel form for casting manholes with the local designer and fabricator.

People first

How was so much accomplished by poor people with such beneficial side effects? The answer lies in the methods employed by the OPP Programme:

1. Community organization and participation in the designing and management of the programme;

2. Appropriating and adapting technology to allow people themselves to carry out the works with reduced costs (by scaling down standard engineering design and practice) and, thereby,

3. Maximizing the use of local resources: personal savings and initiative, manual and managerial skills, complementing and developing them with the provision of expert assistance.

These three aspects of the OPP approach increased people's self-respect and self-confidence as the environment (and property values) improved; along with incentives to co-operate and invest. Conflicts generated by insanitary conditions were reduced, neighbourliness and opportunities for gainful participation were increased.

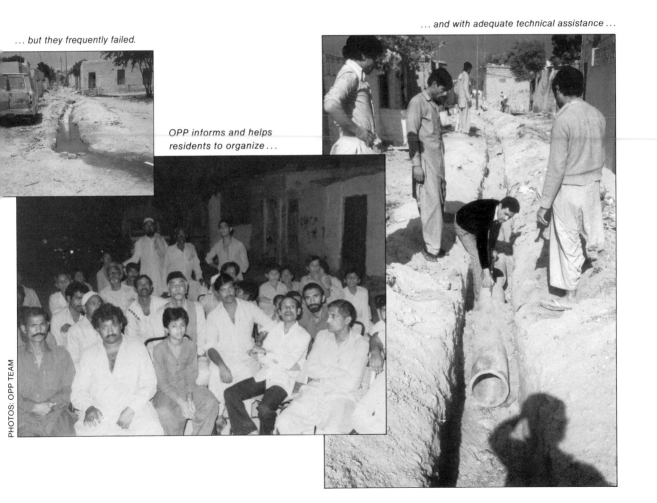

... and with adequate technical assistance ...

... but they frequently failed.

OPP informs and helps residents to organize ...

PHOTOS: OPP TEAM

ORANGI

Small scale organizing produces large scale results

The lanes, with 10-15 houses on each side, were seen by OPP as having the right human scale for the basic units of project organization. This meant that the 20 - 30 households would generally know each other, and fewer problems resulting from mistrust would occur. The existing leadership (mostly the land sellers) functioned at the larger

... the lanes were transformed.

'mohalla', or neighbourhood, level. OPP avoided provoking their hostility by starting at a smaller scale.

The lane organizations are developed in four stages:

1. Public meetings in the lanes. Paid OPP motivators use slides, models and pamphlets to explain the programme and its benefits. They had first to convince the residents that sewer lines laid by city agencies are not a free service and that they could not afford a conventional installation. The lane groups had to be convinced that they could get an affordable system by organizing and with technical assistance from OPP.

2. Lanes organize. The neighbours elect their own leaders who then make a formal approach to OPP for assistance.

3. OPP assists. With help from university students, other volunteers and with the co-operation of the residents, the lane is surveyed, plans and cost estimates are prepared.

4. Lane groups take over. The elected lane leaders, many of whom were women, pass on the information provided by OPP, collect the residents' contributions of Rs1,000 (about one month's income per household) and organize the work. OPP continues to supervise, but makes a special point of never handling local people's money. Maintenance of the improvements has been carried out communally and informally as the need arises, by residents of the lanes.

Initially only those lanes near to gullys (nullas) which are natural rainwater run-off channels, asked for OPP assistance. The programme was endangered, however, unless other lanes too far from a gully got together in order to build shared secondary drains connecting them with the nearest one. OPP promoted the idea by doing a physical survey, using the wards of the KMC (Karachi Metropolitan Council) councillors. Students carried out surveys of each ward, talking to people and involving them in their work, producing a two-way benefit. In this way residents understood the need for secondary drains - and the idea of development through commnity participation was carried back to the universities, resulting in increased professional involvement.

Survey results and OPP literature were given to each ward councillor. Residents, hearing of this at motivation meetings, began to pressure their councillors about secondary drains. This resulted in a large number of neighbourhood lane organizations coming together to ask OPP for technical assistance with secondary drains.

Inverting political relationships

Democratizing local authority
Before the OPP project, the illegal land subdividers were Orangi's self-appointed, exploitative leaders. They have been challenged by the OPP social organizers, lane groups and managers, who have gained the necessary confidence through their project experience, and are forcing the leadership to become more democratic. Three OPP organizers have stood as candidates in local authority elections and one has been elected as a councillor.

In addition to democratizing local representation through people's demands on their ward councillors, OPP has changed relationships between Orangi councillors and the KMC. KMC grants are normally for surface projects only - roads or open storm water drains. In 1984, one Orangi sector forced their Councillor to use these funds for an underground sewer. They wanted to choose their own contractor, but KMC made the choice. The people supervised his work and introduced OPP drain designs.

People appropriating technology

The necessity of doing more with less
Two major obstacles blocked the provision of sanitation by the local authority: their finances were slim and conventional methods inflated costs, making them unaffordable to katchi abadi residents. Experience shows that instalment payments for public services are impractical when users have no responsibility for management and the authority cannot afford proper maintenance. Foreign assistance, when available, could only serve a small percentage of the large population.

Finance had to be found from within the community and made available before development work began. Simple, low-cost designs, an appropriate technology, suitable for local and voluntary labour was needed in order to keep costs and overheads low. And appropriate forms of organization, planning and management also had to be devised if costs were to be locally affordable.

Planning from the bottom up
OPP saw that if lane residents were organized and trained to use the right technical support and tools, they could finance and build an affordable system. The approach was based on local experience and preferences, correcting and developing what people were already attempting rather than introducing alien methods. Experience with sanitary pits and soakaways had been negative. A piped system was preferred and many had installed their own, often with individual pipes running parallel, on or very near the surface, with inadequate diameters, falls and manholes so that they frequently failed.

Underground systems are complex and hierarchic or tree-like: house drains feed into lane or street sewers and these branch into larger trunk mains. It is generally assumed that major works must be planned and installed first to ensure a workable system. But had this orthodox approach been adopted, OPP would have had to start from the top down, risking conflict with local leadership and involving itself with the bureaucracy. A natural drainage system is provided by the gullys which form in the short, heavy rainfall season. Planning and installations were therefore started from the bottom up, using the lanes opening onto this natural drainage system.

Supervision and quality control were not centralized, but carried out by residents. The only way to ensure quality work was to educate people. Confidence in OPP could only develop over time. For this reason, some substandard work was done in the lanes and by mid-1982, there was a lull in the programme. OPP's evaluation of its design concept, specifications and quality of work disclosed the following problems and solutions:

1. Discharged sewerage and excreta occasionally blocked the drains and polluted the gullys which were surrounded by high density housing. Constructing simple one-chamber septic tanks that collected solids, and locating them between every house connection and the lane sewer solved this problem.

2. KMC standard manholes were too elaborate for unskilled labour as well as too expensive. Costs were reduced from Rs400 to Rs120 each by modifiying the design and lending shuttering to lane groups for casting their own manholes on site.

3. Expensive, lightweight, steel-rimmed, reinforced concrete KMC manhole covers were easily broken or removed and manholes were soon turned into garbage pits. These were later replaced by heavy, inexpensive concrete slabs.

4. Sewer lines were laid in the middle of lanes, too near the surface. OPP specified the laying of sewers to one side, to minimize damage by heavy vehicles. Lane groups insisted on placing the lines in the middle, so that

houses would share equally in connection costs, but maintaining the shallow depth acceptable if on one side. Damage to manholes during work-in-progress is avoided by temporarily filling with sand. Experience shows that no damage occurs in lanes, since there is little heavy traffic.

5. Poor workmanship. Despite extension training, proper concrete mixes, curing and drain alignments were not being maintained. These defects were overcome by providing simple tools, such as measuring boxes for concrete mixes, and closer supervision.

One-chamber septic tanks collect solids avoiding manhole and sewer blockages.

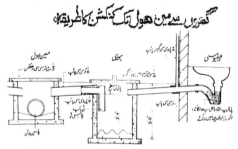

Experts' objections disproved
Between September 1982 and January 1983, officials and professional planners who visited OPP considered this incremental bottom-up planning an invitation to disaster. The international experts could not believe that an overall drainage system could be built up incrementally and empirically, following the natural drainage system provided by the dry gullys and seasonal watercourses.

The drawing up of a master plan at that stage would have involved the bureaucracy, imposing unacceptable costs and undermining the motivation and contribution of the local population on which OPP is based.

The experts recommended that all work should stop until the plan and two other recommendations were put into effect:

1. Excreta should be sealed by changing over to a twin leach pit system with waste water flowing into open drains.

2. Plastic pipes of a smaller diameter (two inches) should replace the more expensive and larger-scale concrete pipes and manholes. Insufficient water existed to

make the larger pipes work, and they were viewed as uneconomic.

OPP disagreed. The residents demanded a water borne system, objecting to the health hazards and maintenance problems of open overflow drains. It was pointed out that leach pits would quickly fill when the water supply increased, with the completion of the Hub River Dam. OPP countered with their own objections to a costly short-term solution ignoring social and political dynamics. Since 1983, adequate water has been provided by the Dam and OPP's prophecy has proved to be correct.

OPP'S and women's horizons expand
OPP no longer needs to motivate people. The demonstration effect has encouraged lanes to organize themselves and to contact OPP, who now concentrate on technical supervision. Relations between the local community and local government have been redefined, along with OPP's scope for future development work. OPP now works on three levels: at the local level, assisting lanes; helping Orangi Council to site secondary drains; and with the Karachi Metropolitan Council, designing and supervising works which they have funded.

Women's expectations have changed and OPP continues to innovate. Eight Women's Work Centres now exist. Women use sewing machines at home, producing articles for sale. OPP delivers material, collects and distributes finished articles, taking on the role of the middle-man. OPP helped women to buy industrial sewing machines. With their faster and better stitching, women have increased their earnings by 30 per cent.

The Women's Welfare Programme is conducted lane-by-lane, using a 'street vendor' approach. Women meet in groups to learn about nutrition, personal hygiene, child growth monitoring, vegetable gardens and family planning. A local woman activist makes her home the centre for these activities. To date, family planning has aroused the most interest.

OPP's programme is now included in the new Orangi Master Plan. The Aga Khan Medical University and the Department of Architecture, DCET, Karachi, use OPP for course work and contribute to the OPP programme. Two Karachi squatter colonies and some large rural villages have asked OPP help in building their own self-financed community sewerage system. The OPP experience in organization and technology goes on, involving local people in transforming their own lives.

Philippino squatters become secure home owners

Documentation:
Sister Lydia Kalaw
Domus Mariae Foundation
Room 205
Marietta Apartments
1200 Jorge Bocobo St.
Ermita, Manila
Philippines

Saarland Village I

Sponsor:
Marian Housing
Foundation
Philippines

Text:
Bertha Turner
AHAS, UK

SAARLAND VILLAGE

357 HOUSING UNITS FOR THE LANDLESS. HOMELESS. SLUM DWELLER FAMILIES.

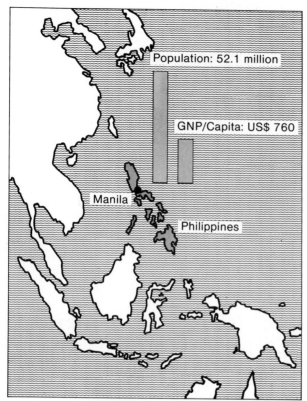

Population: 52.1 million

GNP/Capita: US$ 760

Manila

Philippines

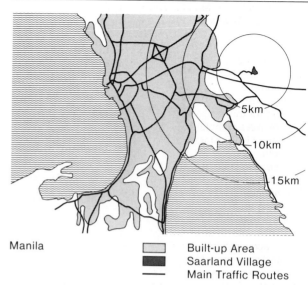

Manila

Built-up Area
Saarland Village
Main Traffic Routes

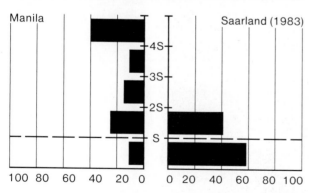

Manila   Saarland (1983)

Percentage Distributions of Population by Income Level
S=when 85% of household income must be spent on food

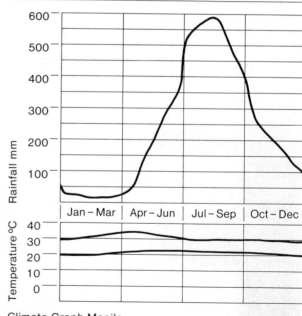

Climate Graph Manila

Population Metro Manila (1980): 5 million
Population Saarland 1 (1986): 1,000

Saarland Village I provides low-cost and secure homes for 110 squatter families from Manila. It is the first project sponsored by the Domus Mariae Foundation Incorporated (DMFI), a non-governmental organization (NGO) especially created for this purpose in 1983. Eight months later, 110 houses were completed and families were moving in. Saarland I is 30 kilometres from Manila near the town of Antipolo.

A second DMFI project has been built nearby and was occupied in 1986: Saarland Village II provides homes for 250 additional families. This is the sequel to Saarland I, providing an important example of co-operation between NGOs and government. A second scheme would not have been possible so quickly if finances had to come from costs recovered from the first scheme. But a government-initiated scheme of home finance and secondary mortgages purchased the Saarland I mortgages and reimbursed DMFI for its expenditures. Those funds then financed Saarland II.

The setting: Metro Manila
Metro Manila, created in 1975, combines four cities, including Manila, and 13 municipalities. It contains 12 per cent of the country's population and 33 per cent of the urban population. In 1980 Metro Manila had 5 million inhabitants and the population is doubling every 15 years.

Between 1 and 2 million squatters
The squatter population of Metro Manila is estimated at between 1 and 2 million people (about 30 per cent of the population). Squatter settlements are the first homes for rural migrants coming to the city to find work and a better life. They offer cheap accomodation, nearness to jobs and a quick orientation to city ways.

Squatters are often violently evicted from sites, to make way for development: private or government. They are dumped onto relocation sites, far from their low-paid jobs, making commuting impossibly expensive. Sometimes they manage to organize, and with help from both NGOs and government agencies, to gain secure tenure and improved homes. More often, they lead a life of continuous harassment, fear and insecurity. After so much struggle and suffering, the focus of the Philippine government is now on renewal rather than relocation.

Abbreviations:

DMFI	Domus Mariae Foundation Incorporated
KMPC	Kaunlaran Multi Purpose Centre
PAG-IBIG	government home finance fund and secondary mortgage system
	literal translation: Love

PHOTO: PATRICK CROOKE

Typical Manila squatter settlement, subject to eradication.

The evolution of Saarland I

Saarland I is located on what was formerly a rural squatter settlement (barangay or barrio) near the town of Antipolo. The one hectare site, donated by Mrs. Orosa, is on a high and hilly terrain and safe from flooding.

From insecurity to Saarland I

The 1,000 residents of Saarland I are made up of 110 families. This includes the family of a community social worker employed by DMFI as resident estate manager. Most people came to Saarland I from the Santa Ana and the San Andres Bukia districts of Manila. Their story is typical of the long struggles of landless, low-income Philippinos to obtain secure and decent homes and therefore defines the context in which Saarland I occurred.

Area A, Santa Ana is a half hectare site in southern Manila where 127 families lived, 18 of them since 1921, 24 who came after the Second World War. 52 families owned their homes while 33 were renters. Ethnically, they were a mix of Tagalogs, Warays or eastern Visayans and Bicolanos.

They built their small shanties of salvaged materials. The only running water was from their leaky roofs and there were no sanitary facilties or toilets. The site was muddy and pitted, with many deep hollows which filled with water during the rainy season. Garbage and refuse were thrown into ravines or 'esteros'. Heavy rains might carry the garbage downstream, but otherwise, it piled up and rotted in the stagnant water, creating a pervasive foul smell. But it was a cheap place to live and near to the job opportunities of Manila, so people wanted to stay there.

Since before the Second World War, Area A residents had paid land rent to the corporation which owned the land. Later, the site was mortgaged to the Philippine National Bank, and in 1968 they foreclosed, refusing to accept the people's land rent. Negotiations began with a buyer, and she began threatening the residents with eviction.

The Kaunlaran Multi Purpose Centre (KMPC) was started in 1971 to work with the urban poor in Manila, enabling them to handle their own land and housing problems.

At this point, KMPC sent a community worker to help Area A residents in finding a solution. They had formed a tenants association the year before, but it was ineffective in dealing with the threats. A core of officers was formed and the community worker conducted leadership training sessions. An election was held and a new constitution and by-laws were drafted and approved.

They appealed to their city councillor who stopped the eviction order. The bank then terminated negotiations with the prospective buyer.

Typical squatter relocation site 40 kilometres from Manila.

In February 1972, the tenants' association petitioned the city government to expropriate the land and to resell it to them by instalment payments. It was officially approved by the city council in December 1975, but no tangible moves were made to carry it out.

By 1976, KMPC's community worker pulled out of the area, feeling that people were now able to handle their own affairs.

In 1977, the tenants' association were informed that a supermarket chain had bought their site to build a new store.

In November 1979, a demolition team arrived with a city permit to demolish the houses. People were shocked and alarmed. They petitioned for postponement of the eviction to March 1980, which was officially approved.

To stop the eviction completely, residents brought the case to court, requesting help from an assemblyman and obtaining certification of Area A as a residential zone.

Still insecure, the residents approached Sister Lydia Kalaw for support. In June 1980, Sister Lydia and His Eminence Jaime Cardinal Sin invited the Vice-Governor of the Metro Manila Commission to a blessing ceremony. Afterwards, tenants discussed their problems with him, and he promised to help. But in August 1980, the second demolition team arrived. Sister Lydia accompanied tenant leaders to the Vice-Governor, pleading with him to suspend demolition, which he did.

Meanwhile, the tenants' association filed a second case in the courts against the supermarket chain. Their lawyer charged a minimum fee and was willing to pursue the case up to Supreme Court level, if necessary.

The tenants' assocation asked both the Mayor of Manila City, Ramon Bagatsing and Metro Manila's Governor, Imelda Marcos, to implement the original resolution already approved back in December 1975 - to expropriate the land and to sell it to them.

The court decided to evict Area A's residents, and to demolish their houses with no relocation or financial compensation. An appeal was made to the Supreme Court. While it was pending, the third demolition team arrived in March 1981. This time, they met fierce opposition when women and children formed a human barricade to stop them. This action, together with a temporary restraining order from the Supreme Court prevented the demolition.

The Supreme Court advised the tenants' lawyer that the evictions would only be permanently stopped by expropriation of the land by the City. The tenants' association asked Sister Lydia to pressure the City Mayor in April 1981. When informed of the Supreme Court's advice, the Mayor finally agreed to expropriate the land, sending an official letter in May.

The City government planned to use Area A for a socialized housing scheme for both house owners and renters.

Cardinal Sin visited Area A and agreed at once that something practical must be done by the Catholic Church. The Domus Mariae Foundation Incorporated was founded in 1983 to develop housing and training for residents of a new scheme, Saarland I. The Cardinal was its Chairman and President, and Sister Lydia Kalaw , its driving force, was Executive Vice-President and Operations Officer. Many residents of Area A applied for housing in the proposed new scheme.

The seed capital
The one-hectare site in Antipolo, donated by Sister Lydia's friend, Mrs. Orosa, became the initial capital investment for Saarland I. Foreign contributions amounting to a total of P2.75 million (Philippine Pesos) were raised by Sister Lydia from Nigeria Hilfswerk-Emmersweiker Stiftung Menshen und Missionare in Not, the German Embassy, the Share and Care Apostolate for the Poor Settlers, the people of Saarland State in the Federal Republic of Germany (for whom the project is named) and a number of local donors.

Selecting the residents of Saarland I
Selecting 110 beneficiaries from nearly a thousand applicants is not easy. Three different levels of criteria were devised to narrow down the applicants. These criteria were housing need and no other house ownership, income sufficient for the monthly payments, 5 years' residence in Manila, character and family acceptability, readiness to participate, number of dependents, family head under 40 years old, members of the government's home finance fund and secondary mortgage system. The final screening prioritized families facing eviction and members of the local network with at least 5 years' residence in priority areas.

Prospective residents attended seminars to educate them for life in Saarland I. The community social worker enforces certain rules to keep up the standards set for the project. Selling or subletting, adding improvements without her permission, having guests for periods longer than one month and other infractions of the rules are dealt with by the community social worker.

Planning the project

DMFI contracted an architect, Fr. Jorge Anzorena, S.J., to do the subdivision and building plans with some advice from voluntary consultants who had experience of low-cost housing development projects in India, Sri Lanka and Thailand.

Site development and construction were contracted out to a professional building firm. Plots are 50 square metres, larger than the minimum 40 square metres, to allow space for extensions. The basic houses are 21 square metres with reinforced concrete hollow-block walls, galvanized iron roof, capable of supporting an added second floor. All houses are built with shared party walls to cut costs. There is piped water, electricity, toilet, shower and sanitary fixtures. Each house cost P25,000 including the land (donated) and infrastructure. Monthly amortization payments start at P230 over a 25-year period.

Participation starts after moving in

Families move into a completed house. The basic core house has one bedroom, and an open space which serves as combined living/dining room and kitchen, along with a toilet and shower. Electricity and piped water are available. Participation comes later when they can afford to add another storey or an extension. Half the families are either extended or combined households averaging 6 persons. Therefore, 69 per cent of residents have built extensions, investing from P11,000 to P15,000.

Sewage is collected in septic tanks and disposal is through a closed pipe system into a nearby creek. Garbage collection remains an unsolved problem, since people dump it in a vacant lot while others throw their waste into the creek, but take the trouble to clear it in the rainy season.

Saarland Village I street: basic units provided shortly after completion.

Sponsors, organizers and Saarland community celebrate together.

A small business set up with a loan to compensate for secondary income lost on moving from previous inner city location.

69 per cent of residents have built extensions, investing on average about a year's income.

Family jobs and incomes in 1983

Most people work in low-paid jobs as labourers, technicians and craftsmen in private business or as clerks in government offices. But 14.7 per cent hold managerial positions or are professionals, while those with the highest income (2.8 per cent) had family members working abroad. Male spouses were 10 per cent unemployed compared to 45 per cent of female spouses.

When they moved into Saarland I in 1983, 58.9 per cent of the families earned between P1,000 and P2,000 per month.

Comparing Saarland I residents' incomes with the monthly incomes in other regions places them among the poorest of the poor. Only 2.9 per cent in the Philippines have such low incomes. The subsistence or poverty line wage is estimated by two government sources at between P1,214.00 and P2,248.50. By contrast, in Metro Manila, the average monthly income is P3,418. (Philippine Pesos 9.17 are equal to US$1.)

To continue to receive an income, Saarland I residents have had to become commuters and they remain more strongly linked with Manila than Antipolo. They travel to their jobs in Manila by public transport along the Sumulong Highway or the Marcos Highway, picking up buses and jeepneys where the two highways intersect. The point is half a kilometre from Saarland I itself, reachable by a rough track which is only negotiable on foot or by tricycle.

Weekend residents of Antipolo include wealthy people from Manila who do not find it difficult to drive there in their cars to enjoy the clean air and to escape the city's pollution at their weekend cottages.

Community spirit

Residents are now organized into a Home-owners Association responsible for maintenance, social projects and helping to collect monthly amortization payments which start at P230 a month for a maximum of 25 years. Membership dues for the Association are P50 a month which goes toward maintenance expenses. The Association has erected a perimeter fence, steel gates and street lights and do night patrols for their common protection. A nursery school was opened in June 1986. Social activities include an annual fiesta, a block rosary, dance parties, bingo socials and athletic competitions.

Evaluating the project for satisfaction
Family perceptions indicate that since moving to Saarland I, they spend 58.8 per cent more money on food, electricity, gas, water, education, children's allowance, clothing, housing, transport, and other items.

Increased income since moving to Saarland I was reported by 31 per cent of residents, due to pay rises, children sending money from working abroad, and small-scale income-producing activities. Decreased income was suffered by 17 per cent due to measures taken by industrial firms during the country's severe economic crisis, and higher transport costs for the journey to work. But 48 per cent of families reported no change in their incomes.

Three years after moving in, residents expressed satisfaction with the physical and social environment, but less with the difficult access and high cost of transport. The half-kilometre of unpaved road presents opportunities for extortion, when tricycle drivers charge the same fare for this distance as a jeepney fare to Manila 30 kilometres away. With their own funds, residents have finally managed to pave some of it but cannot afford the cost of materials required.

Markets, schools, health centres, police and fire stations are within a kilometre, but residents were used to the city's convenience. They missed the city job opportunities where they could earn money as hawkers, sidewalk vendors, shoe polishers, bookers for jeepney and bus passengers. To compensate this loss of income, DMFI obtained finance for small income-generating projects from the government. Twenty-five per cent of families took small loans of P500 to P3,000 to finance small businesses (often in their homes) such as food shops, beauty parlours, bakeshops, cooked foods and sewing for dress manufacturers.

But 96 per cent said that they preferred to stay in Saarland for the rest of their lives. One resident said that moving to Saarland: "...made me feel like a real person. I can now be proud of myself because I have my own house and a lot to show my friends. Weekends are happy events as relatives and friends from the city come for a visit."

NGO and government work in partnership

Saarland I has now been followed by Saarland II. Under the government's PAG-IBIG home finance fund and secondary mortgage system, DMFI sold the mortgages to the National Home Mortgage Finance Corporation, using funds obtained from PAG-IBIG. DMFI was then reimbursed for the initial capital spent and immediately invested it in the second scheme, Saarland II.

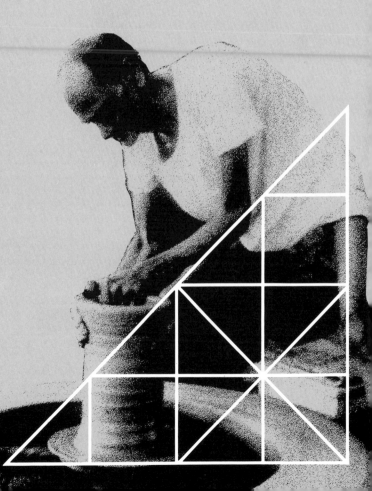

Rebuilding homes and community confidence in rural Indian villages

Documentation:
K. Cappon
Kleine Wynbergstraat 3
8610 Wevelgen, Belgium
and M.A. Windey, S.J.
Director, VRO
Ridge House,
Himayatanager
Hyderabad, India.

Village Reconstruction Organization

Text:
K. Cappon and
John F.C. Turner
AHAS UK.

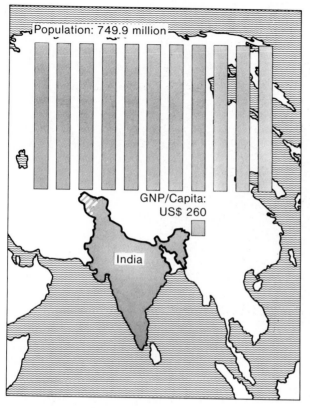

Population: 749.9 million

GNP/Capita:
US$ 260

India

Population of rural regions where VRO works: Andra Pradesh, Orissa, Tamil Nadu (1986): over 100 million 73 per cent of India's population live in its 500,000 villages.

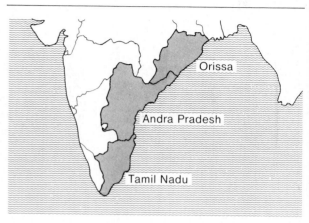

Orissa

Andra Pradesh

Tamil Nadu

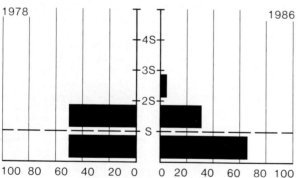

1978   1986

Percentage Distributions of Population by Income Level
S=when 85% of household income must be spent on food

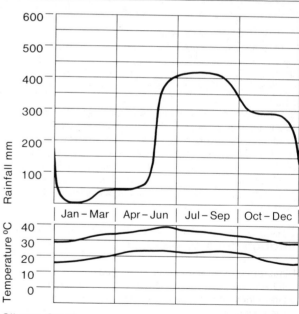

Climate Graph

Flimsy structures cannot withstand cyclones.

The Director of the Village Reconstruction Organization (VRO), Professor M.A. Windey, S.J., describes VRO in these words: "The Village Reconstruction Organization is the result of many efforts to seek a way out of rural poverty and oppression. It is born out of silence, failure and disaster. And out of faith. The silence of 30 years' observation and active participation with the National Community Development (agency), and an analysis of its relative failures; a faith in the future of the village as a way of life in India and the world and in the way of Ghandi as the Indian way to progress and to Christ; and a frequent experience of natural calamities in many parts of the country."

Crisis as a starting point for rural reform through housing projects

Disasters can be blessings in disguise
VRO was started in 1969, after a major cyclone in central eastern India. It has been operating ever since in the three poverty-stricken states of Andra Pradesh, Orissa and Tamil Nadu – an area over 2,000 kilometres long, and up to 400 kilometres wide. The area population is more than 100 million people, 20 per cent of whom are landless and often homeless as well. Most of the poor are exposed to cyclones, floods, droughts, fires and famine. Industrialization is only beginning. Agriculture is treacherous because of the climate, and provides an insecure occupation for the poor, since both the land and the law are controlled by the rich, upper castes.

Surrounded by such hazards and driven by desperation, the very poor are sometimes willing to abandon traditions and the false sense of security that they provide. For VRO, crisis provides opportunities to use village reconstruction projects as stepping stones of progress.

The growth of VRO

VRO's basic unit is the village community. As E.F. Schumacher has said: "World poverty is primarily the problem of 2,000 million villagers . . ." Of the 500,000 Indian villages, which are home to 73 per cent of the country's population, at least 300,000 are in extremely poor and vulnerable situations of the kinds that VRO selects for their projects.

By 1987, VRO had contacts in some 10,000 villages with populations of between 50 and 100 families. VRO has an active presence in 900 villages and integral development projects in 160, of which 140 projects are in varying stages of completion. Selection of villages is done through a detailed survey of several hundred on the waiting list. An average of one village project per month is initiated, giving priority to the lowest-income groups.

VRO has 500 full-time staff and 250 temporary volunteer workers, mostly young graduates, who assist village leaders with the various tasks involved in carrying out a comprehensive programme. These volunteers live and work in the villages, sharing the villagers' lifestyle.

Village access roads are impassable in the monsoon season: VRO test community spirit by requiring the village to improve it.

VRO's aims and approach

VRO's programmes are not primarily housing projects, although they might seem to be at first sight. The focus is on building community. Community is the agent of change. Developmental change is understood as setting in motion a process that has its vital locus in the minds and feelings of the people. All action has to be timed in accordance with the people's consciousness, if it is to develop into self-reliant initiative and financial resourcefulness. Only in this way can rural community life become a 'ruralization movement' in a context which is urbanizing.

The ruralization movement makes use of the special qualities of rural life: its integration of everyday tasks; its closeness to nature; its decentralized energy and technology; its own concepts of space and time. The movement aims at bringing communities together as a counterforce to challenge urban oppression: Ghandi's dream of a non-violent deep structural change. VRO is more oriented to qualitative structural reform than to material construction itself.

VRO projects progress through four stages:

1. When a village applies to VRO for assistance, the villagers' community-sense is tested through encouraging them to improve a road, level a site, dig a well or some other relatively simple task.

2. When a development programme is agreed, work generally starts with improvements to the physical environment: building houses, planting trees, digging wells and so on.

3. Community development through the provision of basic social services and income-generating activities usually follows physical improvements.

4. The final step is the withdrawal of VRO, once the village council is set up and continuing assistance is assured from other villages or the local authorities.

A typical case history

Background

The typical village taken as an example is near the Coromandel coast of India, famous for its frequent cyclones. In 1986, the population was made up of 230 individuals from 25 families who lived in 51 households. While the number of households hardly changed between 1978 and 1986, the population increased by 20 per cent. During the same seven-year period, the income-earning population fell by 18 per cent, from 105 to 89 persons. Due to a decrease in agricultural jobs, the 99 persons formerly thus employed dwindled to only 62. Those employed in higher-paid government and service employment rose from 6 to 19 persons. The number of households living below the poverty line increased from one-half to two-thirds. While this suggests increased rural-urban migration, surveys indicate a decrease. Although figures are imprecise, the period has seen a substantial drop in the number of absent youths and men between the ages of 15 and 25. This may be due to declining employment opportunities in the cities, to increasing expectations in the village, or to both.

The present village site was settled in the 1940s, since it was then the closest available unclaimed land to the nearest town. On the advice of the traditional village surveyor or 'karanum', the village moved to its present, less vulnerable and more convenient location 5 kilometres away. In 1969 the villagers' tenure was secured when the government issued rights of use or 'pattas', to each family, with a nominal rent of one-tenth of one Rupee.

Starting a VRO project
The VRO staff saw this history as evidence of community initiative and selected the village for a project. VRO introduces its approach in two ways: implicitly, through practical actions, starting with the tests; and explicitly, in meetings. The villagers' community spirit was tested by asking them to make an access road from the village to the main road. In a second test, the villagers' were asked to make 1200 bricks. VRO provided a loan for haulage and an artisan to train villagers in making moulds and bricks.

As the community proved its potential, VRO provided a full-time voluntary community worker, the leader of a previous project, who lived in the village. He assisted in setting up a village council, the 'Graham Sabha', which aimed at restoring the community's autonomy. Over the years, local control had been usurped by the district authority, the 'Panchayiti', whose powers over the community should now be turned into services and supports for community initiatives. The first Graham Sabha had 13 members: 5 were traditional elders, 4 were young people and 4 were women, one of whom was also the vice-leader. This council, now a formally recognized body, meets every Saturday. Several years after completion of the project, they can still count on a VRO contact person for advice and assistance.

Had this project been started a few years later, VRO would have used their current community-generating technique: about 15 to 20 experienced village contact persons from different completed VRO projects set up a working camp in a village, preparing for a new project. They donate a week's work without charge to the village, whose only obligation is to provide them with accommodation and food. These experienced believers in the VRO approach serve to animate apprehensive villagers and to give them confidence.

The resident voluntary community worker lives in the model house.

The first village council had 5 elders, 4 youths and 4 women.

Obtaining resources

On condition that its relatively-high building standards are met, government provides up to 50 per cent of financing for village building projects. This presented no problem to VRO, whose standards are even higher. In this case, however, government allocated only 28 per cent, disbursed to VRO after completion. In addition to their labour, each household had to contribute 12 per cent or R1,050 equivalent to 9 months' income for a median income household, and a very heavy financial burden for those living near or below the poverty line. VRO provided 10 per cent and the remaining 50 per cent was provided by the Canadian Mennonite Central Committee of Calcutta.

Additional land was purchased and the villagers agreed to pool and redistribute the land they had previously occupied. As well as enlarged 'patta' plots with hereditary rights of use, and community, income-earning pasture land or 'parambok', some plots were also provided within the village for communal use. Six years later, these were still fenced off and unused.

VRO prepares new village plans, house designs, and house models which are discussed with the community.

Planning and design

In its projects, VRO is responsible for village layout plans, building designs and management of the works. Despite major departures from traditional norms, VRO's layout plan for the village was accepted without question and formally approved by the 13 members of the Graham Sabha. But after being shown a model of VRO's proposed house design and visiting a built example, the villagers rejected it, due to its unorthodox form. A simplified, rectangular design was accepted which the villagers later modified, by adding a shared staircase to the roof terrace and a parapet. Other subsequent modifications, including lean-to additions, have been made by many of the households.

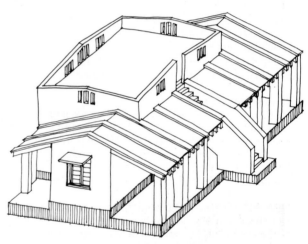

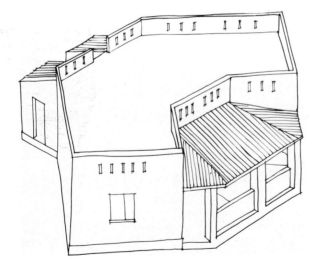

Building

Eight youths were trained in bricklaying, carpentry and rod-bending (for concrete reinforcement) under VRO supervision. Skilled labour was contracted on condition that village voluntary workers would be trained by them. Each household was required to contribute 100 working days.

Following the removal of all existing buildings from the site (most were temporary structures and easily moved), the site was prepared and ceremonially blessed. The model house was built by the trainees with villagers' voluntary help; surface-water drainage prepared; and trees were planted, because 'where trees grow, men will live'.

The building programme, scheduled by VRO to take five months, actually took three years. The main difficulties were over the villagers' own financial contributions, which competed with their need to buy food, and over participation and related benefits. These led to the adoption of mutual-aid building groups, under the principle of 'Building together or not at all'.

All dwellings were successfully completed, and house allocations were made, with first choices given to those who had contributed the most labour. The households moved in while the paint of the first murals was still wet.

Subsequent improvements include a school, a municipal water supply which provides piped water for four hours daily, street lighting and options for domestic connections, and various job-creation schemes.

Management and maintenance

A traditional village, under hereditary leaders, is well able to manage everyday, routine affairs. But they usually cannot cope with complex operations, keeping records and handling large sums of money or negotiating with government agencies. Members of the village councils set up with VRO's assistance are trained during the course of the projects. When these are completed and the resident volunteer leaves, the still-new Graham Sabha can count on VRO assistance at their weekly meetings or on help from experienced people from other villages.

VRO

Village youths are trained in building skills while building the model house.

Village rebuilding in progress.

Lessons learned

It is said that neither governmental nor non-governmental (NGO) schemes can provide durable and secure homes for sufficient numbers of the vast Indian population. The VRO experience challenges this view, showing what can be done on a large scale, by using housing as a vehicle for building community. It demonstrates the need and the value of NGOs building on the capacity for locally self-managed reconstruction, especially when following disasters.

The awakening of a village community and the emergence of its own community-based organization or CBO, can be a slow and sometimes discouraging process. Often, apathy is hard to overcome and the growth of awareness and community spirit is difficult to see. But small, scarcely visible activities may often signify big, internal changes. Modest beginnings in identifying local needs and projects may often provide the starting point for more ambitious projects.

For example, villagers marking their roads with white stones to avoid stubbing their toes at night, or setting up a women's savings club, based on very small individual contributions of a single Rupee a week, has led to the foundation of a community creche. The creche involved the whole community, by demanding land, labour and cash contributions from all the villagers. Community involvement and accomplishments serve to increase villagers' belief in their ability to join together to work out what needs to be done, and to do it. The village then benefits doubly, both from the improvements and from their ever-increasing growth in strength and self-confidence.

New homes and improved lives for Indonesian scavengers

Documentation:
Brother Servatius
Tjondrohartanto, YSS
Jl, Pandanaran
Semarang, Indonesia.

Yayasan Sosial Soegiyapranata

Sponsor:
MISEREOR
Federal Republic of
Germany.

Advisor:
John F.C. Turner
AHAS, UK.

Text:
Bertha Turner and
Andrew Maskrey
AHAS, UK.

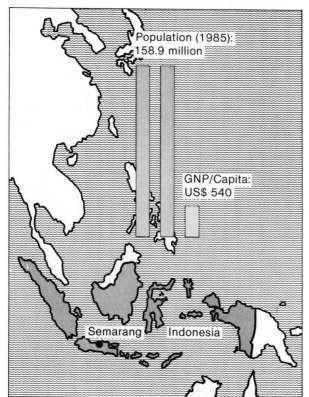

Population (1985):
158.9 million

GNP/Capita:
US$ 540

Semarang   Indonesia

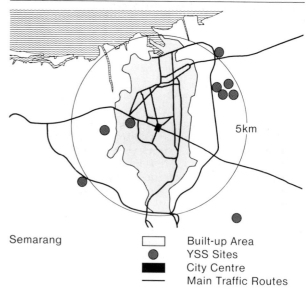

Semarang

	Built-up Area
●	YSS Sites
■	City Centre
—	Main Traffic Routes

5km

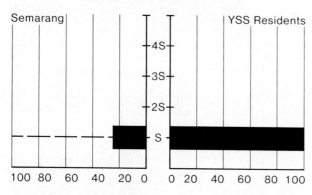

Semarang   YSS Residents

4S
3S
2S
S

100 80 60 40 20 0   0 20 40 60 80 100

Percentage Distributions of Population by Income Level
S=when 85% of household income must be spent on food

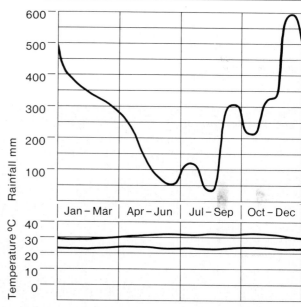

Climate Graph Semarang

Jan – Mar | Apr – Jun | Jul – Sep | Oct – Dec

Rainfall mm

Temperature °C

YSS

106

BUILDING COMMUNITY

Population Indonesia (1985): 158.9 million
Population Semarang (1984): 1.1 million

Yayasan Sosial Soegiyapranata (YSS) is a housing and relocation scheme serving the poorest of the city of Semarang in Indonesia. About one quarter of the urban population are known as 'scavengers'. These are the people who scratch a precarious living from gathering the waste products of industrial society. In Indonesia, they are considered outcasts. YSS views itself frankly as a 'rescue operation'. By providing improved living conditions and social acceptance for the 'scavengers', it hopes to give them better access to employment, education, and services in the city. It is hoped that this will enable them to enter fully into the urban economy.

Living below the subsistence line
Before the YSS programme, the 'scavengers' squatted on public open spaces, beside railway lines or on the garbage

dumps where they worked. With no sanitation, their settlements represented a permanent hazard to family health and safety. They built their houses from plastic and cardboard and whatever other material they could find. They worked as waste collectors, market porters, stall owners, bicycle-taxi (becak) drivers, and other unstable and unskilled occupations. Their incomes were on or below the subsistence line. Because they had no legal, fixed address, they could not hold a Citizenship card and their children could not go to school. The children were often ill through lack of proper and sufficient food.

Before the YSS programme, the 'scavengers' squatted on open public spaces, beside railway lines or on the garbage dumps where they worked.

PHOTOS: BROTHER SERVATIUS, YSS, INDONESIA

YSS

YSS builds 1,604 houses for urban poor

Since the first project of 78 houses was carried out at Gunung Berintik in 1965, YSS have developed over 18 hectares of land in 11 locations of Semarang with 1,604 houses built and occupied. They have invested Rs149,490,000 (US$149,490). More than 2,000 families have been resettled in other islands of Indonesia, in co-operation with the local authorities. Two homes for the elderly have been built, accomodating 56 men and women. Three health centres have been established. With funds from the local authority, YSS also relocated 259 families from areas designated for government public works in 1981/82, at the request and expense of the local authority.

Some win, others lose

Yet YSS itself recognizes that its programme has not been all success. Some families have managed to use their improved status to obtain better jobs, increase their incomes and improve their houses. Others, with less motivation or ability, continued in the same subsistence occupations and were unable to improve their houses.

Housing schemes have follow-up

By evaluating these factors, YSS saw that further help in improving family life and future prospects was needed. They now offer training in vocational skills and lend money for starting small businesses. Related YSS activities also include health services, job creation, homes for the elderly, small-scale production, nutrition improvement, family planning, care of abandoned children, information and motivation services.

Going where the government does not tread

Rural migration swells city population

Semarang is the capital city of central Java. In 1930, it was inhabited by 188,172 people. By 1984, it had a population of 1,086,198. Athough nearly half the area within the city's administrative boundaries was considered as land for agriculture or fishing, three-quarters of employment was provided in commerce, industry, services and public administration. As in other big cities, population growth since World War II has been due not only to natural increase but also to the migration of rural people, looking for jobs and a better standard of living.

Migrants enter the informal sector

Most migrants found jobs only in the informal sector, low in pay, skills and status. In 1978, 24.7 per cent of urban households in Semarang were earning less than US$15 a month, considered as a minimum subsistence level. Twenty-nine per cent earned around US$15 and 22 per cent between US$22 and US$30.

A recently completed settlement of basic dwellings built through mutual self-help.

YSS

Two-thirds of Semarang is 'kampung'

Most people in Semarang build their own houses in illegal settlements called 'kampungs'. Drawing exact meanings from Semarang's housing surveys is difficult: unauthorized, dilapidated dwellings of the poorest people are often not recorded as dwelling units and therefore do not appear in the statistics. But a 1977 survey of the physical quality of houses revealed that: 20.23 per cent were permanent dwellings; 17.51 per cent were semi-permanent and 62.26 per cent were classed as temporary. This indicated that at least 60 per cent of the residential area of Semarang was kampung.

Squatters and pavement dwellers

The poorest amongst the poor are the 'scavengers', stigmatized in Indonesia as society's outcasts. They settle on any available land. Most build houses from salvaged materials, but some do not have any sort of roof over their heads and live on the pavement. By 1965, there were 36 'scavenger' settlements in Semarang where some 2,182 families lived.

Government housing does not serve the poor

Government housing policy in Indonesia has favoured the construction of low-cost housing units by both public and private developers for low-income families. At the same time, different financial mechanisms have been tried to subsidize both developers and buyers of low-cost housing.

Even so, the cheapest price of a low-cost dwelling was US$2,500. To buy such a house, a family would be obliged to spend 20 per cent of their income for 15 years to pay off the mortgage. At that rate, they would have to be earning at least US$125 a month. In 1978, only 7 per cent of Semarang's families were in this income category. The 'scavengers' had no access to these housing schemes, not only because of the cost, but also because of not having Citizenship status.

Rescue operation for the disadvantaged

In 1964, YSS conceived its housing programme, intending it to rescue excluded and disadvantaged people. Thirty-six locations were identified, where most of Semarang's poorest families lived. Of the 2,182 families, 18.5 per cent were classified as 'koelies' or labourers; 10 per cent as 'becak' drivers; 10 per cent were running small business stalls; 22 per cent were waste collectors and the rest were in other informal activities. One per cent were prostitutes and one per cent were beggars. The idea was that once settled in legal settlements by YSS, they could then hold Citizen cards which gave them a recognized social status, and, hopefully, gain access to better jobs.

Unauthorized, dilapidated dwellings of the poorest people are often not recorded as dwelling units and therefore do not appear in the statistics.

YSS

The average income for the people served by YSS is between (the equivalent of) fifty and seventy-five US cents.

Even if incomes do not rise homes improve.

YSS serves the poorest 24 per cent

The average incomes for the people served by YSS is between Rs500 to 750 per day or US$.50 to.75 cents: barely enough for food, placing them in the 24 per cent who earn under Rs15,000 a month.

Twenty years of YSS: starting from a ten-dollar donation

The first project in 1965 resettled 78 families who formerly lived under the bridges, on the garbage dump, and along the sidewalk in front of the YSS office. It started with donated seed capital of US$10 or Rs10,000. By 1986, the average monthly working capital of YSS amounted to Rs7,500,000 (US$7,500). Though most contributors prefer to remain anonymous, the major funding source is the Catholic Church societies, through the Bishopric of Semarang, individual anonymous donors, and some from the local authority.

Finding the people in greatest need

YSS employs about 25 permanent staff and 55 field workers. Every day new housing applicants approach YSS, having heard about it from friends and relatives who are in the YSS programme. Fieldworkers interview them to be sure that they really are the people in greatest housing need, with the lowest income, since people tend to dramatize their situation to get housed.

Buying the land

Sites are selected so that they fit in with the city's master plan, are close to public transportation, and have access to clean water. They must also be free from the threat of flooding. YSS buys land mainly through the conventional market, gaining ownership. Some land was also acquired through institutions such as the railway. Prices varied between Rs1,000 and 1,500 per square metre (US$1-1.5) in 1983.

Houses allocated by lottery

Design layout is carried out by YSS, with local authority assistance. Plots are of 80 to 100 square metres, in conventional urban subdivision layouts, side by side along a vehicular road. They are assigned to people by lottery.

Houses and subsequent improvements and additions are self-built.

People participate
The people clear the site and build the houses themselves. Houses are of simple construction and basic: 4 by 6 square metres, detached or semi-detached, with bamboo walls supported by a wooden frame, with tile roof and earth floors. They do not have ceilings or glass windows.

Residents develop their own infractructure
Infrastructure development was left to the residents. Often, YSS provide communal pit latrines where some families can connect their toilets, or communal water standpipes, in co-operation with outside agencies such as OXFAM.

Tenancy agreements regulate use of houses
The housing agreement between YSS and the residents includes the following rules:

Official YSS permission is required to live in the settlement, in the form of a written allocation letter.

Guests may stay for 24 hours, with permission of the chairman of the neighbourhood association; more than 24 hours requires permission from YSS.

Houses cannot be exchanged between residents except by YSS permission, occupancy rights are not transferrable to another person. Only one house per family. Houses empty for over one month are withdrawn and allocated to someone else.

Houses may not be sold or used to guarantee loans. Gambling, alcoholic drinks or intoxicating substances are not allowed.

All dwellers must obey the rules in the letter of agreement. Defaulters will be punished by cancelling their housing rights.

Houses ten times cheaper than market cost
A YSS house and the plot cost about Rs275,000 (US$25) per unit in 1982, rising over the years due to inflation and the scarcity of suitable land for low-cost housing development. This cost is ten times cheaper than the cheapest low standard house produced in 1978 by subsidized developers.

Repayment generates responsibility
Families were supposed to pay for their houses at a rate of US$1.5 a month (10 per cent of the lowest incomes) over a period of 14 years. This repayment was intended to generate a sense of responsibility towards their dwellings and environment rather than as a method of cost recovery. In practice, although the instalments proved very difficult to collect, most residents did maintain their houses and surroundings as well as possible, given their very limited resources.

Infrastructure development is left to the residents.

Recognizing the benefits and limitations

A charity approach
YSS itself describes the limitations of their own programme as follows: " a typical charity approach, operating on the basis of love and the myth of a nice neighbourhood, seeing their target group as helpless objects."

People's development is their responsibility
Once housing is provided by YSS, people's personal development is left to them. A YSS survey revealed that those who made improvements in their life style were a self-selected, predetermined group. Only those who were already highly motivated made efforts to acquire better skills and took part in productive business to improve their lives. The others accepted the housing as a lucky accident or as a gift. This raised their aspirations for more consumer goods. But, without the means to buy them, their frustrations increased. The survey prompted YSS to extend their programme into improving the skills and capabilities of residents.

Incremental resource accumulation
Some families manage to carry out house improvements and to build extensions over time, and as finances permit, to achieve what YSS calls 'incremental resource accumulation'. However, other families never move above the subsistence line and their dwellings never improve at all. YSS also admits that their dwellings are not designed with future extensions in mind, since the initial house provided would first have to be demolished to make way for a bigger house.

From the 'haves' to the 'have-nots'
YSS are fully aware that their programme is based on conventional charity principles requiring endless donations of resources from the 'haves' to be redistributed to the 'have-nots'. The viability of YSS is dependent on continued donations of funds, the availability of cheap land near to job opportunities and the self-motivation of YSS residents. While it allows YSS to consolidate their property holdings, repayment and revolving funds are not considered to be important in YSS schemes.

Programme replicable only if participation increased
YSS feel the programme would not be replicable unless there was increased participation by residents at an early stage. They state that countries with widespread land speculation could not adopt the YSS approach unless major political changes were taking place to support it.

Training and credit is provided for setting up small businesses.

High-rise management and low-rise, self-build co-operatives

Documentation:
Centro Co-operativista
Uruguayo (CCU)
Sector Vivienda
Dante 2251
Montevideo, Uruguay.

Centro Co-operativista Uruguayo

Sponsor:
Habitat International
Coalition (HIC)
Netherlands.

Advisor:
Yves Cabannes
GRET, France.

Text:
Yves Hardy
GRET, France.

Translation:
C and J Norton
Development Workshop
Canada/France

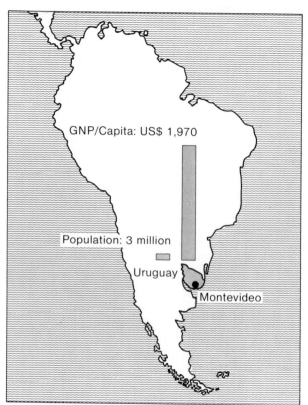

GNP/Capita: US$ 1,970

Population: 3 million

Uruguay

Montevideo

Population Montevideo (1985): 1.5 million
Population Mesa 1: 2,000
Population Complejo Bulevar: 1,600

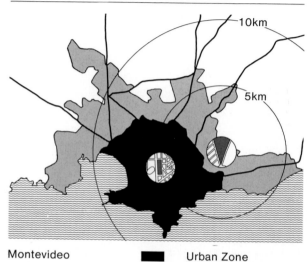

10km

5km

Montevideo

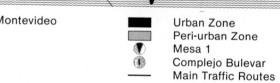

■ Urban Zone
▨ Peri-urban Zone
◍ Mesa 1
◉ Complejo Bulevar
— Main Traffic Routes

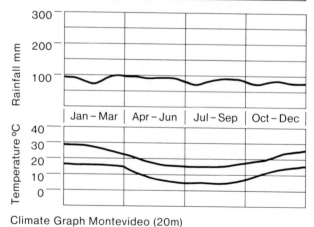

Climate Graph Montevideo (20m)

Montevideo

4S
3S
2S
S

100 80 60 40 20 0   0 20 40 60 80 100

Percentage Distributions of Population by Income Level
S=when 85% of household income must be spent on food

Since 1965, the Centro Co-operativista Uruguayo (CCU) has contributed to producing housing for around 5,000 families who are organized into about 100 co-operatives. Less than one-third of the families were in savings and loan co-operatives. Over two-thirds of the families formed mutual aid co-operatives and made physical contributions to the building work. In both cases, the co-operative members participated in the design and implementation of the works.

Complejo Bulevar: 12 storey buildings housing 1,600 low income and middle class people.

Decent homes for a dignified community

Complejo Bulevar and Mesa 1
Both projects, with the support of the CCU, share the same social objective: to provide quality housing for a population with meagre resources, normally relegated to insecure housing. In 1982, 40 per cent of the families served had only US$220 income per month, the equivalent of three minimum wages.

Both are equally noteworthy for the scale of their operation (26,000 square metres built in each case) and for their technical features: 12 storey blocks of flats in Complejo Bulevar and the use of prefabricated components in Mesa 1.

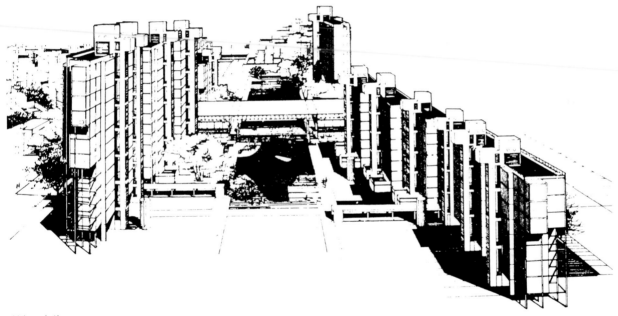

Abbreviations:

CCU	Centro Co-operativista Uruguayo
FUCVAM	Federacion Unificadora de Co-operativas de Viviendas por Ayuda Mutua
COPEVI	Centro Operacional de Vivienda Pobliamento, Mexico
CENVI	Centro de la Vivienda y Estudios, Urbanos, Mexico

	A Savings and Loan Co-operative	A Mutual Aid Co-operative Conjunto Intercooperativo
Location	Complejo Bulevar urban	Mesa 1 peri-urban
Number of Homes	332	420
Surface Area	2.6 hectares	15 hectares
Built-up Area	26,000 square metres approximately	26,000 square metres
Population	1,600 people	1,700 people
Co-operatives	3	5
Social Group	low income middle class	initially working class, later included white collar workers
Housing Type	flats in blocks of up to 12 storeys	flats and apartments of 2 or 3 storeys
Funding	public funds bank mortgages = 80% co-operative members' savings = 20%	public funds bank mortgages = 85% co-operative members' labour input = 15%
Implementation Dates	1970 – 1973	1971 – 1975

Complejo Bulevar: 12 storey apartment buildings have been built through savings and loan co-operatives.

Mesa 1 is planned as a number of small duplexes with either shops or flats on the ground floor.

CCU

Mesa 1, an example of a mutual aid co-operative's achievements. The members' labour represented about 15% of the total cost.

Mesa 1

At the outset of the operation, the majority of the population were of working class origins. By the completion of the building works, 25 per cent of the intended beneficiaries had given up, and were replaced by newcomers, producing a change in the group's social composition. They are now 32 per cent workers, 39 per cent salaried employees, 23 per cent retired, 3 per cent technicians, 2 per cent commercial and 1 per cent unemployed. Typical earnings are about 2 minimum wages as compared to 4 minimum wages in Complejo Bulevar.

Group structure and input

Five mutual aid co-operatives (one organized geographically, the others on the basis of occupation or profession) joined together to build a new co-operative neighbourhood. Its members took part in the project at all stages, from its design to its completion. Co-operative members worked in their 'spare time', an average of 21 hours per week during the house-building phase, spread over weekends and weekday evenings.

The mutual aid co-operative is represented on the central executive, as well as on the various committees responsible for the planning, execution and follow-up of building works. The whole operation benefited throughout from the help of CCU, who provided social, legal and accounting support and appointed specialized personnel (architects and technicians).

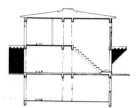

Mesa 1: Plans and facade of 2 storey apartment buildings.

Duplex (2 or 3 bedrooms) on the first and second floor.

Types of Housing

Unit	Number of families	Surface area m²
1-bedroom unit	13	40
2-bedroom unit	230	55
3-bedroom unit	144	70
4-bedroom unit	33	85
Totals	420	26,055

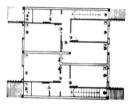

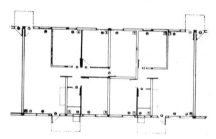

2 or 4 bedroom apartments on the ground floor.

Supplying prefabricated components

FUCVAM (in English, United Federation of Mutual Aid Housing Co-operatives) played an important role in providing the services essential to the co-operative members.

The FUCVAM purchasing department ensured the supply of the bulk of building materials. A prefabricated component factory was installed on the site to produce pre-stressed concrete floor and roof slabs, reinforced concrete beams, door and window frames, and interior staircases.

The housing design chosen is highly standardized, consisting essentially of a small duplex, either built up in groups of individual houses, or in three storeys with the ground floor level set aside either for commercial premises or for dwellings. The programme enabled people to choose from four variations on the design.

Bring your own brick

Total monthly repayments are low, between US$3.5 and US$6.5, one quarter of the payments made by the members of Complejo Bulevar Co-operative.

Thirty-one sites have been set aside for commercial premises, a nursery and a library. The community hall and the school are located on additional sites and sports fields have also been laid out. The co-operative had to overcome several obstacles: a delay of almost 1 year in the completion of the actual work (nearly 3 years, instead of 2) with inevitable repercussions on the costs; problems in establishing an appropriate administrative framework ("The militant spirit doesn't always help in administrative and accounting tasks", acknowledge the co-operative members today); and some poor workmanship.

Nevertheless, the co-operative members declare themselves fully satisfied. Once the housing units had been completed, they continued to make additional improvements to their environment. The spaces between houses have been put to good use by building outdoor cooking facilities (barbecues), workshops or garages. Facades have been repainted and many trees planted.

Mesa 1 neighbourhood has even become a place for a Sunday promenade for Montevideo residents.

A global strategy for CCU

As far as the CCU is concerned, the co-operative movement as a whole must play a major part in the economic and social development of the country. Solidarity and self-management have also taken shape elsewhere, such as in the agri-pastoral sector. Craft, fishing, savings and loan, and consumer co-operatives have also been formed.

All in all, the country is covered by a powerful co-operative network, whose members have an incentive to develop their transactions, and which also, according to CCU officials, fulfills the function of increasing the awareness of co-operative members.

During the dark years of dictatorship (1973-84), the co-operative movement, unlike other popular organizations, especially trades unions, resisted repression relatively well. From the beginning of the 1980s, it was active in promoting the return to democracy.

Despite these successful efforts, (a democracy was set up in March 1985), and many concrete achievements, the co-operative movement is ironically still confronting official resistance to its attempts to recover the freedom of action which it enjoyed at the beginning of the 1970s. The new authorities seem to be in favour of private ownership at the expense of co-operative ownership and organization.

In 1986, in the housing sector alone, 500 families who had organized into 80 co-operatives were awaiting recognition of their status along with government support.

The development of a social project

For CCU and FUCVAM, the role of housing co-operatives does not stop with the building of houses: their activities extend to the provision of educational, cultural, commercial and health facilities.

In Mesa 1 and Complejo Bulevar, from the start it was planned to build schools, libraries, multi-purpose clinics, businesses and sports grounds, along with the house-building activity.

It's not a question of adding years to life but of adding life to years

There are day nurseries for children from 45 days old to 2 years, and children's parks for 2 to 6 year olds have been opened in both neighbourhoods. The Complejo Bulevar children's park has even become a pilot teaching centre, where all the children are introduced to their first foreign language (in this case, French).

Although they number nearly one quarter of the housing co-operative membership, the elderly tended to be left aside. Several types of activity have been put forward to allow them to emerge from their isolation. A mixed group of 50 to 89 year olds, calling itself 'Rebirth', regularly attends gym sessions. Meetings are held in the public halls.

To reinforce the life of the community, the CCU also appoints community workers. One of them says: "No es cuestion de darle años a la vida sino vida a los años." It's not a question of adding years to life, but of adding life to years.

Numerous public facilities, such as sport grounds, were built in Complejo Bulevar.

Particular attention has been paid to children and the elderly, who are often neglected in housing programmes.

The technological debate reopened

Typical of many housing programmes for lower income groups, the CCU aims to lower costs by: mutual aid building, saving about 15 per cent on the cash cost; eliminating intermediaries (building firms, materials suppliers, subcontractors); rationalizing production and introducing innovation, as in Mesa 1, where mutual aid building and prefabrication were combined.

Mesa 1 depended on a prefabrication factory located on the site, making components: floor slabs, light beams, door and window frames. Paradoxically, prefabrication was combined with self-help only for the erection of two- or three-storey buildings at Mesa 1, while at Complejo Bulevar, the twelve-storey buildings were built exclusively with conventional technologies.

The CCU experience revives the question of which technological options can be linked most beneficially to mutual aid.

An inspiring example in Latin America

The Uruguayan experience has spread to several other Latin American countries. In Brazil, the 'Villa Nova Cachoeirinha' programme, Sao Paulo, started on the same principles as Mesa 1. The co-operative system has been carefully studied, in order to maximize the self-help tradition and to produce cheaper accomodation.

The Uruguayan experience of co-operatives has been successfully disseminated, largely due to the architects who followed CCU's operations and trained themselves in the innovations before spreading this knowledge further afield. In Brazil, the architect Pessina worked as a technician with CCU before practising in Sao Paulo and Rio de Janeiro. In Mexico, the architect Carlos Acuña, a former CCU member with experience in housing co-operatives, passed on the benefits to COPEVI and CENVI.

CCU

Peruvians redevelop their inner-city settlement

Documentation:
Gustavo Riofrio and
Marcela Riofrio
CIPUR
Av. San Borja Norte 886
Lima 34, Peru.

El Augustino

Sponsor:
MISEREOR
Federal Republic of
Germany

Advisor:
John F.C. Turner
AHAS, UK.

Text:
Andrew Maskrey and
Bertha Turner
AHAS, UK.

Translation:
Andrew Maskrey,
AHAS, UK.

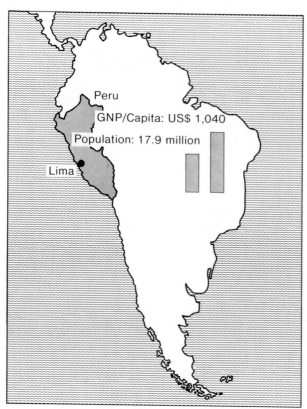

Peru

GNP/Capita: US$ 1,040

Population: 17.9 million

Lima

Population Lima (1981): 4.6 million
Population El Augustino (1983): 6,000

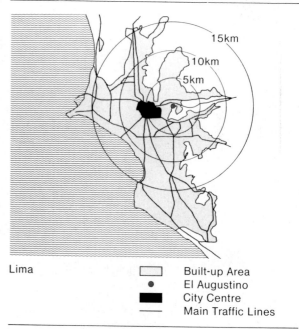

Lima

☐	Built-up Area
•	El Augustino
■	City Centre
—	Main Traffic Lines

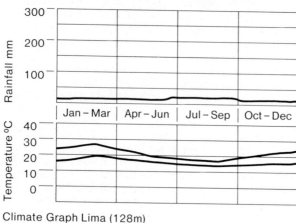

Climate Graph Lima (128m)

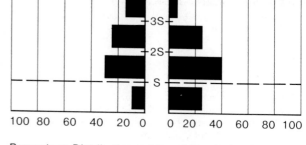

Percentage Distributions of Population by Income Level
S=when 85% of household income must be spent on food

PHOTO: JOHN F.C. TURNER

PHOTO: CIDAP

EL AUGUSTINO

The area in 1964 showing the illegal selling of market garden land for housing (the area in the middle distance and to the right of the main road is the principal city cemetery).

Abbreviations:

CIPUR   Centro de Estudios y Proyectos Urbanos
JNV   Junta Nacional de la Vivienda
ONDEPJOV Oficina Nacional de Desarrollo de los Pueblos Jóvenes
SINAMOS Sistema Nacional de Apoyo a la Mobilización Social
COPRODE Comité de Promoción y Desarrollo

El Augustino is one of the oldest of Lima's 'barriadas' (self-managed and self-built settlements) or 'pueblo jovenes' (young towns) as they are now called. Zone III is one of the six zones into which the large area is divided. Most 'pueblos jóvenes' were formed through the invasion of publicly-owned desert land. El Augustino, however, had its origins in the illegal subdivision of agricultural land. Originally on the periphery of Lima, the city's rapid expansion soon surrounded it, and El Augustino developed into an overcrowded, unplanned inner city area.

El Augustino has been the scene of an interesting and unusual process of settlement remodelling or replanning. In Zone III, the aggregate effect of numerous small subdivisions meant that plots were of irregular shape and size and had been further subdivided over time. Circulation and access were haphazard and the settlement lacked open spaces and community facilities. Remodelling involved drawing up a new layout plan, improving access, regularizing plot sizes and providing open spaces. It also meant reducing density by relocating some of the residents on nearby areas of land.

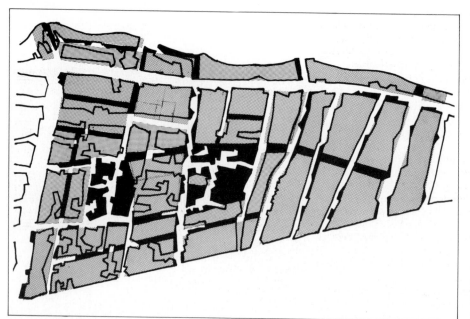

The government agency's remodelling plan: Rejected by the community mainly because it involved an excessive and unnecessary amount of demolition.

Key:

☐ outlines of built-up areas before any remodelling took place

▨ built-up areas in the remodelled layouts

■ areas of building to be demolished or private plots to be taken for streets or open space in the remodelled layouts

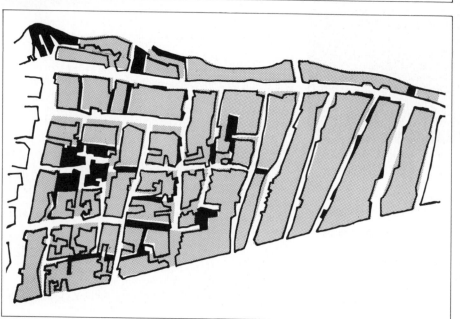

The alternative remodelling plan worked out by the community in collaboration with CIPUR: Far more carefully planned minimizing demolition and relocations.

Residents take over remodelling process

Originally, a government agency promoted the remodelling process, with a passive participation from the residents. Yet when the plan was finally produced, it was rejected by the community. A change of government meant that official support changed to apathy and opposition. In 1979, the residents reorganized themselves and reinitiated the process under their own direction, contracting the assistance of a local non-governmental organization (NGO), the Centre for Urban Projects and Studies (CIPUR).

Although people and their organizations participated actively in drawing up the new plan and in its implementation, the remodelling process stumbled on various obstacles. The lack of support and commitment from government and the difficulty in expropriating the land required for relocating the residents eventually defeated the community's efforts. In 1986, the remodelling process, only 30 per cent complete, ground to a halt.

Despite these set-backs, the experience is both an outstanding example of what low-income people can achieve through their own organization and resources, as well as a demonstration of the need for support from central and local government. It also shows just how effective NGO participation can be, when it is under the direction and control of a community organization.

Rural migrants come to Lima

In the 1950's, Lima grew rapidly, with the modernizing of the urban and the destruction of the rural economies. Lima's wholesale market, established in 1945 at the eastern limits of the city, was a focal point, due to its commercial activities and because it was the terminus for the many bus lines which brought newly arriving migrants from the provinces. Many migrants found work in the market and made their home on a neraby rocky hill, Cerro el Augustino. The demand for housing land soon encouraged tenant farmers, cultivating the fields surrounding the hill, to sell off parcels of this land for housing plots, often in opposition and conflict with the actual landowners.

Selling land you do not own

These subdivisions were illegal, given that the vendor was often not really the owner of the land. Land was 'sold' without planning, urban services or infrastructure. In the area which became Zone III, the northern part was formed

PHOTO: CIDAP

The NGO was approached by the resident's Promotion and Development Committee (COPRODE) who contracted them for advice and technical assistance.

from one single subdivision with regular plots of 150 square metres sold mainly to traders in the market. The southern part was subdivided irregularly and piecemeal, according to the amount each family could afford to pay.

Replanning an existing settlement

Peru has considerable experience in dealing with the formation of new settlements. But it has very little experience of remodelling and improving older settlements. Since 1961, Peru has had legislation specifically designed to deal with existing settlements. The Law of the Marginal Settlements (1961) was intended to stop the formation of new, unauthorized settlements in two ways: existing pueblos jóvenes were to be legalized remodelled and upgraded, while new popular settlements were to be planned to serve the needs of low-income urban families, who could otherwise have no choice but to invade land. Unfortunately, neither of these policies were properly implemented.

The law established that once an existing settlement was officially recognized, government agencies would carry out the following actions: survey the site boundaries;

expropriate the site, which would then be divided into plots for each family; assess the families on a points system to determine who stays in the settlement and who is to be relocated elsewhere; those who owned other property in Lima would have no right to a plot; design a new layout plan; remodel the settlement according to the plan, and reduce density by relocating some families elsewhere; grant legal property titles.

Peru's first official marginal settlements

El Augustino was one of the first pueblos jovenes to be officially declared a marginal settlement. In 1962, the National Housing Board (JNV) began the registration of resident families and initiated expropriation of the site. This gave the residents security of tenure and meant that they stopped paying 'rent' or other 'quotas' to owners and their agents. Over the next few years, the Zone III Co-ordinating Committee (combining what are now Zones II, IV and V) was actively contracting their own professionals to carry out a topographical survey and to draw up a plan of the area. The actual remodelling process did not really begin until 1972.

Pueblos jovenes become respectable
The military regime of Velasco Alvarado seized power in 1968, giving positive support to community organization in the 'barriadas', which were then made more legally acceptable by their new name: 'pueblos jóvenes'. Two government agencies, the National Office of Pueblos Jóvenes (ONDEPJOV) and the National System of Support for Social Mobilization (SINAMOS) promoted block or street committees. These local groups elected in their settlements a Promotion and Development Committee (COPRODE). In 1972, the COPRODE of Zone III was formed. In the same year, SINAMOS decided to implement the remodelling of El Augustino, starting with Zones II and VI.

Reduced density means some must leave
Deciding which residents could stay and which would have to relocate should have stimulated the interest of the people of Zone III. Instead, local participation was passive, leaving the authorities to take the initiatives. The COPRODE leaders worked with the authorities, taking decisions on behalf of the residents without consulting them. This generated discontent when the outcome was known, especially amongst those who would have to move.

Creating space for the remodelling
The key to the success of the remodelling was in acquiring land to relocate the excess families. SINAMOS had already earmarked land: Parcelas A, B, C, D; and the residents of Zone III began negotiating with the owner to buy Parcela A. They even opened their own communal savings account at the bank. At one point, there were enough savings to buy the land outright, but SINAMOS insisted on expropriation, which was accepted by the residents.

Zone III's proposed new layout sought to improve the circulation pattern and to provide plots of regular dimensions. It also sought to avoid demolition of permanent brick and concrete houses, wherever possible. However, the plan generated resistance from the residents. They felt that it clearly favoured the better-off northern sector, which would be left almost untouched. Large areas of the overcrowded southern sector were to be demolished, displacing many families to make way for areas of educational, recreational and community use.

Conflict with authority
From 1976, a new military government sought to repress community organization, first using SINAMOS and then de-activating that agency altogether. The residents began to organize against the remodelling and against the existing leaders, who were collaborating with the authorities. This activity was risky in the context of official repression. Nevertheless, the residents' 'Defence Committee' managed to stop the process and to denounce the leaders for mismanagement of funds.

The residents take charge
From 1979 onward, the residents themselves took charge of the remodelling process, with help from CIPUR. A new COPRODE was elected, which soon had to its credit the following achievements: legal approval of the expropriation of Parcela A, which was later found to have legal errors, making it invalid; update of the registration of residents; invasion of Parcela A to occupy and secure it until the expropriation was completed; tenders invited from professionals and accepting the services of CIPUR.

The community as client

Unlike other NGOs, CIPUR did not approach the residents for altruistic or benevolent motives. It was contracted directly by COPRODE to update the settlement plan, prepare a new layout plan and to supervise the implementation of the remodelling. CIPUR also had to co-ordinate with the government and the municipality who still held legal responsibility for the process. The differences between a conventional consultancy in the private sector and working for a settlement organization were understood by CIPUR. The client group would require lengthy debates for each decision taken, have different technical needs and very limited financial resources.

The settlement plan was updated through a series of lengthy meetings with each of the 27 committees of Zone III. This allowed detailed information to be collected, and also established the confidence of residents in COPRODE and in the professionals whom they had contracted. the new layout plan was jointly worked out, stage by stage, in the presence of each committee. Eventually, the total proposal was developed, acceptable to all the residents, including those of the northern sector.

Planning the layout and remodelling

The definitive layout plan incorporated further changes proposed by the residents. These were approved by the authorities as a modification of the earlier SINAMOS plan. In 1983, the community obtained a grant from MISEREOR, the German Catholic aid agency, which was administered through the local parish, to cover the cost of plans and designs and to initiate the implementation.

The remodelling implementation was planned in four stages, spread over six months, to consist of: adjusting plot sizes to the new layout; relocating excess families and installing temporary sanitary services; demolishing construction which did not fit into the new layout; final adjustments and official handing over of the plots to families by the Municipality of Lima.

Of 1,000 families in Zone III, 848 would remain in the settlement after remodelling, while 152 would move to Parcela A.

PHOTO: CIDAP

After setbacks and the take-over of a less supportive government, the residents reinstated the process of remodelling with NGO assistance.

PHOTO: T.U. HAMBURG – HARBURG STUDY PROJECT

Despite set-backs, arising mainly from the unfulfilled promise of adjacent land acquisition by government for the relocation of displaced by the improvements, much has been achieved by the residents with their own resources.

Implementation brings people problems

Problems emerged in the first stage of implementation. Families scheduled for relocation to Parcela A refused to move there, instead occupying public areas. The legal situation of Parcela A was still ambiguous: although the Municipality had officially declared it a 'pueblo joven', the expropriation was still incomplete.

Despite the efforts of COPRODE, the situation deteriorated further as the other stages of implementation went ahead. It became impossible to keep to the original layout and timetable. The families who refused Parcela A began building in public areas, using permanent materials. Others felt the remodelling was damaging their interests and sued COPRODE leaders for violation of private property.

The end result was the paralysis of the process in 1985, with a complete loss of credibility and prestige for all the people and institutions involved in the remodelling.

Why the project broke down

The two very different experiences of remodelling in El Augustino's Zone III show how much more can be achieved when people themselves are actively in control, rather than being passive beneficiaries of a government programme. They also show that when NGOs are supporting people's programmes and are contracted and directed by a community organization, the NGOs play a much more significant role than when they are acting in a paternalistic way.

Unlike remodelling and upgrading processes carried out in other countries and contexts, in El Augustino government's participation was minimal. The people and their organizations took on all responsibility for a process for which the state was legally responsible. Apart from the grant from MISEREOR, the very low-income people themselves financed the entire programme, including paying the professionals, without even having access to credit.

The eventual failure of the process, however, shows the limits of people with few resources acting on their own. Community organization resolved internal differences to arrive finally at the necessary consensus to start the remodelling. But it was powerless to overcome external constraints. In particular, the problem of land for relocating families and the failure to complete the expropriation of Parcela A was the single most important factor in the breakdown of the process. The length of the remodelling process and the intensity of the involvement required were additional factors which put undue stress on community leaders and the organization as whole, and eventually wore them out.

Partnership between people and government

The experience shows the vital imporance of co-operation between government and local people. The remodelling of El Augustino would have been different if government agencies, such as the judicial system and the police, had supported the people instead of working directly against them.

The story of El Augustino points to the need for a new relationship between people and their government. People should have the responsibility for their own projects, while government provides the necessary and appropriate support. If the roles could be redefined in this way, processes of urban improvement could be carried out which are both highly replicable and cost effective.

Tenement renters buy and rebuild their Mexico City homes

Documentation:
Priscilla Connolly
c/o CENVI
Patricio Sanz 449
Colonia del Valle
Mexico DF 03100, Mexico

Guerrero

Sponsor:
International Development
Research Centre (IDRC)
Canada

Advisor:
Yves Cabannes
GRET, France.

Text:
Yves Hardy
GRET, France.

Translation:
C. and J. Norton
Development Workshop
Canada/France

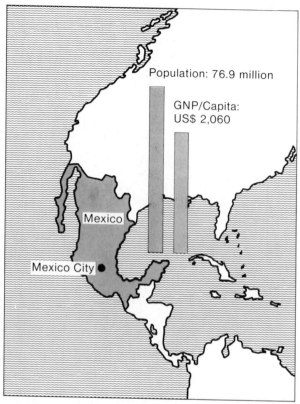

Population: 76.9 million

GNP/Capita:
US$ 2,060

Mexico

Mexico City

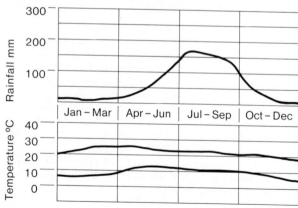

Climate Graph Mexico City (2,315m)

Population Metropolitan Area (1986): 20 million
Population Federal District (1986): 9.5 million
Population Los Angeles District (1970): 25,000

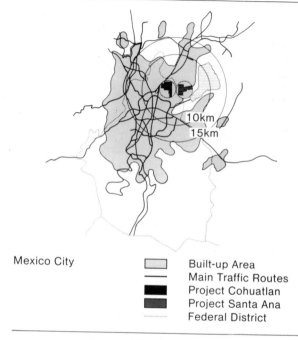

Mexico City

	Built-up Area
	Main Traffic Routes
	Project Cohuatlan
	Project Santa Ana
	Federal District

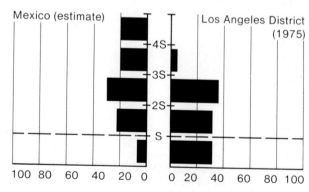

Percentage Distributions of Population by Income Level
S=when 85% of household income must be spent on food

GUERRERO

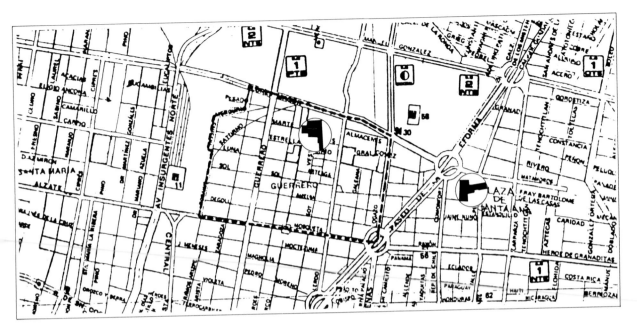

Location of Los Angeles 'Barrio' in Colonia Guerrero, in the centre of Mexico City.

Los Angeles District, location of the Guerrero Housing and Services Co-operative, is a 59.5 hectare area in the centre of Mexico City. From the end of the nineteenth century, the railway industry invested in the area and the population consisted mainly of railwaymen and workers. But in 1950, the government started to dismantle most of the railway installations, and many people left the District. The population declined from 35,400 in 1950 to only 24,900 by 1970.

Abbreviations:

CENVI	Centro de la Vivienda y Estudios Urbanos, Mexico
COPEVI	Centro Operacional de Vivienda y Pobliamento, Mexico
FONHAPO	Fondo de Habitación Popular
INFONAVIT	Instituto de Fomento Nacional de Vivienda de Trabajadores

Genesis of the projects 1974-5

The majority of those who remained lived on low incomes. In 1975, 32 per cent of the residents earned the minimum wage or less.

The majority of dwellings in the District were old, and of the traditional house type known as 'vecindades'. Some twenty (or more) cramped rooms were arranged around a central 'patio'. The 'vecindades' were overcrowded and decrepit, but the tenants preferred to remain there, valuing their location close to the city centre.

INFONAVIT, a state organization, proposed to COPEVI, a non-governmental organization (NGO) that an alternative renovation project be developed, calling on the participation of the community.

In 1975, COPEVI set in motion initial surveys and plans, in collaboration with the future beneficiaries, using an evolutionary housing model.

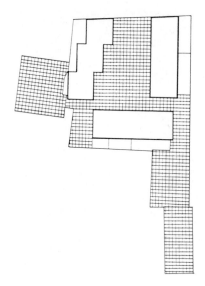

First Project: Cohuatlan 1975-8
60 dwellings in two six-storey buildings and
one one-storey building
Dwelling size: 32 to 86 square metres

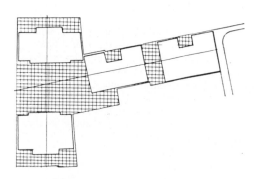

Second Project: Santa Ana 1982-6
32 dwellings in four-storey buildings
Dwelling size: 60 square metres on average

The first project - Cohuatlán 1975-8

In January 1976, the inhabitants officially registered the Guerrerro Housing Co-operative with the aim of providing housing and services. Sixty homes would be distributed amongst 3 buildings of 4 to 6 floors. The work began in 1977 and the 3 blocks were officially opened in 1978. The extra costs of the operation to the residents were covered by public loans.

The second project - Santa Ana 1982-7

The Santa Ana project, separated from the Los Angeles District by a major road, developed along similar lines to that of the Cohuatlán site, bringing together the local residents.

The technical assistance group, CENVI, moved into action. By August 1982, they presented a project proposal to INFONAVIT providing for 32 homes to be built, equally distributed between 4-storey buildings.

Because of the financial crisis, INFONAVIT found its budget axed and the project was held up for two years. The building work finally began in May 1986.

Overcrowded 'vecindad' rooms open onto semi-public patios. Yet, the people want to stay.

PHOTOS: CENVI, MEXICO CITY

"We want to die in Guerrero, but not under a pile of rubble."

More than a project or two, a process
The main virtues of the Cohuatlán and Santa Ana operations are their existence as concrete examples, and that they launched a new process. The two projects (one now inhabited, the other well on the way to completion) show that renovation in an urban centre on behalf of a low-income population is possible.

A triple alliance
In both cases, the dynamic of the process is based on a triple alliance (federal authorities, co-operative members, and non-government organization). The results achieved have contributed to forging new institutional tools, and to modifying urban legislation. The creation in 1981 of FONHAPO (the National Fund for Popular Housing) constitutes an undeniable step forward. This new organization can allocate collective loans to a group of co-operative members or organized users whose incomes are less than two and a half times the minimum wage. The passing in 1981 of a new federal housing law has also provided a more favourable legislative framework for buildings and renovation of 'social priority housing'.

During the implementation of the Cohuatlán improvements, before these legal reforms existed, the triple alliance had to compromise to take into account institutional constraints. At that time, INFONAVIT and the other public financial organizations were only allowed to recognize private property as a valid mortgage guarantee. Meanwhile, the future inhabitants of Cohuatlán were putting forward co-operatively-owned property, as were the technical assistance groups, COPEVI and CENVI. After numerous discussions, an intermediate solution was adopted. The statute accepted the principle of joint property (based on private property). However, the Guerrero Co-operative was granted a pre-emptive right over sales of the Co-operative's housing. In the event of any members dropping out, the Co-operative would designate those to whom new allocations should be made (with INFONAVIT's agreement).

At last, after long efforts, renovation takes place.

An independent local advisory group start working with the local inhabitants.

The benefit and joy are shared by the whole neighbourhood.

The partners also successfully negotiated waivers to the existing planning regulations with the administrative division of Cuahtemoc. The maximum net density allowed was 284 homes to the hectare. Regulations also specified three parking places for every 4 dwellings in 1978 and one for every dwelling in 1982. Reductions in parking spaces were negotiated and agreed: one lock-up garage for every 4 homes in Cohuatlan and two lock-ups for every 3 homes in Santa Ana.

Acceptable extra costs

The Co-operative's members agreed to pay extra for improvements to the Cohuatlán project. Thirty per cent of families paying more than P100 per month are those with the highest incomes, who were not eligible for the highly advantageous INFONAVIT loans. They borrowed instead from another financial institution at 10 per cent interest, repayable over 15 years.

Surface area of homes	Previous housing % of families	Cohuatlán housing
Up to 25m²	30%	0%
26 - 35m²	39%	0%
36 - 45m²	17%	10%
46 - 55m²	10%	15%
Over 55m²	4%	75%
Average surface area	31.80m²	64.00m²
Habitable surface area per person	5.19m²	10.57m²

Services	Previous housing % of families	Cohuatlán housing
Indoor running water	60%	100%
Indoor ventilation	30%	100%
Windows	15%	100%

The guarantees required by INFONAVIT and its financial methods (monthly repayments deducted at source from the co-operative members' wages) excluded from the programme the least well off: the unemployed or those with irregular incomes or undeclared jobs. These restrictions gave rise to debates within the technical assistance groups. CENVI summarizes its position as follows: "One needs to remember that the problem of housing, at least as far as Mexico is concerned, involves not only the poorest of the poor, but also nearly all sectors of the working class. And if one fails to seek a solution to the latter problem, it will be difficult to resolve the issue of the least well off. In any case, if one adopts the criterion of seeking solutions only on behalf of the most needy, then in Mexico, as in many other countries, it would be necessary to direct all resources to rural areas, as it is certainly there that one finds the cases of most extreme poverty."

Monthly payments Pesos/month	Previous housing % of families	Cohuatlán housing
Up to 300	89%	0%
301 - 400	11%	5.5%
401 - 500	0%	25.5%
501 - 600	0%	30%
601 - 1,000	0%	13.5%
Over 1,000	0%	30%

CENVI's dilemma: self-finance or self-destruction

The challenge of an independent advisory group
The two projects highlight the important role played by COPEVI and CENVI, the technical assistance groups.

The time they spent in supporting the community from the beginning to the actual setting up of the co-operative was considerable. Between May 1975 and March 1976, a period of forty-six calendar weeks, the time spent giving technical assistance to the co-operative amounted to approximately three person/years, the equivalent of three persons working full-time with the co-operative for one year.

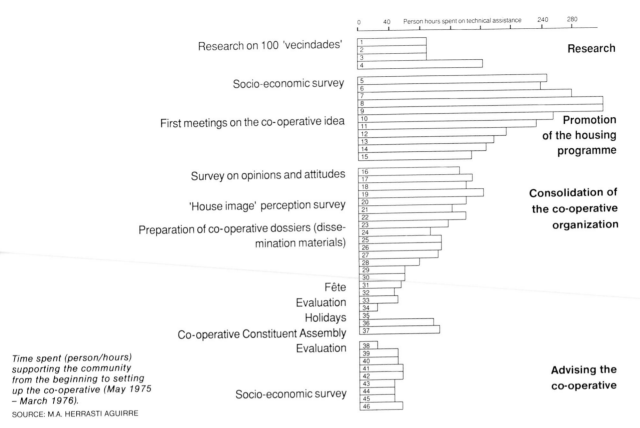

Person hours spent on technical assistance

Research on 100 'vecindades'	**Research**
Socio-economic survey	
First meetings on the co-operative idea	**Promotion of the housing programme**
Survey on opinions and attitudes	**Consolidation of the co-operative organization**
'House image' perception survey	
Preparation of co-operative dossiers (dissemination materials)	
Fête	
Evaluation	
Holidays	
Co-operative Constituent Assembly	
Evaluation	**Advising the co-operative**
Socio-economic survey	

Time spent (person/hours) supporting the community from the beginning to setting up the co-operative (May 1975 – March 1976).

SOURCE: M.A. HERRASTI AGUIRRE

GUERRERO

The activities which took place during this initial period of the co-operative's development included research on 100 'vecindades', socio-economic and attitude surveys, preparation and dissemination of information, liaising with the administrative and financial authorities, social events and meetings of the co-operative, giving advice, and carrying out an evaluation.

It should be noted that apart from the COPEVI/CENVI groups, some universities and their students have participated in the process by collaborating on the socio-economic survey of the District and on the development of housing proposals.

On an architectural level, it is interesting to observe once more, that a non-governmental organization can effectively tackle collective housing.

A particular effort was also made to interest the media (newspapers, magazines), in order to make the achievements of Cohuatlán known, stimulating others and generating a ripple effect. New co-operatives and neighbourhood unions have been set up, leading COPEVI and CENVI officials to keep up their links with the media.

The problem of finding financial resources to remunerate the professionals of non-governmental organizations remains unsolved. Between 1975 and 1978, COPEVI was only able to finance its technical assistance team through donations from a German charitable organization, MISEREOR. From 1979 to 1986, CENVI could afford to finance this assistance from its own resources because the expenses were to be reimbursed, though it took 2 or 3 years for the funds to arrive. These expenses are categorized as 'indirect costs' in the loan granted to the co-operative. But CENVI seems to doubt that this type of technical assistance, high cost both in economic and in human terms, can be offered indefinitely. CENVI staff's assessment of Cohuatlán and Santa Ana states: "...as far as technical assistance is concerned, there are two possibilities. In the first place, one can envisage that part of the assistance tasks would be ensured by means of voluntary or paid work by members of the user group or co-operative. In that event, one would need suitable training. One could also speculate that another series of assistance tasks, notably under financial and administrative headings, might be taken on by the public sector, through its housing finance organizations or by means of new institutions."

The shock of the earthquake

Minimal co-operation
In the case of Cohuatlán and of Santa Ana, the co-operative principle was essentially applied to the management (in the broadest sense of the word) of the housing programme. Actual building work was done by outside firms; there was no self-help building. Three years after the completion of the Cohuatlán programme, it was possible to observe, in the dramatic circumstances of the Mexico City earthquake of September 19 and 20, 1985, the lack of continued involvement of the Guerrero Co-operative. While the Los Angeles District was not so severely affected as other areas, the fact remains that it was other organizations: the neighbourhood union, backed up by students, architects; and 'House and City', a non-governmment organization, which took in hand most of the tasks of clearing and reconstruction of destroyed 'vecindades'.

". . . the community roots of traditional Mexico remain intact."
The seismic tremors of September 1985, which cost the lives of nearly 15,000 people and reduced some 300,000 others to the status of disaster victims, also shattered the regulations on urban development and disrupted the work taking place at the time. Even though the buildings of Cohuatlán withstood the tremor well, building norms were amended. The system of concrete posts and beams with breeze-block infill, intended for use in Santa Ana, now had to be replaced by thin, load-bearing panels of reinforced concrete.

The earthquake finally obliterated many of the old 'vecindades': 13,000 were totally destroyed and 40,000 others needed essential repairs. The new regulations mean that they can only be replaced by buildings with a maximum of three storeys. The institutional framework has also been changed. A new public organization called 'Restoration' has been created.

But whatever the new rules of the urban game, the authorities should reckon with the inhabitants' capacity to mobilize, and the general solidarity which they displayed in September 1985. In this respect, the co-operative 'school' and the neighbourhood groups played a prominent role in increasing public awareness.

As far as the Mexican writer Octavio Paz is concerned, the catastrophe of September 1985 also "...showed that in the depths of society, underground but alive, the seeds of democracy exist in profusion." "For", he observes, "in a matter of hours, popular action spread over and submerged the area occupied by government authorities. It was not a rebellion, an upheaval or a political movement. It was a social tide, revealed peacefully, by the true reality, the historic reality of Mexico. Or more precisely the inter-historic reality of the nation." And it is Octavio Paz who concludes that "the community roots of traditional Mexico remain intact. It was an admirable spectacle, and one on which our governments, and all those who, like many of our intellecuals, idolize the state, would do well to reflect. The historic and social lesson of the earthquake can be reduced to this one sentence: **Render unto society that which belongs to society.**"

Rural migrants gain secure housing in Mexico

Documentation:
Rocio Lombera G
COPEVI, Tlaloc 40
Mexico 17 DF, Mexico.

Palo Alto Co-operative

Sponsor:
MISEREOR
Federal Republic of
Germany

Advisor:
Yves Cabannes
GRET, France.

Text:
Yves Hardy
GRET, France and
Rocio Lombera G.
Mexico.

Translation:
C. and J. Norton
Development Workshop
Canada/France.

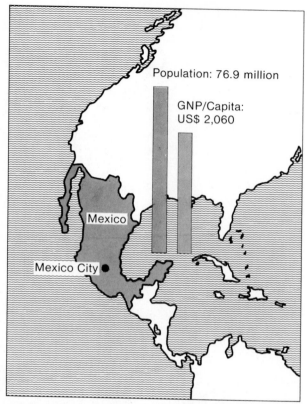

Population: 76.9 million

GNP/Capita:
US$ 2,060

Mexico

Mexico City

Population Metropolitan Area (1986): 20 million
Population Federal District (1986): 9.5 million
Population Palo Alto: 1,330

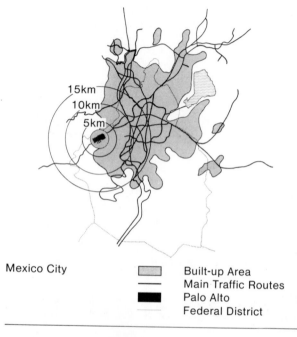

Mexico City

- Built-up Area
- Main Traffic Routes
- Palo Alto
- Federal District

15km
10km
5km

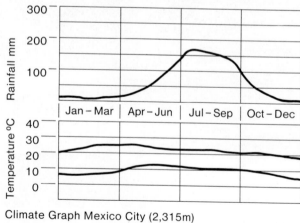

Climate Graph Mexico City (2,315m)

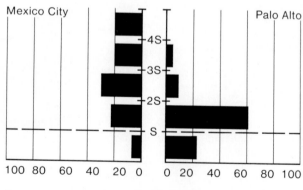

Percentage Distributions of Population by Income Level
S=when 85% of household income must be spent on food

Abbreviations:

COPEVI   Centro Operacional de Vivienda y
           Pobliamento A.C.

Palo Alto: The squatter settlement near sand quarries ... the first houses under construction. In the back, upper class area where luxury housing predominates.

PHOTO: KNA, WEST GERMANY

The Palo Alto Co-operative was organized in 1972, when a group of settlers, formerly from the rural areas, joined together to obtain the rights to land they had occupied for more than 30 years. The co-operative is made up of 317 families, or about 2,250 people. Their average monthly household incomes are the equivalent of US$100.

Palo Alto District is located about 15 kilometres to the west-south-west of the Federal District of Mexico, on the Toluca road. Situated in a very rugged area at an altitude of 2,455 metres, it is higher than the central part of the city. The locality is only partially urbanized: agricultural land covers 57.8 square kilometres of the area, compared to the 15 square kilometres which are urbanized.

Background, from 1940 to 1969

For half a century, Mexican economic development has been accompanied by an uninterrupted migratory flow from country to town, reflected in the staggering growth of the built-up area of Mexico City (nearly 20 million inhabitants in 1987), and in the average density of urbanized space in the Federal District (178 inhabitants per hectare).

From 1940 onward, small groups of peasant families from the Contepec region (Michoacan) began to arrive at the Palo Alto site, seeking jobs in the local industries, particularly in the sand quarries, where they received a minimal wage for working an 11 hour day. Their employer rented them the land they occupied, and they built squatter housing, using locally available materials (stones, mud, roofing felt). Some families sheltered in the abandoned caves left by the sand quarries. At the start, water, electricity, and drains were totally lacking and the new inhabitants used oil lamps for lighting. Lack of contact with the outside world made them unaware that any change in their lives was possible. In their isolation, they endured a life of sub-human conditions and exploitation.

A struggle for land 1969-79

In 1969, the landowner decided to sell, in order to add his land onto a neighbouring estate of predominantly luxury housing: 'Bosques de las Lomas' (Woods of the Hills). Threatened with eviction, and rejecting the idea of being relocated, the inhabitants of Palo Alto united and formed the 'Union de Vecinos de Palo Alto' (Palo Alto Neighbourhood Union). They received the support of a Catholic priest, Father Escamilla, who, together with a few social workers, was already striving to achieve some minimum facilities (a clinic in particular) in the area.

In 1972, they organized themselves into a co-operative and contracted technical assistance from COPEVI (Centro Operacional de Vivienda y Poblamiento A.C.) a non-

PALO ALTO

The inhabitants of Palo Alto consider that their organization into a neighbourhood union (1969) and then into a housing co-operative (1972) is at the root of the successes achieved.

From 1940 onward families from Michoacan arrived on Palo Alto site where they lived as squatters.

governmental organization. The Palo Alto Co-operative was officially registered in the same year, and an area of 46,242 square metres was designated for a project to house 237 families (1,330 people).

In 1973, after two years of negotiations with the authorities, and with the landowner, who made attempts to break up the co-operative, the members took possession of the land. Official recognition of their land tenure had become a reality.

A financial compromise was found with the heirs, who recognized the rights of the occupiers, in return for a phased payment of P200,000 (US$16,000 in 1975), as the total land price.

Despite the progress made, the co-operative members felt that they were living in a hostile environment. The owners of the neighbouring luxury estate, 'Bosques de las Lomas', built a stone wall to avoid all contact with them, and denied them connections with the public infrastructure which served their estate. Other sides of their site are bordered by a busy highway (the Toluca road), a high tension cable, a ravine and a firing range!

The Palo Alto residents, wanting above all to ward off the danger of eviction, preferred to build their houses in permanent, durable materials to increase their security. For the same reason, their homes had to be completed quickly, and before the installation of basic infrastructures. The co-operative members decided to build their homes through mutual aid and self-help. COPEVI was given responsibility for the design and for monitoring the implementation.

A two-storey model house was built first. Then, the neighbourhood was built in 3 stages: 75 homes started in 1976 were completed two years later; 57 homes started in 1978 were completed in 1979; financial preparations for 34 homes began in 1980.

During the intervening two years, 46 additional homes were built by their occupiers, entirely with their own resources, and according to their own methods of building.

By the end of 1985, 189 homes were completed for a community of 237 families. This has satisfied 80 per cent of the demand.

Self-help building brigades were organized by the co-operative members to erect durable houses.

Professional masons were hired to speed up the works.

Housing the next generation

In the remaining 48 plots, 144 housing units are planned, to be built for the next generation. The idea of reserving part of the site for the children of the co-operative members, who would one day be forming their own families, was at first received with mixed reactions. Some were enthusiastic, while others suspected the motives behind it. Anxiety led a few residents to question the principle of co-operatives, as compared to private property. But as the works progressed, their fears were dispelled. The cohesion of the group had been tested, and was quickly restored. The community was even strengthened by adding a new dimension for the original co-operators, bringing security in old age as future generations grew up in Palo Alto.

A clinic, a community hall, a chapel, a dairy, a communal store, a storeroom, and a cement block factory were built, and playgrounds were prepared. Despite difficult beginnings, Palo Alto has become a self-contained neighbourhood.

Basic infrastructure started in 1979 is now complete: water, drains, public lighting. The streets are paved and a few public telephones installed.

Core house with 52 m² floor area that can be expanded to a maximum of 108 m².

First floor

Ground floor on a 9 x 12 metre plot.

Key factors in Palo Alto's achievements

Collective tenure

The legal structure of a housing co-operative unified and strengthened the group by making it possible to hold the land and housing in collective tenure. Permanence on the site was secured. Collective tenure avoided the pitfalls inherent in private ownership of land: speculation, rising prices, changes of occupants and tenancy, which could have weakened the community spirit and eventually caused their organization to collapse.

Community control of land and buildings has protected the interests of the co-operative members. Fifteen years later, the co-operative still controls the property, and the original population continues to benefit — a rare case in a luxury, residential suburb of Mexico City.

'Evolutionary' housing

The co-operative needed to establish their hold on the land by erecting permanent housing quickly. But, lacking the economic resources to build completed houses, they decided to build 'evolutionary' housing, which could be enlarged and completed as time and finances allowed.

Everyone started with the same core house of 52 square metres, as an expression of their unity. It could be enlarged in three stages, to the maximum size of 102 square metres on a 108 square metres (9 x 12 metres) plot. On the ground floor are sanitation, kitchen, living room; the first floor is an area for bedrooms.

The plot size was larger than that provided by the government or the private sector to families of this income level. Yet large families of 6 people or more, who are the majority (40 per cent of the population is under 16 years of age), were concerned with the smallness of the initial core house (52 square metres). Some spoke of a 'doll's house'; the possibility of building extensions was not yet clearly perceived. Shortly after completion of the first phase, many families built an additional room on each level, as a lean-to against one of the walls of the core house. Some went on to build over the entire plot.

The decision to build permanent housing before the services were installed brings into question the wisdom of the conventional sites-and-services approach to housing programmes for the low- and very low-income settlers. Sites-and-services programmes may solve the problems of land acquisition, sanitation, and health, but their costs are usually beyond the means of the intended population, and they often turn into middle-class neighbourhoods.

The legal framework and housing type chosen in Palo Alto were important factors in modifying existing housing norms, which at that time were the same for both low-income settlements and middle-class areas.

The issue of affordable, incrementally-built housing for low-income people has had a major impact on housing policy. It has inspired official programmes of 'core' and 'progressive' dwellings which have been promoted by both non-governmental and government organizations.

Self-help and mutual aid

The democratic structure of the group stimulated active participation. Men, women, and even children took an active part in the decision-making and programme development.

To strengthen community organization and to promote fairness in the allocation of the houses produced, the community labour force was organized into mutual aid and self-help groups.

The building technology adopted had already been successfully used in Uruguay. It consisted of prefabricated elements, including reinforced brick panels and prefabricated concrete beams, covered with a ferrocement screed as roofing. This system provided a more economic alternative to the traditional reinforced concrete slab. The walls were of cement blocks made on the site. The women strongly influenced the choice of this unfamiliar technology, since this building method allowed them to take part in the construction.

Some families, along with some of the professional masons, were doubtful about the earthquake-resistant properties of this unfamiliar method, and so chose to build in the traditional, time-consuming way. Out of a total 189 families, 143 completed their homes through self-help building, using the recommended system. Subseqent extensions were built with a standard, on-site, reinforced concrete floor slab.

Increases in the costs of building materials, particularly bricks, caused some anxiety about the expected economies. But a later survey in 1985 confirmed that the new technology not only reduced costs, but also increased family participation in the building process. Families spent up to 80 per cent of their free time in building their own homes.

From 1977 onward, a production unit was set up to produce cement blocks and metal door- and window-frames, creating eight jobs for co-operative members.

Pioneering alternative finance

It proved difficult to raise the funds needed to start the project, as no banking institution would agree to grant loans collectively to low-income co-operative members. To remove this stumbling block, COPEVI negotiated a grant in 1976 with MISEREOR, a foreign foundation, to create FONVICOOP, a non-profit organization providing building materials loans to housing co-operatives to a value of P14,000 (P15.44 equalled US$1 in 1976). This established the precedent of granting credit collectively. It also led to the government's establishment of INDECO (National Community Development Institute), which granted a loan to the Palo Alto Co-operative in 1980. (INDECO now no longer exists.)

Palo Alto played a pioneering role: it was the first time in Mexico that credit was allocated to a collective, instead of to individuals. This gave hope to many low-income people in squatter settlements, groups denied credit by the banks and, therefore, the opportunity to build permament homes. FONHAPO, 'Fideicomiso Fondo de Habitaciones Populares', or, in English, 'National Fund for Popular (low income) Housing', which evolved directly from INDECO, intended to increase the financing of new housing co-operatives, but increasingly ran into financial difficulties.

Solidarity and democracy

The basis for Palo Alto Co-operative's success lies in its community organization and sustained effort. Their solidarity enabled the inhabitants to withstand the threats of eviction, the attempts to divide them made by the landowner and his heirs, and to find the financial resources to build successfully. They pay tribute to Father Escamilla, who died in 1976. Together with the social workers, he laid the foundations of the alliance between the inhabitants and their collective work. Most of the members credit the shared, organized action as the major factor in their successful struggle for their rights.

Since 1970, the residents have met together in a general assembly at least once a week to debate, plan and co-ordinate community matters. This long experience of direct democracy has ensured collective decision-making and effective implementation. The high level of democracy and participation developed in the Palo Alto Co-operative is not commonly found in other settlers' groups.

The co-operative has also instituted committees for administration, co-operative education, social welfare, communication, technical, and financial matters. This prevents work and power from being concentrated in a few hands, or in an internal bureaucracy, as well as ensuring collective control of information, knowledge and a broader participation.

A modest but long-term social impact

The Palo Alto experience occurred under inauspicious circumstances. There was no significant urban movement capable of paving the way, and the repression of the 1968 movement was still in the air. The new arrivals on the Palo Alto site, coming directly from the very feudal atmosphere of the countryside, were not conditioned by past experience to conduct the long struggle against landowners and administrative authorities in which they found themselves. The relative isolation of the site and the limited number of people involved (237 families, 1,330 people) raised fears that the authorities might easily overpower and defeat the Palo Alto protestors.

Yet forty-five years after the first arrivals, Palo Alto has well and truly taken shape, and the housing co-operative's achievements have also become a landmark, inspiring similar approaches at national policy level. Besides generating integrated development of community self-help and influencing new procedures which made finance accessible to the very poor, it has also helped to develop a more flexible legal, financial, technical, and administrative framework to assist and support projects of other community-based organizations.

Wider awareness of the potential for a higher degree of control by local people over their own homes and neighbourhoods has been generated. Low-income settlement areas, now labelled 'colonias populares' (popular or low-income districts), benefit from a special ruling which helps to resolve the structural problems of these areas.

Palo Alto demonstrates that housing co-operatives can work, even when people have very low incomes, expanding the range of alternatives possible in other developing countries.

Argentinians secure tenure and develop their settlement

Documentation:
Co-operativa 20 de Junio
Diagonal Ica 975
B General Bustos
Córdoba 5001, and
AVE/CEVE/SEHAS
Igualdad 3600
Villa Siburu
Córdoba 5000, Argentina.

Villa Chaco Chico

Sponsor:
MISEREOR
Federal Republic of
Germany

Advisor:
John F.C. Turner
AHAS, UK.

Text:
Andrew Maskrey and
Bertha Turner
AHAS, UK.

GNP/Capita: US$ 2,230

Population: 30.1 million

Córdoba

Argentina

Population Córdoba (1986): 993,000
Population Villa Chaco Chico (1986): 650

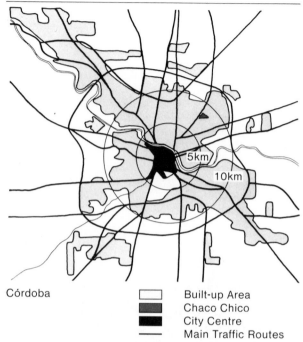

Córdoba

- Built-up Area
- Chaco Chico
- City Centre
- Main Traffic Routes

Average monthly income in Villa Chaco Chico is
US$230 for families and US$182 for heads of families.
The minimum wage is US$121. About 50% of the
people are in the medium-low income bracket, and
about 25% each are in the low and medium brackets.

Abbreviations:

AVE	Association de Vivienda Económica
CEVE	Centro Experimental de Vivienda Económica
SEHAS	Servicio Habitacional y de Acción Social
CEBEMO	Central Agency for Joint Financing of Development Programmes, Netherlands

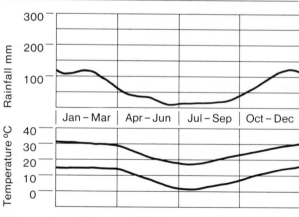

Climate Graph Córdoba (425m)

Spontaneous settlement layout of Chaco Chico, 1969.

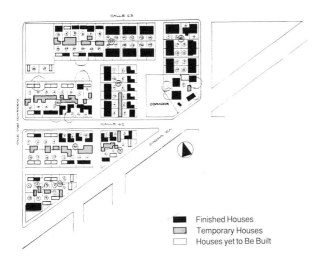

■ Finished Houses
▨ Temporary Houses
□ Houses yet to Be Built

Newly planned layout drawn up by the municipality in 1969, showing plot sizes and house types.

Villa Chaco Chico is a self-built settlement or 'villa de emergencia' in Córdoba, the second largest city of Argentina. Chaco Chico's population is 110 families or about 650 people. Starting in 1945 as a small squatter settlement by rural migrants, it is now a housing co-operative which has built houses for 70 per cent of its families. Its own construction workforce has built 12,000 square metres of floor area, both within and for others outside the settlement. In addition, the community has organized its own layout and planning, and has obtained basic services and community facilities.

Local NGO supports community
The 'Co-operativa 20 de Junio' was formed in 1964. Since 1973 it has been advised and supported by a local non-governmental organization (NGO): Asociación de Vivienda Economica (AVE) and its two associate units: Centro Experimental de Vivienda Económica (CEVE) and Servicio Habitacional y de Acción Social (SEHAS).

Technology as a tool for development
CEVE introduced a light-weight, prefabricated construction system called BENO, which was used to build all of the co-operative's houses. BENO was an important tool to the community in its own development. The community's experience with BENO has provided useful feedback for CEVE, allowing them to adjust and to improve the technology.

Housing before the start of the cooperative.

PHOTO : SEHAS/AVE, CÓRDOBA, ARGENTINA

Supporting community building

SEHAS supported the development of community organization, the consolidation of the settlement and the provision of basic needs. Its aim was to help the community to enhance and to realize its own potential through self-organization and self-management.

Enabling the community

The NGOs involved supported the co-operative's own programme, by using a methodology sensitive and adaptable to changes in priorities and circumstances. This approach enabled the community and its organization to develop a capacity not only for providing houses, but for resolving other basic, local problems as well.

Working together multiplies resources

The houses were built by the co-operative, some working together in organized teams on each other's houses (mutual aid), others by their own construction workforce. They were financed by both central and local government. A contribution from CEBEMO, a European aid agency, allowed the co-operative to develop and to consolidate the construction workforce. By organizing and working together toward a common objective, the community has produced results to a value far exceeding the resources obtained from governmental and external sources. This was done by making good use of external finances and careful administration, the recovery and reinvestment of funds and the input of formal and informal resources by the families involved.

Interchange and exchange

Previously, Villa Chaco Chico was considered inferior by residents of the surrounding higher-income neighbourhoods. Today, people from outside come into the settlement to use its community facilities. Ideas and methods originating in Chaco Chico are now being taken up in other similar areas. 'Co-operativa 20 de Junio' has links with other settlements, both locally and in other parts of the country, to exchange experience, thereby enlarging the network of exchange.

From squatter settlement to housing co-operative

Argentina, in the middle of the present century, has experienced large scale migration by people from depressed rural zones into the cities. This migration has given rise, in many cities, to the formation of squatter settlements called 'villas de emergencia', on both public and private land.

An unserviced squatter island

Most of Chaco Chico's people came from the north of Córdoba province, and some from neighbouring provinces. Initially, 10 families moved onto an isolated brick field. The irregularly-shaped site was flat, as is the wide zone which surrounds it. Gradually, the surrounding areas were built up with houses for people of higher incomes, and with all services installed. Over time, Chaco Chico became an unserviced squatter island set in their midst. The site area was originally 5 hectares (now reduced to 2.5 hectares) and became the property of the Municipality in 1954. By 1964, it was inhabited by 145 families.

Students help to set up co-operative

In 1964 a group of university students contacted the community and helped them to form a provisional committee, preparing for the future co-operative. It was called 'Co-operativa 20 de Junio' in honour of the date it was established in 1964. Its objectives were to obtain the land; to provide housing; to obtain credit; and to organize consumer units and social services. Forty families were the founder members, and they produced and printed an information bulletin to generate wider interest. Among their goals were: to devise standing orders and guidelines for running the co-operative; to obtain the land and to build houses; to find work; and to organize a consumer section. The co-operative was formally and legally registered in 1965.

Co-operators raise levels of awareness

In 1969, the Municipality donated the site to the community, under the condition that the co-operative would build 50 per cent of the total houses within five years. The Municipality itself drew up the layout plan. The co-operative's own housing plan began in 1969 by building two houses with used and donated materials. One was to be occupied by a group of nuns who came to live there, the other was for a member of the co-operative. These first houses raised the residents' awareness of the co-operative's potential. They soon adopted a slogan: 'The site belongs to the co-operative.' At the same time, people began to organize themselves into mutual aid building

PHOTOS: SEHAS/AVE, CÓRDOBA, ARGENTINA

The make-shift homes of the
first settlers were without
electricity and water. In 1964
the tenants formed a
co-operative which was able,
by means of a simple building
system and mutual support, to
build 70 of the 96 planned
new homes by 1986. Today
the settlement is supplied with
water and electricity and has
long since lost its poor
reputation.

groups. The first technology experiments were also carried out with CEVE's construction system, BENO, later to be improved, due to this experience.

Obtaining the first funds
In 1970, the first funds were allocated by the Ministry of Social Welfare for the 'purchase of materials to build 40 houses'. The actual funds did not arrive until 1974, in the form of a loan. The funds were badly eroded by inflation and were barely enough to build 33 units. However, it allowed for the prefabrication of the first BENO panels.

Thirty-three houses built by mutual aid
By 1973, thanks to mutual aid construction, 33 houses were completed, including their sanitary installations. Families who received houses were required to use their own resources to enclose their plots. After this experience, modifications to the BENO system were carried out and the house designs were changed, reducing their size.

Forming the construction workforce
In stage two, the goal was to produce a further 19 houses. The government promised funds for the seond stage including paid labour. This enabled the co-operative to form paid construction gangs, who later became their construction workforce. Funds did not actually arrive until 1975, and by that time were sufficient for only the foundations and walls of 13 houses. The new layout for the settlement began, a process which lasted for 3 or 4 years. Families were relocated in stages, to allow for new street layouts and the installation of electricity and water.

Workforce takes on outside jobs
By 1976 the co-operative's construction workforce began to take on outside work, as they continue to do up to the present day. In the city of Córdoba and in others in the province's interior, they built houses, rural schools, workshops and shops. At the same time, the workforce carried on building in Villa Chaco Chico, as resources permitted. By 1978, new government funds allowed the completion of the 13 houses from stage two, and the construction of 6 more.

Consolidating the organization
The community's social organization was also becoming consolidated. All the families took part in defining the internal rules for regulating their particular neighbourhood, as well as the policies for allocating housing, repayment and reinvestment of funds. The construction workforce strengthened its internal organization and clarified its rules. In 1981, with funds from CEBEMO, the co-operative's construction workforce decided to focus on income-earning work for external bodies and upgraded its plant and equipment to include a workshop and a lorry.

Stimulating other groups
Over the next few years, the workforce suffered the effects of high inflation. Despite difficulties, they built more than 12,000 square metres of floor area, both for the co-operative and for outsiders. During the peak period of work, 15 people were employed permanently, with 35 others on a temporary basis. Of the total 96 houses which were proposed, 70 houses had been built by 1986. The co-operative has consolidated its organizational structure, stimulating other groups and communities, who see it as a model.

A process of consolidation

The community has always directed its own development. This was accepted by the various non-governmental organizations who worked with them. But participation by families was erratic. At the start, few people were convinced that the co-operative would succeed. Certain crucial events, such as the first stage of the housing plan (1970-73) or when plots were being allocated and occupied, evoked a higher level of participation. Those co-operative members who had been part of the construction workforce naturally formed a stronger and more cohesive group than the community in general.

Tensions between leaders and community
The first phase of building brought together a group of responsible, capable leaders. Some tensions arose between those being housed in the first phase, and the rest of the community who were waiting for their houses. Both leaders and families experienced a lack of confidence when events did not keep pace with their expectations.

Lack of resources threatens participation
Similar problems arose in the second stage, when the 13 houses could not be finished due to lack of funds. People

became dispirited and discouraged. Other financing methods were tried. Self-financing did not work, given the variations of income within the community along with inflation, which quickly devalued people's savings. Other families tried to build individually, but with their low incomes, houses generally ended up unfinished and without sanitary installations. The co-operative's basic democracy was even challenged, but it was eventually agreed that the problems were really external and due to lack of resources.

Community implements new layout

The implementation of the new layout presented its own problems. In the first phase, 33 plots had to be vacated. These families were relocated to another part of the settlement, which increased densities there.

The second phase suffered as well from many complications: the co-operative could not afford to build temporary houses for the relocated families; all relocated families could not be guaranteed a new permanent house; some families whose houses would be demolished were not co-operative members, and therefore had to move to another place; some relocated families had already moved previously, and it was difficult for them to make yet another move.

Families were required to position themselves to the rear of their new plots, to allow their permanent houses to be built at the front. The AVE team willingly took up ideas generated by the residents, and the new layout was implemented without excessive resistance from the families who had to move. The entire process provided a very rich exercise in participation for every family, strengthening the community's organization.

Building community confidence

Building houses showed the residents just how much they could achieve by organizing and working together toward their common objective. The people of Villa Chaco Chico gained confidence in themselves. Through their achievement in resolving their shared housing problem, they gained the capacity to do many other things.

Planning together

The result: new homes for the families

Self confidence and external acceptance

Changing Chaco Chico's image
Health and education were always priorities for the
community, which they dealt with over the years. The co-
operative also succeeded in inverting outside, negative
prejudices which existed against its members in the early
years. Then, the settlement was considered a refuge for
thieves and prostitutes; their children had difficulties in
attending the local school and there was little access to
the public health service. Now people come in from
outside the area to make use of the modern medical
centre, night school and training courses which are
located in one of the co-operative's own buildings.

People define their priorities
Villa Chaco Chico's people defined their own priorities.
Because the community was in charge, problems such as
legalizing land titles, obtaining services and building
houses drew a high level of community support and
participation. The community maintained an independent
stance, and a relationship of equals with political parties,
the state, NGOs, funding and other agencies. Its own
vision and control has guided the process of change and
development.

Development as community learning
The community was able to take control of its own
development process, dealing with problems gradually.
This allowed a real learning process to take place, through
a constant interplay between thought and action, a
gradual consolidation of the community. Villa Chaco
Chico's people have shown that they are capable of
formulating their own plans, projects and programmes.
The role of the state should be as enabler and articulator
of people's initiatives, encouraging a 'bottom-up' process
of planning and management, rather than taking a
technocratic role and imposing its ideas on people.

Low-income Peruvians build a new township

Documentation:
Andrew Maskrey
CIDAP, Lima, Peru.

Villa el Salvador

Sponsor:
International Development
Research Centre (IDRC)
Canada.

Advisor:
John F.C. Turner
AHAS, UK.

Text:
Andrew Maskrey and
Bertha Turner
AHAS, UK.

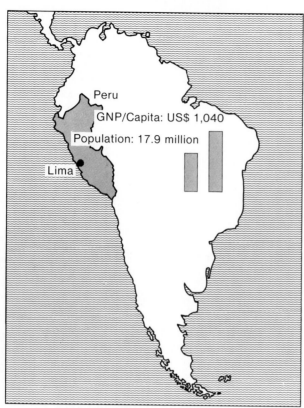

Peru

GNP/Capita: US$ 1,040

Population: 17.9 million

Lima

Population Lima (1981): 4.6 million
Population VES (1986): 168,000

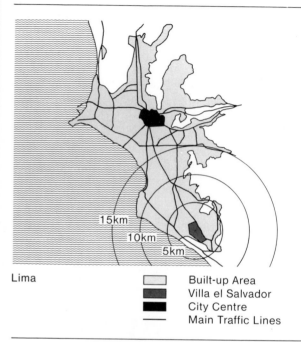

Lima

15km
10km
5km

	Built-up Area
	Villa el Salvador
	City Centre
—	Main Traffic Lines

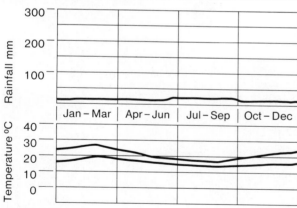

Climate Graph Lima (128m)

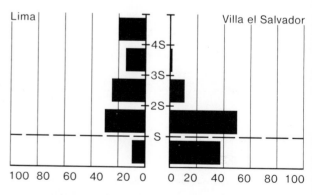

Percentage Distributions of Population by Income Level
S=when 85% of household income must be spent on food

Villa el Salvador is Peru's largest squatter settlement or 'pueblo joven' (young town). What was a large area of state-owned desert land only 15 years ago, is now a thriving, self-governing community where nearly 200,000 low-income people are permanently settled. By 1984, there were 31,034 housing plots: 15,827 had permanent brick and concrete houses; 22,586 had electricity connections; 17,938 had domestic water and sewerage connections, while a further 8,038 were served via external standpipes. The desert has blossomed with many trees and gardens, the main roads are paved and bus services provide access to central Lima, some 20 kilometres distant. All basic commercial and community services have been set up. The majority of these investments have not been made by government, but by the people themselves (and their organizations), paid for from their own low incomes.

A typical 'pueblo joven' population
Villa el Salvador (Villa for short) shares many characteristics with other Lima suburban squatter settlements. Over 1.5 million people or a third of the population of the rapidly growing metropolis live in such settlements. The average annual household income in Villa was about US$1,000 in 1984. Nearly two-thirds of this was spent on food and one-tenth on transportation to and from work, leaving about a quarter for all other expenses. About one-third of the population have incomes at or below subsistence level and must spend all their income on food and fuel to maintain good health. Like most similar settlements, Villa was settled and is being built up by former inner-city slum dwellers and former tenants of loaned or rented rooms in other 'pueblos jovenes'. Most adults settling in Villa were resident in the city for 10 years or more, but were originally migrants from villages and provincial towns.

Abbreviations:

VES	Villa el Salvador
CUAVES	Communidad Urbana Autogestionaria (the self-managed urban community of Villa el Salvador
SINAMOS	Sistema Nacional de Apoyo a la Mobilizacion Social (National system to support social mobilization)
UNICEF	United Nations Children's Fund

Learning as a process
Although helped by a radical military regime in the early years and now supported by its own municipal government, Villa's achievements stem largely from the struggles and sacrifices of its own people. They have learned, through a difficult and painful process, to overcome internal and external divisions and interference. Only in the last few years has local self-government emerged as a viable alternative.

Community organization assumes responsibility for development
CUAVES (Comunidad Urbana Autogestionaria, or in English, the Self-managed Urban Community of Villa el Salvador) is at the heart of these achievements. CUAVES is Villa's own community organization which shares with the Municipality responsibility for block and neighbourhood development and for the planning and management of the whole settlement. CUAVES shows that self-government and devolution of power to a local level can and does work.

Over fifteen years houses have developed from unserviced cane matting shacks to two storey brick and concrete structures with water, sewage and electricity connections.

PHOTO: ANDREW MASKREY

Government participates in people's decisions

In Villa, government policy has oscillated between appropriate support of local initiatives and overt repression; between allocating land, encouraging the setting up of CUAVES and suppression of community action by imposing curfews and prohibiting meetings. Nevertheless, Villa's inhabitants have consistently asserted the right to determine their own future and have forced the state to participate in and to support their own decisions and actions, instead of being pushed into government decisions taken on their behalf.

Suggestions for a viable policy of government support

On balance, both government and local authority have played important roles in enabling the settlement and its development to take place. This experience suggests that a support policy is viable when it encourages and respects the evolution of the creative imagination of local people and their own organizations' initiatives.

Working together to transform the desert

Villa has evolved from a squatter land invasion to a large city with a unique system of self-government and a flourishing community. From its beginnings until the formal legal agreement was made between CUAVES, the community organization, and the Municipality of Villa el Salvador (which was officially constituted in 1984), Villa's evolution can be traced through six distinct phases.

PHOTO E. DURAND

The beginnings of Villa: organizing to meet basic needs.

People, shacks and sand, the desert settled: May, 1971.

April-May 1971

During preparations for an international development conference, hosted by the government in Lima, 200 families invaded desert land on the city periphery. A flood of almost 9,000 additional families spilled onto adjacent, privately-owned land nearby. Unsuccessful attempts by armed police to evict them resulted in the deaths of two people. This event led, at first, to the involvement of a local priest and, later, of the Bishop of Lima. His subsequent arrest embarrassed the military junta which was professing a policy of support for local action. The Minister responsible was dismissed and the authorities negotiated an alternative site with the squatters and helped them to move.

May 1971-November 1973

After two months, 20,000 households were living in cane-matting shacks on the desert sands. The Ministry of Housing planned the 3,140 hectare area, dividing it into seven sectors, each providing 140 square metre plots for a total population of 30-40,000. The squatters formed their own organizations to resolve problems of education, transport, water and so on. SINAMOS (in English, National System to Support Social Mobilization) helped these organizations to join together, forming CUAVES. With support from SINAMOS and other agencies, CUAVES would then guarantee the participation of local people in the planning and development of Villa el Salvador.

November 1973-February 1976

CUAVES and SINAMOS planned to finance housing and services through the development of an ambitious community-owned industrial and commercial development programme, funded by an autonomous local savings and loan bank. The electrification of Villa was initiated in 1975 by government agencies, 160 classrooms were built and several commercial enterprises were started, but the programme failed. The bank was never authorized or financially assisted by the government, and local savings margins were too low to provide enough credit to get enterprises started. The government never recognized CUAVES as an autonomous body, making it dependent upon SINAMOS. Following a right-wing coup in 1975, government support for CUAVES rapidly evaporated, leaving the industrial estate and other projects unused and useless.

February 1976 - April 1978

CUAVES asserted independence from SINAMOS and demanded legal recognition, materials and staff for locally built schools, and the provision of a domestic water supply and sewers. Government responded with fierce repression of the neighbourhood organization. With the collapse of the community enterprises and the bank, CUAVES was seriously weakened.

VILLA EL SALVADOR

PHOTO: NICHOLAS HOUGHTON

April 1978 - June 1983

In the new CUAVES executive, elected in April 1978, national party politics prevailed at the expense of grass-roots interests in local development. This further weakened and divided the neighbourhood organization and, without local support, CUAVES lost control over Villa's development. Community land reserved for public areas was taken over by government and by squatters. However, the community did manage to assert its control over education and health programmes which were assisted by UNICEF and to restart some community enterprises. To compensate for the executive's neglect, there was a resurgence of local neighbourhood organizations, together with demands leading to the formation of Villa el Salvador as an independent municipality in 1983 together with the election of the CUAVES executive.

July 1983 - July 1985

After the preparation of a development plan for Villa by CUAVES and the Municipality, joint actions were carried out: the relocation of squatter communities in a new planned expansion; the installation of a new trunk drinking water pipeline following pressure on the government; a self-census of the settlement; the implementation of a health plan; tree planting; the asphalting of roads and the construction of various community facilities. In July 1985, elections for the CUAVES executive were held.

The desert transformed: May 1986.

PHOTO: ANDREW MASKREY

Making the state participate

Squatters and commercial developers

Lima squatter settlements generally occupy state-owned desert land not legally available for commercial development. Developers compete for the shrinking supply of accessible, privately owned building land, affordable only to those with higher incomes. While for many years 'pueblos jóvenes' had the advantage of a large supply of free land, many recent settlements are now forced out to distant, inaccessible or inadequate sites, where infrastructure is difficult and costly to install.

Government housing policy serves middle-income groups

Since Peru's urbanization process took off in the 1940s, three policy trends for low- and moderate-income housing have evolved. Two of these are common to other mixed economies: directly subsidized housing construction for rent or sale and the promotion of commercial finance systems, designed to serve a wider spectrum of the population. Both have sometimes been combined with directed self-help construction to reduce costs by using unpaid labour. Neither these nor even sites-and-services projects are affordable by the low-income sectors who became 'pueblo joven' dwellers.

Towards a support policy for locally organized housing

The third trend from which Villa's experience evolved began in 1955, with the setting up by the government of OATA (Oficina de Asistencia Técnica a las Urbanizaciones Populares de Arequipa) to provide technical (but not financial) assistance to the squatter settlements of Arequipa, Peru's second largest city. In 1961, the government passed a law granting security of tenure to plot holders in all improvable 'pueblos jóvenes'. It made provision for the installation of utilities and community facilities, and for excess population by providing serviced sites or tracts of unserviced land. This anticipated by ten years the promotion of such policies by the UN, the World Bank and many bilateral aid agencies.

Few administrations, however, had done much more than talk about this third and clearly most effective 'support' policy, with the partial exception of some 'pueblo joven' improvement programmes. Little attempt had been made to guarantee a supply of well-located land or to plan basic infrastructure provision for low income families.

The emergence of a third option: Villa el Salvador

One exception is Villa el Salvador. By 1970, the supply of desert land at a convenient distance from the city was nearly exhausted, tempting squatters to invade better-located private building land. In the case of Villa, the government was forced to make a large area of land available, together with site planning, infrastructure and assistance with organizing the community. Although two other areas were allocated to similar invasions in subsequent years, support of this kind was not given. Only in the last three years, with the formation of three planned settlements by the Municipality of Lima, has the spirit of the 'pueblo joven' support policy materialized into effective programmes, with the emergence of a third option, different from both government-organized sites-and-services programmes and from unplanned squatter settlements.

Joint management with the municipality leads to locally planned and controlled development.

VILLA EL SALVADOR

PHOTO: ANDREW MASKREY

Support locally organized housing, don't provide it
Villa el Salvador is not a model scheme, meant for identical copying or replication. Instead, it offers a rich source of inspiration for locally organized housing in other contexts, with important lessons to be learned on several key issues, as well as expressing the creative imagination of its own people.

Organizing ourselves is the key to local development
The existence and development of Villa el Salvador can only be explained by the enormous capacity which its people have developed for managing their own affairs, through their own autonomous organizations based on CUAVES. When government agencies are able to support rather than substitute for local action, substantial quantitative and qualitative improvements are possible in the built and social environment. Villa demonstrates the difference between people participating in governments' actions, as occurs in many sites-and-services programmes, rather than government providing essential resources to support locally organized housing. It also shows the considerable range of difficulties communities face in organizing themselves and in obtaining government support.

Central planning works with local control
The rapid development of Villa owes a great deal to the provision of land, site planning and to the programming of infrastructure installation by the government. In spite of the constraints imposed by poor location and delays in the provision of water and other services, Villa's development has been relatively orderly and well planned, compared to other 'pueblos jóvenes' developed without government support. Experience also shows that the necessary counterpart to central planning is local control over development, which is essential for the maintenance of orderly growth and, once again, emphasizing the complementary roles of government and community.

Self-financing requires external support
Villa, along with the other 'pueblos jóvenes' in Lima, demonstrates just how much can be achieved with so little when very low-income people manage their own housing programmes. The aggregated investment is far greater than any low-budget government could possibly provide. It also demonstrates the unrealistic and impractical nature of expecting an adequate self-financed development to be achieved by low-income people with very small or no margins for saving and with no access to external credit, as in the case of Villa's community bank.

Skills and employment for Jamaican women

Documentation:
Ruth McLeod, Director,
Construction Resource
and Development Centre
(CRDC)
166½ Old Hope Road
Kingston 6, Jamaica, W.I.

Women's Construction Collective

Sponsor:
Planning Committee for
NGO Activities:
World Conference on UN
Decade for Women, USA.

Advisor:
John F.C. Turner
AHAS, UK.

Text:
Bertha Turner and
Andrew Maskrey
AHAS, UK.

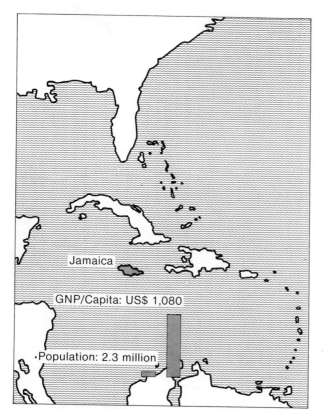

Jamaica

GNP/Capita: US$ 1,080

Population: 2.3 million

Population Jamaica (1985) 2.3 million
Population Kingston (1982): 524,638

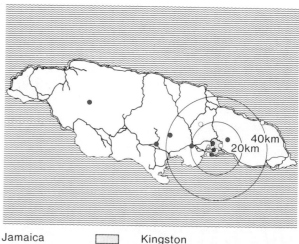

Jamaica

Kingston
○ Feeder Communities
● Places of Work (Project Areas)
— Main Traffic Routes

Minimum weekly wage in Jamaica is J$56 (US$10).
Typical weekly pay for female workers employed as
domestic help is J$50 (US$9). Subsistence minimum for
food only is J$30 (US$5.45) per person. Most Kingston
households headed by women contain at least one
child, and are often several generations: an extended
family.

Abbreviations

CRDC   Construction Resource and
        Development Centre.
JLP   Jamaican Labour Party
VTDI   Vocational Training Development
        Institute
WCC   Women's Construction Collective

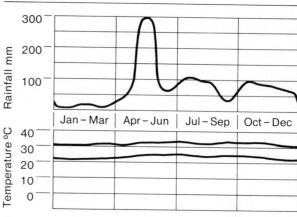

Climate Graph Kingston (12m)

The Women's Construction Collective (WCC) started in October 1983, with ten women from Tivoli Gardens - an inner city area of Kingston, Jamaica. The original aims were to help women to find employment at trade level in the building industry and to provide a mutual support group for on-going training. WCC is affiliated to the Working Group on Women's Low-Income Households and Urban Services in Latin America and the Caribbean, as are other groups in Peru and Mexico. WCC, a project of the Construction Resource and Development Centre, a non-governmental organization, is now a registered, non-profit company, managing its own day-to-day affairs and funds. WCC activities have evolved and developed. Adjusting to a slump in the construction industry, it expanded into other communities and took on new tasks, such as small-scale building and repair work.

Women excluded from training and jobs

The collective began as a response to four main factors:

1. the construction industry was booming and trade workers were in demand;

2. several contractors were willing to employ skilled female labour if it was available;

3. unemployment for young women in western Kingston was around 75 per cent;

4. government vocational training policy had changed to exclude women from building trade training programmes.

Low-income women would be trained by the collective in basic building skills and in carpentry. The tools necessary to start work were provided through a revolving loan fund. Contractors initially employed the women as labourers. But because they were highly trained and had their own tools, most were soon promoted to being trade helpers, earning much more than they could earn in conventional women's jobs.

Violence decreases and productivity increases

The building industry has responded positively to the WCC project. Contractors find that with women on site, violence goes down and productivity goes up. Another achievement of the collective is its ability to move women across political borders. Women from communities associated with one political party were placed on sites identified with the opposition party with no serious problems. Contractors who have employed WCC members now have confidence in employing women and are employing others. In its three

WCC

PHOTOS: RUTH MCLEOD, WCC, KINGSTON

year existence, the collective has demonstrated how mutual support amongst local women can work: creating earning opportunities for low-income women in the male-dominated building industry; breaking down rigid political divisions; changing established structures and building up confidence and ability.

Sophistication and squatters

Jamaica is the third largest of the Caribbean Islands, with an area of about 4,000 square miles and a population of about 2 million. The population of Kingston, the island's capital, has grown rapidly from 202,000 in 1943 to 472,321 in 1970.

The high-rise buildings of Kingston's financial centre and the luxury hotels of the north coast are evidence of the island's modernity and sophistication. Kingston's squatter settlements and urban ghettos present the underside of Jamaica's identity. Characterized by high unemployment, political partisanship and poor living standards, these densely populated areas suffer from a complexity of social, economic and political problems.

In Kingston, 5.6 per cent of the urban population live in spacious splendour on 41 per cent of the residential land, at an average density of 0.1 persons per room. Meanwhile, 74 per cent of the urban population are crowded into 33 per cent of the residential area, living at average densities of 2 persons per room.

Unemployment and teenage pregnancy

Over one-third of Jamaica's households are headed by women, rising to nearly half in urban areas. Women's unemployment is nearly double that of men, reaching 75 per cent in areas of western Kingston. Teenage pregnancy is very common amongst unemployed females, given that becoming a 'baby mother' gives them adult status in the community. Yet most teenage mothers continue to live in the homes of their own mothers, who are the female heads of low-income households.

Women excluded from the building industry

In 1982, the Jamaican building industry was booming. However, of 32,000 people employed, only 800 were women, none of whom had the status of trade workers. Very few of the estimated 1,000 women trained in building skills between 1976 and 1980 had found jobs. Moreover, women had recently been excluded from the government's building and construction training programme at the trade level. The Working Group on Women's Low-Income Households planned to attack the problem simultaneously at both industry and community levels.

Male dominance and political partisanship

There were difficulties to overcome before women could enter the construction industry. Most trade work was carried out by subcontractors hired on a task basis and working with informal trade gangs. Entry into these gangs occurred through a male network of friends, relatives and workers who had met on previous jobs. Territorial political rivalries presented additional complications. Building sites in areas with party political affiliations are expected to give party followers exclusive rights to jobs. Those from other parties enter at their peril, unless they have a scarce skill or a strong tie to the main contractor.

A community-based programme

In May 1983, the Working Group on Women's Low-Income Households received a grant to select and train 10 unemployed women from western Kingston, to place them in jobs and to monitor and document their experiences. The women were chosen by a community liaison officer, with help from local youth leaders, based on literacy and numeracy tests. They were from Tivoli Gardens, an area of four-storey apartment blocks and terraced houses which provide homes for 1,000 households. This community was developed during the 1960s as part of an upgrading scheme, when the Jamaican Labour Party (JLP) was in power. In addition to being highly politicized, it also has high levels of teenage unemployment and teenage pregnancy.

Locating a training agency

A first step was to locate an agency to provide training. CRDC often develops experimental training programmes for adult construction workers. It also had previous experience of working in co-operation with the Vocational Training Development Institute. VTDI trains vocational instructors for Jamaica and other islands in the Caribbean. It also provides short-term courses to upgrade skills in a wide variety of industrial fields. The WCC was able to work with both organizations, and the staff of VTDI provided technical and moral support on an informal but ongoing basis.

Starting training

Trainees began with a basic five-week masonry and carpentry course. Each woman had to build a concrete wall, rendered correctly and finished neatly, in between sawing wood to make building formwork and making a correctly jointed stool. When the women first arrived, some fashionably dressed in nylon stockings and high heeled shoes, they resembled anything but a potential gang of construction workers. Five weeks later, they were prepared to start work as trade helpers on large construction sites.

Job auditions

Originally, an agreement had been reached with contractors to place the women on a market upgrading project being funded by the government. It was located in an area sharing the same political allegiance as Tivoli Gardens. This project was postponed indefinitely. Faced with a prospect of no job placements, the collective developed a strategy of 'job auditions' - offering to work on site on a trial basis, at no cost to the employer. Soon the first contractor responded, taking two women on trial. One week later, they became part of the workforce. Before long, all the women were in regular work, earning two times the minimum wage and more.

Rising demand leads to expansion

Soon the rising demand from contractors justified expansion of the collective. Building on its existing base in Tivoli would have tied the collective into being politically identified with the Jamaican Labour Party. Instead, it was decided to work with two new communities: Nannyville, a housing settlement built within Kingston city limits in the 1970s by the PNP government; and Glengoffe, a rural community some 15 miles outside Kingston. The collective now held its monthly meetings on politically neutral ground at the CRDC offices, rather than as previously, at Tivoli's community centre. Suggestions that each community should form their own, separate collectives were firmly rejected by members, who wished to avoid being divided by local politics.

Project hit by building slump

Thirty-four women had been trained by June 1984. However, there were clear signs of a slump in the building industry. The collective faced the problem of no job placements for its members. However, there was a market for some small-scale building repair and extension work and the women decided to explore the market further. By June 1985, the collective had launched itself as a small business.

Training continues through repairs and maintenance
Their first job was to build a wooden house for Jamaican potter, Ma Lou, in Spanish Town. With the small profit from that job, the women built a lean-to workshop at the back of the CRDC offices and began to offer carpentry services to the general public. Outside funding allowed the collective to buy tools and two vehicles to take on jobs in other parts of Kingston and surrounding areas. A local carpenter was hired as instructor for the workshop. Women, now unemployed as a result of the slow-down in the building sector, continued their training, upgrading their building skills in the workshop, and learning administrative skills by taking an active part in the day-to-day planning and running of the project.

New developments: education and extension
New developments of the collective include research on traditional building techniques, such as thatch, masonry and carpentry. In May 1986, they signed their first major contract for work on a primary health clinic. Within two weeks, two further contracts were signed. Linkages were established with a new community and a batch of new trainees entered the collective. An education campaign was launched to strengthen wooden houses in three communities. The work of the collective is having widespread effects, as they help to set up similar groups in other parts of the island - a recognition of its success.

Self-confidence and independence

Community base brings mutual support
The high placement rate achieved by the collective is largely due to its focus on skills. But the human concerns were equally important, laying the foundation for confidence and cohesion among the women who joined the group. The transition from unemployment to non-traditional employment in the male-dominated field of construction required mutual support. Since family support was necessary, but not always forthcoming, the collective itself took on this role. Women were able to share their experiences and to build up confidence together.

From dependence to independence
Expansion led to a redefined role for the collective and to the creation of a new organizational structure. The goal was to increase the collective's ability to govern itself by increasing each woman's ability to take on responsibility. The collective has gradually moved toward independence from its parent non-governmental organization, the CRDC. Originally, most of the key policy decisions (selection, training content, job placement, etc.) were made by CRDC. Later, two trainee managers were selected from the collective's women to take over the book-keeping, placement, site monitoring and other organizational tasks, assisted by a newly appointed Executive Committee. Finally, the collective became formally registered as a company limited by guarantee. They moved into their own offices and adopted a new organizational structure. The collective has evolved toward creating its own work opportunities, repairing and maintaining wooden houses. This move has given experience in self management, significantly increasing the collective's independence.

Supporting people building
Over thirty competent young women entered the building industry at trade level. This had an impact on the industry, when it began to recognize that woman could play an important role. Decreasing violence, increasing productivity and overcoming the traditional political boundaries and conflicts were some of the side effects of the collective's work. However, the importance of WCC goes beyond obtaining placements on building sites. In the collective, the women can come together to discuss their problems and develop solutions through mutual support. Women have become conscious of their own capabilities and have an opportunity to put them to use. WCC builds at several different levels simultaneously: it builds skills, buildings and people in their local communities.

A mediating role
The collective plays a mediating role. It helps women to realize their full potential and brings changes to the structures which surround them: in the building industry; in political relations; in perceptions of women's roles and in income distribution. By building community among women, WCC is creating a capacity for change far beyond its original objectives.

Issues and Conclusions

Main Conclusions

The cases reported through the HIC Project, together with others which are well documented, lead to three basic conclusions:

a) that there is a grossly underestimated and underused potential in non-commercial, community-based and non-governmental organizations (CBOs and NGOs) which assist and support the people who already build the great majority of homes and neighbourhoods in low-income countries;

(b) that government policies which attempt to compensate for the market's failure to provide for lower- or even middle-income households by building housing projects must change from supplying ready-made housing from a central source to supporting the efforts of self-managed, community-based organizations and their helpers in producing their own homes and neighbourhoods;

(c) that in addition to their roles as community developers, innovators and motivators, NGOs have an essential role to play as third-party mediators, in the development and implementation of such supportive and enabling policies which involve changes of relationships between people and government.

Changing Over from Supply to Support Policies

The Necessary Order of Development

The change-over from 'supply' to 'support' policies demands that we recover the traditional order of development to modern conditions wherever it is practical and demanded: the authorization of land uses by local government, the self-organization of future residents who are able and willing to take responsibility for the works and their implementation. This is precisely what many national and international NGOs, bi- and multi-lateral agencies and even an increasing number of national and state governments are now promoting, stimulated by the direct action of low-income people who find themselves excluded by regulations and market prices. In five of the six 'resettlement' cases (Villa El Salvador, the Village Reconstruction Organization programme, Yayasan Sosial Soegiyapranata, Saarland Village I and the Centro Cooperativista Uruguayos projects), land was obtained before the residents organized for building. And where people organized before land was obtained or its use authorized, as in the abortive land invasion that led to the Villa El Salvador success and in the long-term development of Palo Alto, severe conflicts often arise involving avoidable suffering and even loss of life. Other serious social and economic losses result from centrally-administered housing projects which reverse the traditional or historically normal order by building before the residents are even known. Since this procedure eliminates personal and local initiative in the planning and construction stages, a vital contribution is also lost: that of the people most concerned and highly motivated, who collectively possess the most resources.

Three levels of action

The necessity and nature of the changeover from supply to support policies can be clearly seen when the three levels of government intervention are identified and the potential values added by the other sectors are recognized. There are no abrupt divisions between the three levels described below; they are clearly different levels in a spectrum in which one level shades into another (see Figure 1).

Figure 1
Increasing the Returns on Public Investment

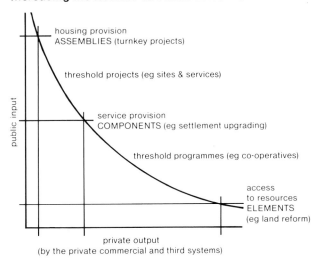

housing provision
ASSEMBLIES (turnkey projects)

threshold projects (eg sites & services)

public input

service provision
COMPONENTS (eg settlement upgrading)

threshold programmes (eg co-operatives)

access
to resources
ELEMENTS
(eg land reform)

private output
(by the private commercial and third systems)

(a) Housing provision or assemblies:
An 'assembly' is used to indicate a completed project, an assembly of the components that make up a habitable place. In order to live somewhere, there must at least be a site, access routes connecting the site to the other places on which the residents depend for their livelihood, a water supply, and shelter. This is the absolute minimum of four components, but each can take many different forms, so that the variety of even the simplest settlements is immense. Modern urban developments, tending to be much more standardized than traditional settlements, can still have over seventy components, including telephones and cable television networks, nursery schools, dental clinics, and swimming pools, and a wide variety of dwelling types. These components can range from primitive shelters to North American-style ranch houses with three-car garages or penthouses in multi-storey blocks of flats. Assemblies or housing developments are local by definition and, with rare exceptions, are of neighbourhood scale or smaller. Residential developments are complex and, over time, they change, usually a great deal when their forms allow. Every assembly is a unique complex of physical structures and infrastructures, sustained by invisible social and economic structures. The provision of a ready-to-occupy or turn-key housing simply cannot be afforded without a subsidy by low-income people in low-income countries. Housing supply policies, based on intervention at this level, are clearly ineffective in low-income countries where the governments have very low per-capita budgets. Saarland Village I is the only case in this book where minimum, modern-standard homes are provided before the land is occupied. While it illustrates the economic and social advantages of NGO promotion and management, Saarland Village I also demonstrates the impossibility of NGOs substituting for government action on a significant scale.

(b) The provision of components.
A component is used to indicate an independently variable part or sub-assembly, such as water and electricity supply systems, drainage sytems, roads and public transport, fire protection, health services and so on. They are also simpler than whole assemblies, of course, and most are extensions of larger systems. A component can generally be modified or replaced without major changes to the other components. Some components, such as dwellings or parts of dwellings and other buildings, are complex sub-assemblies, not extensions of larger systems. But, as long as their design and construction permits, even large components such as dwellings can be altered, demolished or replaced without major disturbances to the rest of the development. Although relatively large, the number of (independently variable) components is limited and, with the partial exception of dwellings and other buildings, their forms do not vary anything like as much as those of whole assemblies or developments. Settlement up-grading programmes provide services and stimulate investment, as illustrated by the cases of Ganeshnagar and Kampung Banyu Urip. Sites-and-services schemes, which often accompany settlement upgrading in order to accomodate those displaced by the improvements, may also generate high levels of housing investment by low-income people, as in the case of Klong Toey. High levels of private (or third sector) investment do not always follow, however. When such schemes are administered to provide only one choice of location, restricting eligibility to narrow categories of users, or imposing costly procedures or standards, investment may be long delayed. This has occurred in the case of the Karachi Metrovilles (government-sponsored and managed sites and basic services schemes), which are developing at a far slower rate than the unauthorized 'katchi abadis' or self-built settlements, such as Baldia and Orangi.

(c) Increasing access to resources: the elements of building. This term 'elements', is used as in chemistry, to designate the parts common to all components and, therefore, to all assemblies. No component or assembly can be built or even modified without using space, and therefore, land; working time and skills; materials, tools and energy and unless their users have sufficient control over them, whether *de jure* or *de facto*. Compared to the number of possible components, elements are very few, and their natures are identical or similar, even in very different contexts. When elements are subject to national law (as in the case of land) or to markets and exchange systems, they can be seen as extensions of very large, even worldwide systems, as in the case of a material like cement or a fuel such as oil.

Essential elements for building exist in all contexts
Constraints on building and maintenance are rarely due to absolute shortages of basic resources. They are primarily due to social and institutional constraints: mainly to the structure of authority, to the law and its administration and to the exchange system, usually finance. Ignorance of

locally available alternatives or unwillingness to use them are also common constraints, especially where social values identify more costly forms and technologies with modernity. All the significant and affordable improvements achieved in the cases documented have been due mainly to institutional changes, often provoked by direct action. Few or no major community-building improvements have been due entirely to the increased supply of funds, to the introduction of innovative technics, or to the streamlining of conventional, centrally-administered programmes.

Increasing the effectiveness of public investment

Most government housing policies are identified with public housing projects and, therefore, with a top-down, directive approach. At this level of intervention, the per capita costs are high and the returns are low or even negative: 'good money' is only too often thrown after badly invested money, in vain attempts to solve the consequent problems. A more effective level of government intervention is the provision of infrastructures and services that facilitate building. Sites-and-services and settlement-upgrading projects, providing essential components, cost governments substantially less per capita served, and the returns can be very much higher, especially if the value and returns on private investments are added.

Even more cost-effective is the removal of institutional constraints on the investment of available material and human resources. The most important is generally the provision of secure tenure, where low-income people are able and willing to invest in improvements, as in the programmes in which HUZA operates, in Ganeshnagar, Klong Toey, Guerrero, Palo Alto and Villa Chaco Chico. Providing alternative sites for those willing and able to move away from locations where they cannot improve their living conditions or realize their expectations, is the necessary complement, as in the cases of El Augustino, HUZA and Klong Toey. The simplification of regulations is important in all cases and vital in most. The only cases where official standards were adhered to are those that were either subsidized or undertaken by relatively high-income groups: Saarland Village I, the Centro Co-operativista Uruguayo and Guerrero projects.

The geometric increase of cost-effectiveness sketched in Figure 1 does not automatically follow from the shifts of public investment from one level to the next, however. Sites-and-services projects can fail to serve their intended beneficiaries for the same reasons as many turn-key projects also do: they are unaffordable; too far from workplaces and sources of livelihood; imposed mortgages have undermined security of tenure; building design and use regulations inhibit future improvements or income earning uses.

Maintaining the continuity of a community is important, especially for the poorest whose survival is most precarious. But the provision of secure tenure only for individual building plots can be counter-productive, especially when land values are rising more rapidly than the incomes of the residents. There are fears that the exceptionally strong Klong Toey community, highly supportive of its most vulnerable members, will be broken up, as residents sell off to new, higher-income residents at inflated prices, or rent their land, charging high costs for the improved environment. The members of the Palo Alto, Guerrero and Urugayan co-operatives have ensured the survival of their existing community through shared ownership and management, but possibly at the sacrifice of transferability.

The assessment of returns on investment in publicly-funded projects is conservative, as they are often negative, even though the unit cost is very high, usually higher than the majority of the population can afford and out of reach to low-income people, even with substantial subsidies. Experience proves what common sense suggests: that as the level of public investment penetrates more deeply, first with the provision of infrastructures and services and then to change the invisible structures of the controlling institutions, there is a proportionate increase of production. Some may suppose that this would be socially regressive, but evidence shows that this policy would be progressively redistributive and far more supportive for the poor than conventional policies of supplying housing. Even tentative steps toward this policy, such as the sites-and-services or settlement upgrading programmes, have led to significant benefits to low- and very low-income people in many countries: many more were served than could have been housed in earlier conventional projects. Where government intervention has provided community-based organizations with rights to land, to control of their own development programmes and/or with infrastructures they can pay for, but cannot install themselves, the cases show how much more can be achieved with available funds. Villa El Salvador and the Baldia and Orangi sanitation programmes show that when communities are in charge of their own development, the financial costs of direct provision can be reduced by as much as 80 per cent.

Thresholds of policy change

Only by radically changing the distribution of government investment between these 'levels of action' can a quantum improvement of low-income housing conditions be achieved by governments with limited and inelastic housing budgets, as illustrated in Figure 2. If governments are to make effective use of their limited budgets for housing, then they must minimize expenditure on direct construction, increase investment in the provision of infrastructure and services, and give the highest priority to institutional changes that increase local access to resources and which guarantee personal and local freedom to use them properly.

A start has been made with the introduction of sites-and-services and settlement up-grading programmes endorse sites-and-services projects, residents control the construction of their own dwellings, but little else. External agencies usually make the key decisions on location and selection of residents, the forms of tenure, land-use and infrastructure planning, and financing. The provision of

'sanitary cores' or even complete core units for future extension is sometimes compulsory, leaving little to the initiative of the occupiers, as in the case of Saarland Village I. The threshold between providing ready-made assemblies pre-packaged by the suppliers, or providing components selected by the users is crossed when up grading programmes for established communities are carried out in close co-operation with the residents through their own organizations, as in the case of Kampung Banyu Urip.

Recent evaluations of World Bank assisted sites-and-services and settlement up-grading programmes. In typical this analysis. In general, the latter have proved to be substantially more cost-effective, even though they tend to reduce rather than increase the overall housing stock. This is a limitation that need not apply when land for those displaced, as well as for the increasing population, is made available concurrently, as in the HUZA case.

Crossing the main threshold between centrally-administered housing supply policies and support policies for locally self-managed development demands major changes in institutions, attitudes, and in the relationships of the essential partners. On the one hand, central authorities and the professionals who serve them must recognize the relative capacities and limitations of their own government- and market-based organizations and those of local communities. Respect must be mutual, based on a recognition of mutual dependence. Due mainly to the highly visible and massive evidence that governments are unable to house significant numbers of their low-income people have attitudes begun to change. People who are forced to house themselves, unsupported and often harassed by government, are well aware of their need for assistance. It is mainly in the higher-income countries that many people are unaware of their own capacities for self-management. Authoritarian decision and control systems, legislation that protects material property rather than human rights, exchange systems based on financial rather than social capital: all these combine to suppress and even pervert the use of essential and renewable resources.

Once strangers meet and begin to know one another, they begin to develop a relationship. As this is the starting-point for institutional change, attempts to ignore and jump over the first threshold may be counter-productive. As the analysis below suggests, the relatively paternalistic projects managed by external agencies for people may be

Figure 2
The Changing Distribution of Public Investment

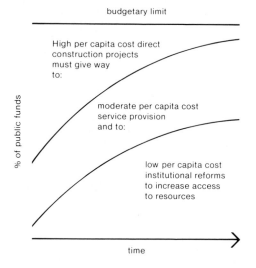

budgetary limit

High per capita cost direct construction projects must give way to:

moderate per capita cost service provision and to:

low per capita cost institutional reforms to increase access to resources

% of public funds

time

the only socially practical and politically feasible way in which well-intentioned but culturally-distant professionals can learn how to work as enablers. The increasing emphasis on social and economic development, reflected in the Yayasan Sosial Soegiyapranata and Saarland Village I cases, highlight this point. Cases differ greatly when the NGO has assumed a governmental role or when CBOs are in charge, as in Ganeshnagar, Ukanal Fé and Villa El Salvador. The case studies summarized in this book can only indicate what the detailed background materials confirm: that the key mediators are experienced individuals who understand the difference between directive and non-directive approaches and who are able to bring about the necessary negotiations between the CBOs and authorities willing to support local initiatives.

NGOs in the Third System

Defining NGOs and CBOss

The conventional, two-dimensional splitting of society into 'public' and 'private' sectors leads to confusion in defining and understanding the term 'NGO'. As the Introduction states, it is much easier to see and to understand changing reality in a three-dimensional perspective. When the semi-autonomous existence of non-governmental and non-commercial motives and activities is recognized, the meaning of non-governmental and community-based organizations becomes clear. 'NGOs' and 'CBOs' may seem esoteric terms or jargon to the general public and can be especially confusing to the people of planned or command economies and many one-party states. Confusions are compounded by the wide variety of types and scales of organization which are non-governmental and non-commercial. It is not unusual that well-informed people from African and Asian countries often identify NGOs with Christian churches or with foreign organizations. There are also many overlaps between governmental, commercial and community-based organizations. This is especially so at the local level, where many community-based organizations, although oriented mainly to locally self-managed self-service, overlap with decentralized political structures, as in the cases from Ethiopia, Tanzania, Zambia and by Kampung Banyu Urip in Indonesia. Most local artisanal enterprises are commercial, even if organized co-operatively. Nevertheless and as long as it is accepted that motivation and the scope of an organization are the main

determinants of its social value and resource economy, it makes sense to include them in the 'third system', whether they are technically legal or not.

Readers will notice that the term 'informal sector' is not used. In this context, it is not a helpful concept, as it is too closely identified with illegality, often in grossly unjust legal systems, and all too often assumed to be synonymous with poverty. While the 'third system' is naturally stronger in contexts where centralizing institutions and technologies are weaker, it is vital everywhere. As suggested in both the Preface and the Introduction, the recognition and strengthening of the community base is a universal necessity, and a more difficult task in urban-industrial countries, where it has been so badly eroded.

CBOs and NGOs are the principal types of third system organization, as suggested in the Introduction. At the Limuru Symposium in Kenya, where the Declaration included in this book was formulated, it was agreed that NGOs of the kinds most commonly referred to are supra-local organizations working for or with people locally, either directly or through their own CBOs. These are not only another kind of third system organization, but also provide the basis of NGO authority and their potential for influencing policy change. This dependency of NGOs on CBOs is obvious, in the worldwide view of what people do without the help of NGOs. In Indonesia, for instance, with exceptionally few NGOs, people and their CBOs have built about 90 per cent of all homes and neighbourhoods, largely to acceptable standards, with little or no intervention by NGOs.

CBOs are distinguished by the important fact that they are self-organized by local residents, whereas NGOs are organized by outsiders, usually from higher-income social sectors based in major cities and often by foreigners. At the NGO Workshop during Habitat Forum Berlin in June 1987, it was recognized that CBOs can federate and provide the same kinds of services as do NGOs organized by outsiders. The Duang Prateep Foundation, based in Klong Toey, is a case in point.

The sizes, scopes, scales of operation, and the nationality of NGOs are major factors in their relationships with other organizations. Therefore, it is essential to know in particular situations, whether the NGOs are local, national or international. 'Nationalizing' international NGOs or their branches, as in the case of the American Friends Service Committee of Zambia which handed over to

Zambians to become Human Settlements of Zambia (HUZA), is a precedent of increasing importance. In most cases, the cultural or political affiliation of an NGO must be taken into account: whether it is of or sponsored by a religious body, a secular charity, a university, or other institution; and what political associations the NGO or its parent body may have.

When applying any set of categories, there are always overlaps and marginal cases, as well as a wide variety of types within the category, as indicated in Figure 3. Local authorities are at times classified as NGOs, or as state organizations or institutions. Which is most appropriate depends on the scale of the authority in question and its relative autonomy. Swiss communes, New England towns in the United States, or exceptional municipalities in more centralized states, like that of Villa El Salvador, are local, direct democracies. Most local governments in most countries are decentralized branches of national or state governments, however, and cannot therefore be described as NGOs.

Figure 3
NGOs Scope for Roleplaying by Level of Intervention

DIRECTIVE ⟵——— ROLES ———⟶ NON-DIRECTIVE

Relative potential for NGO roles:
+ + = Very high
+ = High
+ – = Fair
– = Low
– – = None

LEVEL OF INTERVENTION	Surrogate	Manager	Community Developer	Community Organizer	Consultant	Mediator
ASSEMBLIES (turnkey projects)	+ –	+ –	–	– –	– –	– –
threshold projects (eg sites & services)	+ –	+ –	+ +	+ –	–	–
COMPONENTS (eg up-grading)	–	–	+ +	+ +	+	+
threshold programmes (eg co-operatives)	– –	– –	+	+ +	+ +	+ +
ELEMENTS (eg institutional and financial measures to increase local access to resources)	– –	– –	+ –	+ +	+ +	+ +

The overlaps with the second, market system are evident at the local level of commerce, especially in the so-called 'informal sector' or 'petty commodity production'. The point or scale at which a local or community-based enterprise is seen to move fully into the commercial sphere, where increased profits are the aim, rather than the support of home and neighbourhood life, depends on the circumstances and viewpoint. One suggestion is that a self-managed activity, dependent on a local clientele and not owned by shareholders (i.e. non- or pre-capitalist formations) should be considered as a predominantly third-system organization. In a debate over qualifications for membership of the newly re-structured Habitat International Coalition in 1987, it was agreed that while commercial real estate firms should not qualify, their not-for-profit associations may. Similar discussions will take place, if they have not already, over the place of political organizations. In reality, motives, relationships and the systems they generate are mixed and the balance is often difficult to assess especially when it is a dynamic equilibrium in constant change.

NGO tasks and roles in human settlement
As the HIC project cases show, CBOs and NGOs are contributing more than any other kinds of organization to the key task identified by Dr. Arcot Ramachandran: '... to find the necessary capacities to apply these (above defined) enabling strategies ...' which can multiply the cost-effectiveness of public investment. NGOs and federated CBOs can make a strong contribution to this essential policy change. To clarify this potential, identification must be made of the kinds of NGO, together with a simple, useful definition of the range of actions and positions taken by them: their basic relationships with CBOs on the one hand and with supra-local organizations of state and market-based, national and international kinds, on the other. This basic range can be infinitely elaborated if the different kinds of local or supra-local organizations are taken into account, along with the kinds, scales, or levels of action with which they are involved.

What NGOs can or should do in particular circumstances to develop enabling strategies is influenced by several factors relating to the NGOs scale and level of action: involvement in building or improving homes and neighbourhoods as a whole, with groups of people and relatively small organizations; or with infrastructures at a larger district or municipal level; or at regional or national levels with those responsible for institutional changes affecting local access to resources. NGO activities, roles, and relationships vary according to their involvement with central state or large-scale commercial organizations, local government and commerce, people in their own communities and their own local NGOs, therefore, have three key tasks.

(a) At the local level, to assist people in the management of their own home and neighbourhood development programmes, supporting the structuring of their own community-based organizations where necessary, and often in co-operation with the local authorities.

(b) At central, national or international levels, NGOs can promote support policies in every way possible, from protesting the abuse of power, as in the still frequent evictions of low-income communities, to advising governments on ways and means of implementing support policies.

(c) The third and most important task is carried out by NGOs acting as mediators between the conflicting interests of central and local organizations, a supporting role that is frequently needed by CBOs in their negotiations with government.

The scale and influence of NGO programmes

The cases in this book illustrate the ways in which NGOs assist in local projects, from highly managerial to consultative roles. Where CBOs already existed or where they initiated the projects, NGOs have also supported their development. But the majority of NGOs working in the settlement field concern themselves only with local projects, for which criticism is often voiced, as at the Limuru Symposium, the Berlin Forum and other meetings. While some hold the opinion that great achievements start from small beginnings, there is a common concern that many NGOs aim only to produce an inevitably limited number of dwellings and/or to develop selected communities.

Limiting one's aims to exclude the relation to a broader societal change might be reasonable if NGOs were able to succeed where governments have failed, by increasing the subsidization of low and very low-income housing to the required scale, within existing institutional frameworks. Collectively, NGOs do contribute a significant proportion of external development aid (US$2.9 billion in 1985 or 10 per cent of the total contributions of the OECD countries). But even if a much higher proportion were invested in housing, it would make very little difference and would still be insignificant compared to the aggregate investment made by unaided, low-income people. The main value of the NGO contribution is in the leverage it provides for increasing pressures for policy changes, leading to far more cost-effective uses of the limited amounts of financial aid that can be obtained.

The focus of the issue for NGOs, along with international agencies and national governments should be on their longer-term objectives and the ways in which they are carried out, rather than on the inevitably limited scale of their projects. One participant aptly quoted a traditional English saying 'Great oaks from little acorns grow.' But this only happens if live seeds fall on fertile ground. When small, experimental seed projects are carried out, only when the experimental stage has passed as a demonstration of alternatives, can the seeds then take root and reproduce. The constraints that NGOs have to overcome in order to realize their full potential are discussed on page 178.

Innovation and Promotion vs. Housing Provision by NGOs

NGOs increase the housing supply in three principal ways: through housing provision programmes of various kinds; through projects or programmes testing or demonstrating innovations for adoption by other kinds of organization; and through motivating those who have underused capacities. Some large-scale quasi non-governmental organizations or quangos, as they are called in Britain, are major housing suppliers in some European countries. The state-funded British housing associations, for instance, are providing a growing proportion of subsidized housing in much the same way as government agencies. Although these quangos could use their powers to support and work through self-organized co-operatives, few yet do so. Ever since the suppression and co-option of the little-known but widespread housing co-operative movement in Austria and Germany by the Nazis in the 1930s, European co-operative housing organizations have tended to be excessively large, centralized and more like state agencies than CBOs of the kinds presented in this book.

When NGOs assume responsibility for the supply of housing, as an alternative to the market or the state, they inevitably inherit many of the limitations of corporate organization. Even when organized co-operatively, large NGO housing ventures relate to their tenants in much the same way as public and corporate private landlords — usually limiting tenant responsibilities to the care of their own private space and expecting hired management to cope with everything outside the tenant's own space, including minor repairs. Supra-local NGO developers and builders may be more efficient than government agencies who are subject to direct political pressures and administrative discontinuities. Depending mainly on fiscal policies and subsidies, quangos may also reach much lower-income levels than commercial builders and developers. But the evidence does not suggest that they can compete economically, let alone socially, with large numbers of smaller community-based building organizations when the latter have access to sufficient resources or are adequately supported by NGOs or government.

If the long-term goal of constructing or improving homes or neighbourhoods is to build a supportive community, then the achievement of locally self-managed projects is even greater. The quality of peoples attitudes and relationships is apparent to an observer, though it may not be explicitly stated or accurately measurable in formal surveys. Few would deny that the sense of community is far more commonly built and maintained in environments where residents are responsible for them, than when the environments are provided for them, whatever the material standards. Mutually supportive personal relationships can be more important than material conditions for those who depend on family and neighbours for social or emotional security, and take precedence over any social status which higher standards might confer. It could even be argued that if the sense of community is not built along with the material improvement, then the latter is meaningless.

In low-income countries, the purpose of NGO direct intervention in low-income housing should be to innovate or motivate in economic ways, maximizing opportunities for community building. The direct provision of houses for passive consumers is more expensive and socially detrimental. NGOs should avoid building for people wherever more creative and participative options are available. Some building must take place, in order to demonstrate innovations that might be taken up by organizations with greater capacities for production. But the quantitative aspects of projects: numbers of units produced or people housed are not ends in themselves. Constructing dwellings or installing services should be

used as means to introduce more effective approaches or policies. This is clearly shown by the impacts of the initially small sanitation projects in Baldia and Orangi towns in Karachi, the experimental land-sharing projects in Bangkok, the participatory Kampung Banyu Urip improvement project in Surabaya and most of the NGO initiatives documented in the HIC project. all have different scopes and limits. The following overview focuses on the common denominators, making only passing references to these important variations.

The principal advantage of all NGOs is their third party status in relation to people, government and other corporate organizations. Being detached from state and market interests, NGOs are well placed to communicate and to stimulate communication, to mediate and, occasionally, to co-ordinate the sectoral activities of government agencies. Principal constraints on realizing these potentials are lack of public awareness and of self-awareness by the NGOs, their dependence on limited voluntary funding and, sometimes, their own constrained policies.

NGOs possess four intrinsic advantages, whether they make use of them or not:

(a) **Communication**

The 'communicator' role is not included in the descriptions and tabulation of roles above. This is because NGOs are less constrained and suspect than either state or market organizations and they generally have access to modern means of communication and the media. Within limits set by censorship, the laws of libel and extra-legal political threats, NGOs are relatively free to say and publish what they will, whatever roles they play. With the partial exception of the surrogate position, described above, NGO staff are not constrained by the necessity to justify public policy; as they are not generally party to internal government affairs, they are not usually subject to official secrets acts. As literate individuals, they often have personal contacts with journalists, broadcasters and publishers NGOs have far greater opportunities to disseminate. When they are able to afford postal charges and have access to electronic communications, they have extraordinary possibilities for sharing experience and information.

Apart from the costs of communication and travel, and the high cost of modern time, other major constraints on communication and dissemination by NGOs are their own policies. The HIC project team, while gathering the case materials used in this book, was refused information by at least one NGO on the grounds that money spent on documenting their experience fully (with warts and all) would mean a reduction in the number of houses they could build. Since the NGO in question distributes copious amounts of expensive, glossy, public relations literature, the real reason for refusal probably has more to do with an intrinsic constraint on charities. Most are dependent on voluntary contributions, motivated by pity rather than by understanding. Another larger NGO with many years of worldwide experience to its credit, makes very limited efforts to record and share it, even with its own staff. This is partly due to the NGO's focus. The pressures of dealing with emergencies distracts attention from both the causes of disasters and the longer-term consequences of short-term actions.

Political constraints deserve special attention. Sharing information can endanger lives where political violence is widespread, and it can endanger personal freedom, where paternalistic states attempt to monopolize communications. As lightweight, electronic communications (telematics) become widely available, it is debatable whether policing may become more easily evaded, or information exchange may be more easily monitored. But even without constraints of this kind, few are yet aware of the actual potential for networking and information exchange — internal constraints that must be rapidly overcome.

(b) **Networking**.
NGOs have a relative freedom of communication, making it far easier for them to identify and contact individuals, groups and local organizations with similar aims and views. NGOs can organize meetings of people they want to meet, rather than having foisted upon them selected representatives chosen by authorities. This comparative advantage enables NGOs to generate far more exchange at much lower costs than organizations which have to work through governments. Large and costly international meetings are occasionally necessary, but a consensus is growing that more is learned at lower per capita cost through small exchange visits between practitioners. Reports of exchange visits by local community members from different continents suggest that language difficulties are greatly overcome when they can show each other what they do and how. Smaller, regional meetings of people carrying out NGO and CBO projects and programmes are increasingly common and effective ways

of strengthening mutually supportive networks. Jorge Anzorena, a roving networker circulating his reports among the practitioners he visits, has probably done more to stimulate and generate local initiatives than any other individual. NGOs circulate many networking publications such as the SINA (Settlements Information Network, Africa) Newsletter of the Mazingira Institute in Kenya. Those who speak one or more languages in international use usually have access to the rapidly developing telematic systems of electronic communication through which they can or soon will communicate instantaneously, and at much lower cost than travelling or communicating by mail.

Most NGOs make too little use of their advantages for networking. Over the past 11 years, inter-regional meetings have increased since the first global meeting of NGOs at Habitat Forum in Vancouver in 1976, but there are still far too few exchanges. Although less costly and easier to arrange, little effort is made in most countries by neighbouring NGOs and CBOs to exchange experience and ideas and to co-operate on joint campaigns. The common preference of re-inventing the wheel instead of making efforts to learn from ones colleagues, especially if they are close neighbours, may be difficult to overcome. As the efforts of some networkers and NGOs show, a great deal more can be achieved at low cost when exchanges take place free from the other main constraint: attracting unwelcome attention from hostile political forces. Shortly before going to press, it was reliably reported that about 600 local community leaders have been murdered by politically motivated gangs in Colombia, a country where CBOs are particularly strong and from which many who actively support them are fleeing in fear of their lives.

(c) **Mediation**
NGOs are in a far better position to be trusted by those suffering from oppression or poverty, given their relative independence from both state and market forces. Besides their access to communications, most NGOs are sponsored and staffed by individuals with more than average access to the corridors of power, to financial institutions and to commercial corporations. Bi- and multi-lateral NGOs which predominate often have even greater influence when based in a country on which the nation is dependent for trade, aid or political protection. Whether foreign or national, NGOs are uniquely placed to act as mediators between sectors that distrust or fear each other

and which, coming from different social strata, are often mutually ignorant and hostile.

As for communication, a major constraint on networking by NGOs are their own policies. While they are changing, stimulating those of governments, the overall impression may be over-optimistic. Even though there is a strong and general trend away from directive approaches, many NGOs still continue to promote them. This is not due only to conservatism and the outdated but still strong paternalistic tradition of elitist charities. It is also because most NGOs depend on voluntary contributions from the general public — the wealthy of poor countries and the general population of wealthy countries. Donors and their agencies want to see results: the material products which they deem to be solutions to the problems or crises that move them. There is a long jump to make, maybe through years of public education, before there is sufficient understanding that people must have a meaningful input in working out the solutions to their own problems, the only way to finally resolve them.

(d) Co-ordination

The advantages of NGOs in communication, networking and mediation can make it possible for them to achieve the elusive: co-ordination of public agency roles in project development. This can be done directly when NGOs act as managers or as community developers, or indirectly, when they act in the non-directive, consultative and mediating roles. Unlike government ministries and agencies, NGOs are free to act in different sectors and are therefore able to respond more rapidly to the different demands and activities of a local community, such as generating employment; education and health care. Once again, NGO policies are a major constraint on their own realization of their potential for co-ordination. Although they are not locked into the administrative divisions of labour by sectoral ministries of state, NGO policy makers generally share the Cartesian view. This maintains the theoretical separation of activities that are not separable in real life. Building or improving a house does not have a lower priority than health care, or food production, especially if either releases and leads to the investment of otherwise wasted resources: to the regaining of health or of self-confidence and initiative and to personal investment in income-generating demands for local goods and services.

NGOs' Comparative Disadvantages

NGOs suffer from three main current disadvantages largely beyond their control:

(a) Low Profile

NGOs are principally limited by the fact that, as Third System organizations , they do not have the status or visibility of the other two. Quangos, such as British housing associations, are seen as extensions of the private sector or some combination of commerce and government. Self-managing, autonomous NGOs and CBOs do not belong to a commonly recognized category. Without a public face as familiar as that of the state or the market, their direct influence on policies is reduced, however great their actual contributions to society may be.

(b) Low level of political participation

When the identity of the Third System is not clearly recognized, NGOs are at a disadvantage in competing for access to the corridors of legislative and financial power with national political parties or industrial and commercial corporations. This weakness exposes even federations of NGOs and of CBOs to the natural tendency of the other powers to co-opt them for their own agendas. When NGOs and CBOs are effectively taken over, they lose their Third System identity or membership, further weakening their status, influence and potential.

(c) Limited and insecure sources of income

Until public demands and awareness bring about the restructuring of policies, currently preoccupied with centralizing power in the state, the market or in an exclusive alliance of the two, NGOs and CBOs will remain dependent on the donor public and the generally marginal contributions from central and local government budgets. As economies and budgets shrink, governments pursue conventional policies, naturally giving priority to their own, and sacrificing the 'troublesome' people and organizations of the Third System. These constraints can only be countered if NGOs make fuller use of the advantages summarized above: by using their access to communications and the media and their capacity for networking. Through their own national and international coalitions, together with CBOs and their coalitions, a great deal more can be done to raise public consciousness of facts such as those published in this book, by closer co-operation for lobbying for peoples rights while protesting evictions and other abuses by the market or the state.

Key Positions and Roles for NGOs and Specialists

This paper identifies three key positions occupied by enabling NGOs in relation to government and to people in their own localities. Each provides NGOs with a major advantage over other kinds of organization:

(a) as **enablers** (whether community developers, organizers or consultants) alongside self-managing groups;

(b) as **mediators** or advocates between the people and the authorities which control access to resources or goods and services which they need; and

(c) as **advisors** or consultants to the controlling authorities on ways and means of changing decision-making structures, rules, finance systems or other uses of government authority that increase local access to resources and their freedom to use them in locally-determined ways.

This interpretation assumes the repeatedly observed necessity of separating responsibilities for programming projects (i.e. working out courses of local action) from responsibilities for enabling them to take place through the institutions of government.

Three Priorities for Action

In November 1987, shortly before going to press, the three priorities for action set out below were agreed by the International Workshop on a Global Strategy for Shelter to the Year 2000. The workshop, convened by the German Foundation for International Development (DSE) and Habitat Forum Berlin, was attended by representatives of 35 NGOs who are members of Habitat International Coalition, from 27 countries on all continents. The outstanding but under-used advantages that NGOs have for communication and networking, together with the increasing frequency of emergencies and the escalating necessity for enabling policies, indicate the three priorities for action outlined below.

Information and networking

The clearest advantage that most NGOs and/or independent specialists have worldwide is their capacity and freedom to communicate with each other and on behalf of people who have little or no access to the means, however skilled or articulate they may be. Communication is the key denominator of all three of the above-mentioned programmes and, as information is power, HIC's influence depends, above all, on networking,

exchanging and disseminating experience and knowledge.

There is a lack of exchange between communities and their CBOs, even when within easy reach of one another. As it was accepted that NGOs' influence rests on the communities that they serve, the strengthening of that base through local inter-communication and the growth of associations and coalitions of CBOs is vitally important.

This summary of issues and conclusions reflects the growing awareness among NGOs of their wider roles and potential for path-finding exploration and innovation. Many NGOs still assume the sterile and ineffective role of surrogates for state or market provision. As most of the cases in this book and the Limuru Declaration confirm, there is a wide and growing recognition of the fact that NGOs are not very useful as pseudo-state agencies or pseudo-commercial developers; that their potential can only be realized when the necessity of enabling policies is generally accepted and the role of NGOs in the change-over is clearly understood.

In order to contribute effectively to the search for enabling strategies, the first priority of NGOs is to build up national and regional coalitions. This demands greatly increased numbers of exchange visits by local practitioners and of regional meetings; it also requires a tiered and decentralized database for the deposit and dissemination of information at all levels; it demands the widespread publication of materials for practitioners and, therefore, a great deal of translation. And, finally, an emergency communications network must be set up in order to assist members confronted with crises and disasters.

A campaign against evictions

Overt and covert threats of eviction, as well as actual displacements and dislocations, create more suffering and do more damage to low-income people, their communities and fragile economies than anything else. It is the most common catalyst for community organization and, therefore, the most frequent opportunity for community-building and for generating effective demands for policy change. Evictions also generate public sympathy and support through media coverage, providing excellent opportunities for consciousness-raising and public learning and even policy changes.

This urgent need must be seen as part of a campaign for the right to habitat: the right we share with all creatures to an environment in which we can thrive.

Strenuous efforts must be made to protect people from perverted interpretations of this right, by those who would exploit it for commercial or political ends. It must be understood that people have a right to house themselves, and a right not to be housed by powers over which they have no control. It must be understood as a right of access to resources and enabling services, rather than a right to receive identical manufactured products, as indistinguishable from one another as a row of army barracks. The right to habitat must insist on the essential characteristics of a home and neighbourhood: affordable; access to sources of livelihood; the requisite security and transferability of tenure and, of course, sheltered space and privacy adequate to maintain physical and mental health.

By highlighting the issues of residential displacement and dislocation, whether from disasters, wars, rural impoverishment, commercial or political exploitation, a campaign against evictions will increase awareness of the broader and deeper issues.

Eviction takes many forms. Residential displacement and consequent social and economic dislocations are suffered by refugees from wars and other disasters, as a result of rural impoverishment; and from specious relocations as well as blatant evictions by commercial or political interests. All these undermine household economies and break up flourishing communities. And the threat of eviction can be as damaging as the reality. Anxiety resulting from deliberately or unnecessarily sustained insecurity of tenure often has disastrous effects on hope and health; when these are undermined so is initiative and investment. The most effective defence of individually powerless people is collective action, as shown not only in the Latin American experience, but also in Thailand in the case of Klong Toey and others. Current events in Colombia remind us that even where traditions of community action are well established, the defence of these rights is urgent. The fact that 600 Colombian activists, mainly local community leaders have been assassinated during 1987 should be headlined worldwide. As NGOs influence rests on the base of community organization, active defence of people's rights to organize and to protect themselves from overt harassment and assassination, as well as from covert disruption, is a prerequisite for the right to the traditional and necessary custom of incremental building and local improvement.

The search for 'enabling strategies' will get nowhere without the active defence of people's rights to habitat and self-defence.

Promoting Support Policies
Campaigning against evictions will make no headway against the perpetrators without putting forward practical alternatives. All the issues raised underline the need to both anticipate and rapidly react to emergencies, in ways that stimulate structural change. Although campaigning against evictions may be seen as negating a negative action, and therefore positive, it will only appear negative to those who implement policies that involve eviction. Whether sincerely or hypocritically, the interested parties will defend evictions in the name of progress. Alternative kinds of development that minimize eviction and ensure viable relocation must, therefore, be part of any effective campaign.

'Enablement' is a new and apparently threatening concept for many on whom its implementation depends. It is therefore essential to promote the precedents and their advantages. This book and the HFB wallnewspapers provide a nucleus of well-documented precedents for alternative and enabling policies, as well as illustrating the barriers that have to be overcome. They provide powerful arguments for the changes needed as long as they are properly used.

There is, however, a dangerous and counter-productive tendency by NGOs, as well as by government and international agencies: to search for the 'magic bullet', a programme which can be replicated wholesale, adopted and imposed. To redirect efforts in the search for 'the necessary capacities to apply enabling strategies', a clear understanding of the need for devolving decisions and controls over local projects to local communities is required. A clear understanding must also evolve of the complementary roles and responsibilities of government: the provision of utilities and services that local communities cannot provide for themselves.

The twin hazards of abstract generalization by harping on principles, and the vain search for the 'magic bullet' replicable programme, can be avoided by focussing on methods, that neglected link between general theories and particular practices. Top priority must be given to identifying transferable, adaptable community-building methods or 'tools', the means by which the principles of enablement can put into practice and become better understood.

CONCLUSIONS

180

BUILDING COMMUNITY

What can one do

Finally, there is one activity in which all concerned citizens can and should take part, whether employed by government, industry, NGOs or oneself: the promotion of enabling policies and the defense of the millions threatened with eviction whether by market- or state-based interests. Everyone in almost all countries can form or join pressure groups and ensure that these associate with regional organizations forming the global Habitat International Coalition.

John F.C. Turner

For more information about HIC's activities, constitution and membership, please write to:
The Secretariat
Habitat International Coalition
41 Wassenaarseweg
CG2596 The Hague
Netherlands

For information on the Habitat Forum Berlin 'wallnewspapers' on cases and urban processes, please write to:
The Secretary
Habitat Forum Berlin
Trabenerstrasse 22
D 1000 Berlin 33
Federal Republic of Germany

To order this book by mail or to enquire about translation and reproduction rights to this book or parts of it, please write to:
The Directors
Building Communities Books (BCB)
5 Dryden Street
London WC2E 9NW
United Kingdom

A Directory of Sources

A selection of some key references to sources of information useful to the enablers and the managers of community-based programmes.

Note: The services and items listed are available or published in English (Eng.) only unless otherwise stated. French and Spanish abbreviated Fr. and Sp. Other languages in full. When more than one language is listed the order indicates the relative frequency.

Directories and Catalogues

Appropriate Technology Sourcebook
Volunteers in Asia, AT Project, PO Box 4543, Stanford, CA 94305, USA.
An 800 page catalogue/guide to practical books for village and small community technology. Written and revised by K. Darrow and M. Saxeman in 1986. Reduced price for local groups in developing countries.

Building Communities Bookshop
By mail. PO Box 28, Dumfries DG2 0NS, Scotland, UK.
A worldwide mail-order service for books, pamphlets, information packs and videos on community architecture, planning, development and technical aid. Catalogue on request.

Campaign Housing Index
CED, 3 Suleman Chambers, 4 Battery Street, Bombay 400 039, India.
A directory jointly compiled by documentation centres in India, listing references to and locations of documents on housing methods: from leaflets to reports.

CIDSE Brochure
International Co-operation for Socio-economic Development, 1-2 Avenue des Arts, B 1040 Brussels, Belgium.
A Directory of Catholic agencies worldwide who support Third World development work. 130pp approx.

Directory of Information Sources
Appendix 4 in *Community Architecture*: N. Wates, C. Knevitt; paperback, 208 pp; Penguin, London, UK, 1987. Lists of organizations, mainly in the UK, providing information and advice, nationally and internationally, on community architecture. Mail-order from: Building Communites Bookshop (see above).

The Foundation Center
888 Seventh Avenue, New York, NY 10106, USA.
A clearinghouse for private funding foundations in the USA: provides directories and information on funders. General list of publications available in English. Charges made for printouts relating to specific grant needs.

IDRC Communications Division
International Development Research Centre, Box 8500, Ottawa K1G 3H9, Canada.
IDRC supports research projects identified, designed,

conducted and managed by developing country researchers in their own countries. Publications on paper or microfiche, of interest to village technology workers. Free to local people in developing countries.

IT Publications Catalogue
Intermediate Technology Development Group, 9 King Street, London WC2E 8HW, UK.
A mail-order service to all parts of the world of publications dealing with appropriate technologies.

Planning Bookshop Catalogue
Town and Country Planning Association, 17 Carlton House Terrace, London SW1Y 5AS, UK.
Books and publications of interest to the planning community. Mail-order service at home and abroad.

SATIS Publications Catalogue
Socially Appropriate Technology International Information Services, PO Box 803, 3500 AV Utrecht, Netherlands.
Title: **How to: Tools for Developing Your World,** 238pp. Eng., Fr., Sp.

UNCHS Habitat
PO Box 30030, Nairobi, Kenya.
Three directories:
UNCHS Habitat Trilingual Thesaurus in Field of Human Settlements, Eng. Fr. Sp. HC/91/86/EFS. 126pp.
UNCHS Bibliography, Vol. 4, HS/102/86/EFS.
Habitat Directory in the Field of Human Settlements, HS/106/86/EFS. 385pp.
Mail orders: IRB, Nobelstrasse 12, D 7000 Stuttgart 80, Federal Republic of Germany.

Urban Self-Reliance Directory
UNU/IFDA Urban Self-Reliance Project, IFDA, 4 Place du Marché, 1260 Nyon, Switzerland.
214 organizations worldwide, concerned with: energy; urban planning and agriculture; housing, management; environment and resource management; local development, employment. Compiled by C. Cordova-Novion, C. Sachs as part of the IFDA/UNU Food Energy Nexus Programme, 1987.

Vision Habitat
UNCHS Information Office Europe, Palais des Nations, Room E47, 1211 Geneva 10, Switzerland.
Audio-visual materials on human settlements.

Women's Issues

ICRW Publications
International Centre for Research on Women, 1717 Massachusetts Av. NW, Suite 501, Washington DC 20036. Research documentation and publications on ICRW housing projects demonstrating roles and options for women.

INSTRAW News
UN International Research and Training Institute for the Advancement of Women, Cesar Nicolas Penson 102-A, PO Box 21747, Santo Domingo, Dominican Republic. Women's role in development: issues, research, publications. Four issues per year; Eng. Fr. Sp.

National Congress of Neighbourhood Women
249 Manhattan Avenue, Brooklyn, New York, NY 11211. Various articles or publications relating to their activities across the U.S.A.

SEEDS
PO Box 3923, Grand Central Station, New York, NY 10163, U.S.A.
A newsletter on women's issues and activities.

WIN News
Women's International Network, 187 Grant Street, Lexington, MA 02173, U.S.A.
A worldwide communication system, for and about all women, disseminating information on women's issues, publications and activities.

Women and Environments
c/o Centre for Urban and Community Studies, 455 Spadina Avenue, Toronto, Ontario M5S 2GB, Canada. Published jointly by the Centre for Urban and Community Studies, University of Toronto and the Faculty of Environmental Studies, York University.

Newsletters and Journals

Appropriate Technology
IT Publications, 9 King Street, London WC2E 8HW, U.K.
For and about people working in appropriate technologies.
IT is a subsidiary of the Intermediate Technology
Development Group founded by the late Dr. E.F.
Schumacher. Four issues per year. Back issues available
on microfiche.

Asian Action
Asian Cultural Forum on Development (AFCOD), 232/9
Nares Road, Siphaya, Bangkok, Thailand.
The ACFOD newsletter links groups in Asia and the Pacific
region participating in integral development. 6 issues p.a.

AVE Informativo
Igualdad 3585, Villa Siburu, 5000 Córdoba, Argentina.
Journal of the activities and projects of AVE, SEHAS,
CEVE in developing economical housing and participating
communities with groups of low-income people. Sp.

Boletín medio ambiente y urbanización
CLACSO, Corrientes 2835, 6 B, Cuerpo A, 1193 Buenos
Aires, Argentina.
Low-income housing experiences and issues in Latin
America. CLACSO/IIED/CIDA. 4 issues p.a., Sp.

Carta Informativa Latinoamericana
c/o SUR, Estudios, Documentación, Educación Casilla A
323V Correo 21, Santiago, Chile.
Information on low-income housing in Latin America. Sp.

CEUR Bulletin
Corrientes 2835, Piso 7, 1193 Buenos Aires, Argentina.
Newsletter on human settlements, distribution Latin
America. Sp.

Community Network UK
Town and Country Planning Association (TCPA), 17
Carlton House Terrace, London SW1Y 5AS. U.K.
Newsletter on community planning, architecture, design
and technical aid in the UK, jointly published by the TCPA,
ACTAC, the RIBA Community Architecture group, London
Planning Aid Service and Manchester CTAC. 6 issues p.a.

Co-op Housing Bulletin
Bulletin of the International Co-operative Alliance,
published in 1987 by Centraluy Zwigzek Spoldzicki,
Budowuictwa Mieszkaniowego, ul. Marchlewskiego 13,
00.828 Warsawa, Poland.
News of housing co-operatives around the world.

Cuadernos Ciudad y Sociedad
Ciudad, Casilla Postal 8311, Quito, Ecuador.
Notes on the city and society. A Catalogue of Ciudad
publications is available. Sp.

DESWOS Brief
DESWOS, Bismarckstrasse 7, 5000 Koln 1, Federal
Republic of Germany.
News on co-operative housing in Third World countries.

Dinámica Co-operativa
Centro Co-operativista Uruguayo (CCU), Dante 2252,
Montevideo, Uruguay.
Activities of Uruguayan co-operatives. Sp.

Dinámica Habitacional and
Cuadernos de Dinámica Habitacional
COPEVI, Tlaloc 40, Mexico 17 DF, Mexico.
Low-income participatory housing in Mexico. Sp.

D & C Journal
Development and Co-operation, Hans Bocklerstasse 5,
D-5300 Bonn 3, Federal Republic of Germany.
Contributions to development policy. Published by the
German Development Foundation (DSE) in collaboration
with Carl Duisberg Gesellschaft (CDG). 6 issues p.a. Eng.
Fr. Sp. and German.

Development Dialogue
Dag Hammarskjold Foundation, Ovre Slottsgata 2,
S-752 20 Uppsala, Sweden.
A journal of international development. 2 issues p.a. Eng.
Fr. Sp.

Ecodevelopment News
54 Boulevard Raspail, 75270 Paris 06, France.
Information on the environment and development.
Published by MSH/CIRED. 4 issues p.a. Eng. Fr.

ENDA Bulletin
Environnement et Développement du Tiers Monde,
PO Box 3370, Dakar, Senegal.
News on environment and development in the Third
World. Fr. Eng. Sp.

FEDEVIVIENDA Newsletter
Federación Nacional de Organizaciones de Vivienda Popular, Diagonal 60, No. 23-63, Apartado 57059, Bogotá, Colombia.
News on human settlements in Colombia. Sp.

Habitat International Journal
Pergamon Journals Ltd., Headington, Oxford OX3 0BW, U.K.
Journal for the study of human settlements. 4 issues p.a.

Habitat et Participation Newsletter
1 Place du Levant, Louvain-la-Neuve 1348, Belgium.
A bulletin on human settlements and participation, published by the Catholic University of Louvain-la-Neuve. 4 issues p.a. Fr.

IFDA Dossier
International Foundation for Development Alternatives, 4 Place du Marché, 1260 Nyon, Switzerland.
Current articles on development alternatives. 6 issues p.a. Eng. Fr. Sp.

IRED Forum
Development Innovations and Networks, 3 rue de Varembé, Case 116, 1211 Geneva 20, Switzerland.
Communications link for 350 organizations working in the field. Published/distributed with financial aid of CIDA.

IULA Informa
International Union of Local Authorities, Casilla 1109, Correo Central, Quito, Ecuador.
Development news for capital cities of Latin America and for training and development centres. 4 issues p.a. Sp.

Lettre Urbaine
ENDA-RUP, Post Box 3370, Dakar, Senegal.
Links research and action in human settlements in Africa, Asia and Latin America. 4 issues p.a. Fr. Eng. Sp.

NGO/UNICEF Forum
NGO Liaison Office, 866 United Nations Plaza, New York, NY 10017, U.S.A.
Publicizing the work of international voluntary organizations and their national affiliates in implementing UNICEF-aided programmes.

NGO News
Habitat International Coalition (HIC), 41 Wassenaarseweg, The Hague, Netherlands.
Information for and about NGOs working in the field of human settlements; prepared in collaboration with UNCHS and distributed as an insert of UNCHS Habitat News, P.O. Box 30030, Nairobi, Kenya. 4 issues p.a.

Open House International
School of Architecture, University of Newcastle-upon-Tyne, Newcastle-upon-Tyne NE1 7R, U.K.
Current research and practice in housing and the built environment: theories, tools, practice. 4 issues p.a.

Participation Network
c/o CONTEXT, 10 West 86th Street, New York, NY 10024, U.S.A.
A newsletter in English, produced periodically by and for persons working toward increasing community participation.

Planners' Network
1901 Que Street NW, Washington DC 20009, U.S.A.
A network of professionals, activists, academics, students in urban and rural areas, promoting people-oriented environmental planning. 6 issues p.a.

PRISLIHA News
Private Sector Low-income Housing Association, PO Box 64, Greenhills, San Juan, Metro Manila, Philippines.
A news service on current, low-income housing issues and developments in the Philippines.

Revista Interamericana de Planificación
Sociedad Interamericana de Planificación (SIAP), Apartado Postal 27-716 06760, Mexico DF, Mexico.
Planning issues in Latin America. Free to SIAP members, others by subscription. 4 issues p.a. Sp. Eng.

SELAVIP News
Latin American and Asian Low-income Housing Service, Casilla 871, Santiago, Chile.
A newsletter on low-income housing theory and practice. 2 issues p.a. Sp. Eng.

SINA Newsletter
Settlements Information Network Africa (SINA), c/o Mazingira Institute, PO Box 14550, Nairobi, Kenya.
Linking people who work with settlement projects in Africa: self-build, education, health, nutrition, skills training, employment, community organizing. 3 issues p.a.

TRANET Newsletter
Transnational Network for Appropriate Technologies,
PO Box 567, Rangeley, ME 04970, U.S.A.
A newsletter-directory in English of, by and for those who
are actively developing appropriate or alternative
technologies, worldwide. 4 issues p.a.

Trialog Journal
Ploenniesstrasse 18, D-1600 Darmstadt, Federal Republic
of Germany.
Planning and construction in developing countries. 4
issues p.a. German, Eng.

UNCHS Habitat News
UN Centre for Human Settlements, New York Office Dc2
Room 946, United Nations, New York, NY 10017, U.S.A.
Contact New York for addresses of local UNCHS offices,
providing free subscriptions. 3 issues p.a.
Eng. Fr. Sp.

Urban Edge
Subscriptions: Johns Hopkins University Press, Journals
Division, 701 W 40th Street, Suite 275, Baltimore, MD
21211, U.S.A.
Practical approaches to urban problems in developing
countries. 10 issues p.a. Eng. Fr. Sp. published by the
World Bank. Free to developing countries.

The Limuru Declaration April 1987

We, the participants from 45 Third World based NGOs and 12 international NGOs, have convened in Limuru, Kenya, committed to reversing current trends toward ever increasing homelessness, over-crowding, lack of basic services and other forms of social and economic deprivation. More than a third of the world's population is seriously affected. Poverty is our constant emergency. Adequate, affordable shelter with basic services is a fundamental right of all people. Governments should respect the right of all people to shelter, free from the fear of forced eviction or removal, or the threat of their home being demolished.

Governments should also respect urban citizens' right to a land site on which a house can be built, to credit, infrastructure, services and cheap building materials. Their right to choose their own forms of social and community organizations in building, planning and use of materials should also be respected.

Adequate shelter includes not only protection from the elements, but also sources of potable water in or close to the house, provision for the removal of household and human liquid and solid wastes, site drainage, emergency life-saving services, and easy access to health care. In urban centres, a house site within easy reach of social and economic opportunities is also an integral part of an adequate shelter.

As a group, we declare our opposition to people's forced eviction from their homes, neighbourhoods and communities. Such forced evictions are taking place on an ever-increasing scale. Forced eviction is an intolerable breach of human rights, most especially when those subject to such evictions are already suffering from inadequate income, inadequate access to social services and other manifestations of poverty.

The scale of evictions worldwide is but one reflection of the inequality in resource distribution and of the powerful forces and vested interests whose policies and actions infringe on each person's right to adequate shelter. It also reflects urban housing and land markets, and the norms and codes of building and planning standards, which exclude the poor majority from the possibility of buying or renting an adequate shelter. Governments should support institutions and inititatives to defend people's right to an adequate shelter against land speculation and developers — and NGOs have an important role in providing legal advice to those facing eviction.

Low income people as city builders

Worldwide, it is low-income people who are responsible for the planning and construction of most new houses. In cities, most additions to the housing stock are undertaken by low-income groups and the community or neighbourhood organizations that they form. In many nations, Third World based NGOs play significant supporting roles in working with the community-based organizations and in helping such organizations' development efforts. Such NGOs also play important roles as originators, enablers and implementors of new ideas and models. Their research has contributed much to our understanding of the scale and nature of shelter problems. And their collaborative efforts as coalition builders is now evident in many nations, as such coalitions seek to influence government policies and priorities.

Governments should recognize the intrinsic right of people everywhere to form community-based organizations and NGOs to address their own needs and to demand secure tenure for housing and basic services.

Governments as Enablers

Governments should recognize that appropriate support for individual households and the community-based organizations that they form, and the NGOs with whom they choose to work in their efforts to improve shelter and environmental conditions, represents the most innovateive and effective strategy to reverse existing trends. Government programmes to build houses 'for the poor' misunderstand their needs. Such programmes waste scarce resources to little effect. Governments' role is to ensure that land sites are affordable and freely available in appropriate locations, and that low-income households have access to credit and cheap materials. Their role is to ensure that all houses and residential areas have the services and facilities noted earlier as being integral parts of adequate shelter. And their role is to ensure that such enabling policies are backed with appropriate legislation, norms and codes.

Community-based organizations and NGOs cannot solve all the problems of homelessness and inadequate shelter. But supported by the enabling approach outlined above, much can be achieved. It is heartening to note that certain governments have changed their policies toward such enabling approaches.

The unmet needs of women and children

The housing needs of women and children have been ignored or given too little consideration. Yet women, children and youth usually account for around three-quarters of the total population. Women and children are the most intensive users of housing and the people who suffer most from defficiencies in structure, services and facilities. Special note should be made of the shelter needs of de facto women-headed households. These often represent a high proportion of all households, especially among the poorer households. Often they are denied secure tenure of land sites, access to low-cost housing schemes, acccess to construction skills, employment and credit.

The multisectoral approach

One of the strengths of NGOs working to improve housing conditions is that their approach is usually multisectoral. The causes of poverty and ill health and of environmental degradation fall into many sectors; so too do successful actions to reduce them.

Relations between NGOs, CBOs and Governments

Some basic principles

The group notes that there is often a gap between governments' positions and the aspirations of low-income groups and the community-based organizations they form; it is within this gap that NGOs work and have a role.

NGOs define their lines of action based on an understanding of one essential principle: that all people have the right to control their own destiny, with a preference for shelter solutions based in their own community.

After 20 years' experience from all over the world, NGOs have arrived at a point from where they can reflect upon past work and achievements. New guidelines are now being drawn up, based on systematic evaluations of past experiences. This collective reflection has been much helped by exchanges of experience at local, regional and international levels.

Definitions of NGOs and CBOs

An NGO can be distinguished from a community-based organization by the fact that its sphere of action goes beyond the local level. Many NGOs work as technical advisors, linked closely to community-based organizations. NGOs' actions are usually small-scale, based on a 'step by step' approach, so as to respect and follow the slow consolidation process of community-based organizations.

In some instances, community-based organizations which have gone further in their process of autonomous consolidation, have an evolution similar to that of NGOs. But they need support from specialized NGOs.

NGOs play an intermediary role between the demands of community-based organizations for adequate shelter (or other needs) and the local authorities, to whom these demands are addressed (usually municipal authorities). This role is translated into action by promotion, mobilization and technical, social, legal and administrative assistance.

NGOs' action must aim to promote the rights of community-based organizations to obtain access to practical decision-making and planning processes, with the aim of finding solutions to their collective problems. NGOs have a duty to pass on to community-based organizations their knowledge and resources.

Practical problems between NGOs and CBOs

NGOs, moving from a position of interventionist management to a position of support for community development, must work out a positive way of relating to CBOs to avoid paternalism and its resulting dependency. NGOs that accept what government policies are doing risk adopting a top-down approach.

In NGOs area of activity and considering their level of resources, there are various possible dangers:

—the manipulation of CBO initiatives —having their actions shaped to serve the interests and influences of political and economic power; and
—breaking or at least weakening the strength of CBOs.

Conditions for the implementation of human settlement projects rarely give enough attention to the identification of wider issues and to the specific needs of CBOs. This can lead to confusion between NGOs' socially-oriented objectives and the everyday survival needs of the CBOs.

CBOs can be supported in solving their own specific problems with concrete solutions. NGOs' precise actions do not in themselves help the slow process of a CBO becoming autonomous. To achieve this progressive consolidation, integrated methodologies on how NGOs' knowledge, resources, contacts, training and planning skills can be passed on have to be devised. The process of passing on such knowledge and techniques requires work plans for which the results may not become immediately obvious. The relationship between NGOs and the funding agencies does not always help this process of CBOs becoming autonomous.

Relations between NGOs and Government

Government is one of the key social actors with whom NGOs interact, but the way in which NGOs relate to the state at national or local level is quite different from nation to nation. Such relations are influenced by widely differing historical, cultural and economic contexts, and the organizational experiences of NGOs in their relations with government take many forms. But they can be divided broadly into four categories: cooperation; complementarity; critical appraisal; and open confrontation or conflict.

NGOs and (where they exist) their federations, have widely varying levels of influence in different nations. And the nature of the relationship between government and NGOs working in human settlements is also dependent on the characteristics of NGOs and their networks or federations. When discussing relations between governments and NGOs, perhaps the key question is: who is responsible for meeting social collective demands which include all the elements of an adequate shelter, like secure tenure for housing and basic services and facilities? The answer is clear. These are the responsibility of governments — as are the definition and implementation of the legislative and institutional framework to enable collective social needs to be met. NGOs can demonstrate alternative solutions to meeting such needs through specific projects or programmes. In turn, these can point to approaches which have a wider application. Of course, for the right kind of development, NGOs are guided by the low-income groups with whom they work and the community-based organizations that they form. This incorporates a political democratic process that goes beyond any particular context. For this purpose, it is also important that NGOs work with those municipal governments which are representative of the citizens within their jurisdiction. NGOs can help strengthen such local levels of government through working with community-based organizations to define needs and priorities and through helping to train community-level workers.

The relationship between the state and community-based organizations that tend towards organized movements is characterized by points of tension and potential conflict. In such instances, NGOs have a key role to play. They have to help translate social movements into political presence, but not on a party basis.

NGOs and community-based organizations should act and influence government policies in the short, medium and long term. They must be autonomous vis-a-vis the state and they should be wary of their possible co-option by the state. Such co-option can mean repression of community-based organizations and NGOs, but the former are likely to suffer most. Strong relationships between community-based organizations and NGOs should be developed as a protection against such co-option.

This is a special moment in terms of trying to take full advantage of the International Year (of Shelter for the Homeless, 1987) to seek international support for Third World based NGOs working to increase the proportion of people with adequate shelter. Such international support can help neutralize national factors which prevent or inhibit NGO action at a local level. For this purpose, NGOs must build coalitions with other pressure groups such as trade unions, neighbourhood movements, professional associations, women's movements and human rights movements, in pressing the government to meet their social responsibilities in regard to shelter.

NGOs who work with low-income communities must go beyond the community level. This implies a relationship with local and central government, and with other actors in society. NGOs should become more vocal publicly, but always as catalysts for lower-income groups and their community-based organizations. NGOs should not seek to replace the voice of the homeless or of those with inadequate shelter or indeed of any underprivileged group in society.

International donor NGO strategy for the future

1. In relation to total aid flow from the North to the South, the amount devoted to improving shelter conditions and tackling homelessness is insignificant. According to the United Nations, for the period 1980-84, just 5 per cent of concessional aid (grants and soft loans) and 6.5 per cent of official non-concessional loans went to projects which sought to improve shelter. Thus, the sum of all projects for housing, urban and community development (including upgrading existing houses), water supply, sanitation and garbage disposal, and building materials represented around one-twentieth of total flows.

2. This percentage represented around US$3 billion a year. But only a very small percentage of this went to NGOs.

3. Given the scale of homelessness and the number of people with inadequate shelter, and the positive role that thousands of Third World NGOs play in human settlements, NGOs have a responsibility to raise the awareness of the international donor community on how to establish far more effective and efficient shelter programmes for the poor.

4. First and Third World NGOs need to develop a dialogue and seek a more effective partnership in this area with the donor community and with local governments.

5. NGOs should try continuously to mobilize international technical and financial support from a variety of sources. This can allow them to go beyond relatively small-scale and experimental scales of action in working with community-based organizations to improve housing and living conditions. Nonetheless, there is a real danger that NGOs might be pressurized by international agencies to move beyond their capacities, limits and nature. This danger grows when governments or state agencies refuse or are unable to assume their responsibilities in shelter and basic services.

6. Donors and NGOs should be clear that the ultimate aim of their co-operation is to contribute to integrated development and to the promotion of social and structural changes needed to achieve this. Much can be achieved through support for new models of community development that can work with the poor and homeless in the achievement of adequate shelter and the replication of such approaches by those institutions responsible for ensuring that solutions to inadequate shelter and homelessness are found.

7. This requires technical and professional excellence combined with the social commitment of the NGOs. This is a necessary but not a sufficient condition. Technical aid and learning must go both ways between NGOs and donor agencies. There is also the need to strengthen NGOs' institutional capacity and their ability to have long-term perspectives and programmes and not have their work load continually fluctuating as they rely on project-by-project funding.

8. A trend towards donor suppport for NGOs moving away from grants or soft loans to loans at higher rates of interest is one we view with disquiet. Social goals must not be threatened by the interest rate demanded by the international donor or by the conditions the donor places on the NGO for on-lending to project beneficiaries. A real home is a social good to which all people have a right. It should not be commodity to which access is determined by market forces.

9. A World Fund for NGOs is needed to provide funds direct to Third World based NGOs working on human settlements projects and programmes.

10. Increased training is much needed at the following levels:
—Grassroot and craftsperson or artisan training, to allow the development process to continue after NGOs end their work with low-income communities.
—Technical and social 'cadres' from NGOs to allow a more effective financial and administrative management of projects.

The ultimate aim is for training instititions to be set up at regional and continental levels, throughout the Third World.

Research and Action

The following are the primary problems related to the development of appropriate research potential among NGOs and the action steps that the working group recommends:

Credibility of NGO Research

1. We urge donor agencies to examine the non-traditional, action research approaches that are appropriate to NGOs and to make funds available for this research and the dissemination of its findings.

2. There is a need for funds to document non-traditional research methodologies and their role in NGO activity in human settlements.

NGO and donor relations

3. We urge donor agencies to assist NGOs working in human settlements to strengthen their organizational structure and institutional capability through the support of research.

4. We particularly urge donor agencies to support integrated, non-sectoral research approaches to human settlements issues.

Local Resources (Research and Training)

5. There is a need for the development and sustaining of research-action capacities through training at community, NGO, governmental and donor levels. Training should be viewed as a standard element of the research process.

6. NGOs must recognize that research is an integral part of action and that all members of an organization should have the capacity to participate in research processes.

Dissemination

7. We urge donor agencies to incorporate funds for the publication and dissemination of NGO research findings — especially in South-South networks.

8. We urge UNCHS (Habitat) to provide NGOs with a research clearinghouse facility that includes NGO research, appropriate technical assistance, and information for research development.

NGOs and communities

9. NGOs must define their research in terms relevant to the communities they work with and in direct reference to programmes for action.

10. NGO research findings must be presented in languages and in ways that are accessible to community participants in research, as well as to academic, governmental, and donor constituencies.

NGOs and Governments

11. We urge NGOs to make serious efforts to involve governments in their research activity — including funding, training, and the dissemination of results.

Plan of Action

1. For those evicted or threatened with eviction, the right of appeal at international level.

The aim is to investigate the possibility of support from international law and from the UN Charter for those being evicted or threatened with eviction. The NGOs and national committees for the International Year of Shelter for the Homeless will:

—monitor and publicize widely the cases of current or threatened evictions, forced relocations and demolitions in both the North and the South.

—keep a record of the legal battles that took place over evictions and the final results, to provide precedents on how to fight evictions.

2. Media Campaign

To draw the attention of the world's peoples and to raise awareness among donor agencies of current trends towards ever increasing homelessness, overcrowding, lack of basic services and other forms of social and economic deprivation, and to highlight the present and the potential role of NGOs in addressing such problems, especially in the context of appropriate government policies.

A strategy to interest the media in such subjects will be launched. Such a strategy will be carried out by each national co-ordinating committee for the International Year, by the Habitat International Coalition (formerly Habitat International Council) and by each NGO.

3. Strengthening the partnership with international agencies

The aims are:

—to demonstrate the credibility of NGOs and the advantages to donor agencies of partnership with NGOs

—to discuss in detail at policy level how such a partnership can be developed and to define together a framework for this

—to increase the flow of funds channelled to Third World based NGOs working in shelter, services and community development.

Steps to be taken include:

—The preparation of a widely-based information package, to show the potentials, roles and requirements of NGOs. This information package will be widely circulated through the donor community.

—Letters sent to donor agencies, especially those ready to open a dialogue with NGOs. Such letters will request donor agencies to invite NGO representatives to attend a meeting to define together NGOs' policies and roles in the field of human settlements. The identification of on-going projects and programmes which need funding and support for joint presentation to funding agencies. Invitations by Third World based NGOs to senior officials from donor agencies to visit them, to allow a better understanding of their achievements and their aims and potentials in the future.

4. The creation of 'project pools' at regional level

The offices of most donors are too distant and remote from the context within which Third World based NGOs operate. Intermediate instititions at regional level should have the task of identifying NGO programmes that require funding, and providing NGOs with technical backup and help in formulating requests. These instititions would build a 'catalogue' of projects in need of funding. This would help donor agencies to identify and fund good projects and programmes without spending too long on project identification. Such institutions would facilitate links between locally-based NGOs and donor agencies and could provide the mechanism through which funding flows could be increased.

Networks and Coalitions

The Working Groups on Networks and Coalitions discussed the objectives of national, regional and international NGO networks and issues relating to their establishment and strengthening. It proposes the adoption of the following resolutions:

Considering that NGO networks at the national level are important because they are or could fulfil the following functions:

—to bring together people and NGOs with similar objectives;

—to act as a clearinghouse for the exchange of information;

—to reinforce weaker groups;

—to stimulate the creation of more networks;

—to fulfil an advocacy role in contacts with government agencies at all levels;

—to act as pressure groups, sometimes in coalitions with other groups and popular organizations;

—to co-ordinate production and marketing of building materials for the use of households and base groups;

—to promote participative action research;

—to disseminate information;

—to carry out training programmes for groups at different levels, including that of community-based organizations;

—to strengthen the links with community-based organizations;

—to fight for the introduction and application of just land rights;

That in their establishment the following factors are taken into account:

—that they are based on common issues

—that they work through existing frameworks

—that responsibilities and tasks be decentralized among members of the network

—that sub-committees be created on a sub-national or thematic basis

—that the network responds to priorities which are established together with community-based organizations.

Further considering that regional networks are important for the following reasons:

—they are the support services and facilitators for activities at the national and international level and the basis for a definitive consolidation of networks at all levels;

— they can define priorities and programmes on specific schemes and allocate tasks among their members;

—they can establish data banks, undertake training, exchange information between different actors, undertake joint publishing services, carry out services to national networks and promote the exchange of technical staff and know-how with other regions.

Recommends

1. That for the above mentioned reasons, national and regional networks should be created and strengthened where possible.

2. That in doing so, the specific situation of each country and region should be taken into account.

3. That in some countries and regions, the formulation of coalitions with other established groups, can be a useful method of promoting networks.

4. That international NGOs should promote the formation of local groups, especially in continents such as Africa where they are still few in number.

5. That networks be promoted in Northern countries because, among other things, this would facilitate the transfer of experience from other parts of the world confronted with problems of homelessness.

6. That regional networks can be promoted (among other ways) in the following manner:
—the publication of periodical bulletin on specific themes
—the creation of regional publications and translation funds
—the establishment of technical assistance and of an operational fund for disaster and crisis interventions.

Considering
—that there is a need for a mechanism for South-South and North-South relations;
—that there is a need for an international pressure group to deal with human settlements issues; for instance, a world-wide coalition against the existing problems of eviction and demolition;
—that there is a need for a global coalition built up on the basis and collective aims of national and regional networks.

Recommends that the Habitat International Council be transformed into that global coalition and for this purpose:
—the composition of the Board should reflect the incorporation of national and regional networks into its membership;
—under these conditions, HIC acts as spokesperson in contacts with international organizations such as UNCHS (Habitat) and provides information and other services to its members with the purpose of reinforcing national and regional networks;
—the name of HIC be changed into the Habitat International Coalition —NGO Alliance on Human Settlements.

Participants were present from the following organizations:
ADAUA (Association pour le Developpement Naturale dun Architecture Africaine), Burkina Faso.
AHAS (Appropriate Habitat for Another Development), United Kingdom.
AIAI, Mauretania.
ASAG (Ahmedabad Study and Action Group), India.
AVAS (Association for Voluntary Action and Services), India.
BEAU (Bureau d'etudes d'Amenagement et d'Urbanisme), Zaire.
CCU (Centro Co-operativista Uruguayo), Uruguay.
CDG (Carl Duisberg Gesellshaft), Federal Republic of Germany.
CEBEMO (Catholic organization for joint financing of development programmes), Netherlands.
CEDEC (Centro pour le Développement Auto-Centre), Cameroun.
CENVI (Centro de la Vivienda y Estudios Urbanos), Mexico.
CIDAP (Centro Investigación, Documentación y Asesoría Poblacional), Peru.
CLACSO (Latin America/Urban and Regional Development Commission), Argentina.
Community Development Trust Fund, Tanzania.
CODE (Consultants for Community Development), Netherlands.
COOPAN (Co-operative des Artisans de Nylon), Cameroun.
COPEVI (Centro Operacional de Vivienda y Poblamiento), Mexico.
CRAU (Centre de Recherche Architeturales et Urbaine), Ivory Coast.
CRDC (Construction Resources and Development Centre), Jamaica.
Development Workshop, Angola and Canada.

ENDA (Environment et Dévéloppement du Tiers Monde), Senegal.
ENDA, Central Africa.
ENDA, Latin America, Colombia.
FEDEVIVIENDA (Federación Nacional de Organizaciones de Vivienda Popular), Colombia.
Freedom to Build, Philippines.
FUNDASAL (Fundación Salvadorena de Desarrollo y Vivienda Mínimia), El Salvador.
GRET (Groupe de Recherches et d'Echanges Technologiques), France.
Habitat Forum Berlin, Federal Republic of Germany.
Haquabtir Somali Voluntary Organization, Somalia.
HIC (Habitat International Coalition) c/o IULA, the Netherlands.
Horizons Development Agency, Canada.
Human Settlements Centre, Thailand.
HUZA (Human Settlements of Zambia).
ICA Housing Committee, Sweden.
IDESAC (Instituto para el Desarrollo Económico Social de América Central), Guatemala.
IIED (International Institute for Environment and Development), United Kingdom and Argentina.
Indian Federation of Building and Woodworkers, India.
International Solidarity Foundation, Finland.
ITTA (Institut Tunisien de Technologie Appropriée), Tunisia.
IYSH Trust (International Year of Shelter for the Homeless Trust), United Kingdom.
KKNSS, India.
Lagos Group for the Study of Human Settlements, Nigeria.
Mazingira Institute, Kenya.
Mustard Seed Communities, Jamaica.
NCCK (National Council of Churches of Kenya).
Rooftops Canada Foundation, Canada.
SERVIVIENDA (Fundación Servicio de Vivienda Popular), Colombia.
SGHAS, Department of Architecture, University of Khartoum, Sudan.
SouSou Land, Trinidad and Tobago.
Sudanese Group for Assessment of Human Settlements
Taller Norte, Chile.
TCPA (Town and Country Planning Association), United Kingdom.
Unnayan, India.
Urbatech, Mali.
World Council of Churches, Central Africa, Kenya.
York University, Canada.
Zimbabwe Project, Zimbabwe

Observers were present from the following organizations:
CIDA, (Canadian International Development Agency) Canada.
DAEI, Ministry of Housing, France.
GATE (German Agency of Technical Co-operation), Federal Republic of Germany.
Government of the City of Berlin, Federal Republic of Germany.
GTZ (German Agency of Technical Co-operation), Kenya.
IDRC (International Development Research Centre), Canada.
JICA (Japanese International Cooperation Agency), Japan.
NOVIB (Netherlands Organization for International Development and Co-operation).
UNCHS (UN Centre for Human Settlements), Kenya.
UNICEF East and Southern Africa, Kenya.
USAID (United States Agency for International Development), Kenya.
World Bank, United States of America.